The Book of the
IVATT CLASS 2 2-6-0s
46400-46527

By John Jennison

Irwell Press Ltd.

ISBN 13 978-1-911262-26-8

First published in the United Kingdom in 2019.
by Irwell Press Limited, 59A, High Street, Clophill,
Bedfordshire MK45 4BE
Printed by Akcent Publishing, UK

Contents

Introduction and Acknowledgements

The Ivatt Class 2 moguls and tanks were the amongst the last new LMS designs and although intended for secondary duties to replace a variety of ancient pre-grouping specimens, they incorporated all of the refinements developed over the previous decade and honed by Ivatt on his post-war Black Fives. The two classes were developed together, sharing as many components as possible, using the same boiler, and they were very much complementary. Operationally, they worked mostly in different areas and on different duties, and hence the story of the tank version is covered separately in the Book of the Ivatt 2-6-2Ts.

Terry Essery in his book Steam Locomotives Compared provided an indication of how those who operated and maintained them viewed the 2-6-0s, 'not only did the 2MT offer new and wider possibilities to the operating department, they were also very acceptable to their crews whether out on the road in traffic or being serviced on the shed. Locomen are traditionally conservative by inclination and new engines have to earn their respect. That these little Ivatt Moguls did so on pure merit in a short space of time is ample testimony to the excellence of their design. The reasons for this general acceptance are not hard to find. They were lively performers having excellent powers of acceleration, pulled well on banks and yet ran freely at speed while at the same time giving a tolerable ride. Their spacious cabs offered almost tank engine-like protection from the elements and allowed first class vision both fore and aft. Firemen too were well catered for since, if operated correctly, they steamed freely without excessive physical effort. And when it came to disposal, that onerous task was rendered almost pleasant since they were perhaps the simplest of all LMS locomotives to service'.

Michael Bentley, who was a fireman at Buxton and worked on the engines in their last few years in service, remembers his driver on a local freight working to Friden remarking 'if we put some curtains up and had a geranium plant it would be like being at home'.

Their light axle loading meant that the 2-6-0s could go almost anywhere on the system and they certainly did that, reaching Scotland, Wales and Eastern England as well as almost all of their native LMS lines; the only area where they did not work was the Southern Region. The only negative that could be said about them was that they arrived on the scene far too late and hence were cut-down while still in their prime by the onset of dieselisation and rationalisation.

Unlike previous LMS volumes in the Book of series, there are many gaps in the surviving Engine History Cards and Engine Record Cards which I have attempted to fill from a number of sources, backed up by reference to a large number of photographs. I would record my thanks especially to Rail-Online, Michael Bentley, Rail Archive Stephenson, Colour-Rail and Initial Photographics for the use of their pictures.

REFERENCES
In addition to the Engine History Cards, Engine History Sheets, Engine Record Cards and Repair Statistics, I have consulted magazines including The Railway Gazette, The Railway Magazine, Steam Days, Backtrack and The Railway Observer, the latter providing much contemporary information on the workings of the class.

Left. **46404 has been repainted and fired up again after completing a Heavy General in Crewe May-June 1961.**

Below. **6410 on 12 March 1950 at Blackpool Central. It was the first of four which went new to the shed in 1947. It stayed there until November 1953, moving to Newton Heath.**

As the **LMS** press release explained, *The new L.M.S.R. locomotives, however, although of small size and light weight, incorporate every modern development which has been found successful on the larger main line types.* They had self-cleaning smokeboxes, manganese steel axlebox liners, rocking grates and hopper ashpans. Externally, the high running plate and outside cylinders contrasted with the rather ancient looking large diameter chimney. The tender cab and inset tanks were designed for tender-first operation. The injectors on the first twenty engines were horizontally mounted under the cab but from 46420 onwards they were positioned vertically.

1. Modern Secondary Service Locomotives

When the contemporary railway press announced in January 1947 the arrival of the new LMS Class 2 engines, they highlighted that these were designs produced specifically for secondary work: *Since grouping the L.M.S.R. has built new locomotives to a strictly limited number of basic types, but stagnation in development has been avoided by introducing successive modernised versions of these basic types, in which were incorporated the latest improvements in the art as they were available.*

Two of these [eleven] types are new designs, namely, the Class 2 2-6-0 tender and 2-6-2 tank engines. The first examples of both types have just been completed at Crewe Works to the designs of Mr. H.G. Ivatt. They are of special interest in that it has not hitherto been the general practice on British railways to design and build new types for secondary services on cross country and branch lines. Old locomotives have usually been employed for this purpose or even newly built locomotives to an old design. The new L.M.S.R. locomotives, however, although of small size and light weight, incorporate every modern development which has been found successful on the larger main line types. It is clearly desirable that secondary service locomotives, equally with main line, should be capable of the highest attainable mileage between repairs, that they should be quickly and easily serviced at the sheds, and that they should be economical to run. Since their prospective life may be over 30 years [sic], they should also be capable of good acceleration and relatively high maximum speed so as to be able to meet any future speeding up in branch line services, which is a matter that has been sadly neglected in the past.

These two new classes are identical in design, except that one has a separate tender, and the other carries side tanks and coal bunker on its main frames, Both are intended for Mixed Traffic work but the 2-6-0 engine is intended more for light main line and cross country freight and passenger working where greater coal and water capacity is required, whereas the 2-6-2 Tank engine is intended more for branch line working including Push and Pull services. In both types attainment of very low axle weights has been essential in order that they could run practically all over the system, including minor and lightly laid branch lines.

Design deliberations

E.S. Cox in *Locomotive Panorama* provided some of the background to the new engines, albeit in a somewhat flowery language: *The third phase of [LMS] design activity turned out to be the application of all that the preceding years had taught about locomotives for secondary services, but the initiation of this project stretched backwards over many years. By Stanier's advent the continued breaking up of Class 2, 3 and 4 pre-grouping engines, which hitherto worked these services, was beginning to establish the need for new construction in this waveband, which had by no means been* wholly satisfied by Fowler's Class 4 0-6-0s and Class 3 2-6-2 Tanks.

Deadlock persisted in translating this need into action, because the motive power people wanted straight replacements of the old Class 2 and 3 0-6-0s, saturated boilers, slide valves, the lot. Successive C.M.E.s and their designers, on the other hand, could not yet again bring themselves only to tinker with the pre-1900 designs, as had been the case with the abortive 0-4-4 Tank in 1931. So nothing was done except the creation and discussion of a lot of engine diagrams from 1932 until 1944, while the battle swung to and fro between inside cylindered front coupled engines, and outside cylindered machines with pony trucks. In the final stage from 1941 onwards, Coleman [the LMS Chief Draughtsman] and his few people still on this kind of work must have got a good deal of amusement out of letting their hair down and in becoming quite uninhibited in what they put down on paper. Bar frames, wide fireboxes, inside Walschaert gear driven from outside return cranks, and stovepipe chimneys were rampant, and to the dustbin with running plates, fall plates, splashers and all the clutter of 100 years of previous design!

Throughout the design deliberations, there were questions about the economic case for fitting superheaters to engines which would spend much of their time on local freight work and would rarely run for long under steady conditions. In 1944 Derby Drawing Office produced a report on the

The Class 2 moguls and tanks were the amongst the last new LMS designs and although intended for secondary duties, they incorporated all of the refinements developed over the previous decade and honed by Ivatt on his post-war Black Fives. The two classes were designed together, sharing as many components as possible, using the same boiler, and they were very much complementary.

The whole batch of ten engines, 6400-6409, built in December 1946 were lined up outside the Crewe Works Paint Shop to pose for the official photographer.

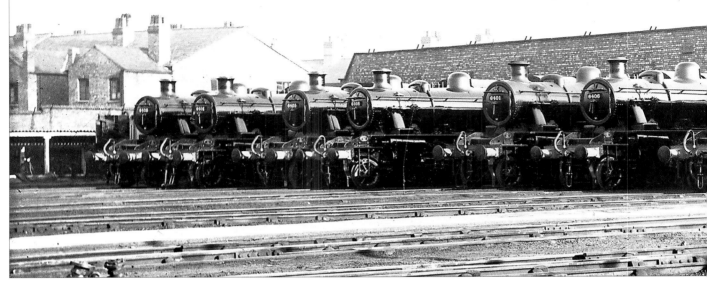

comparative costs of saturated and superheated engines on freight work which showed that the extra cost of the superheater was more than covered by the saving in coal, and thus settled the argument.

In 1934 outlines for a light weight Class 2 engine in both 0-6-0 tender and 0-6-2 tank versions had been sketched out. They had taper boilers, 5ft 0in. coupled wheels, 16½in x 26in cylinders and inside valve gear. By the time a decision was taken on the definitive designs in 1944, Cox had shown that, if inside-cylinder and outside-cylinder

versions of the same engine were compared, the maximum forces on the axleboxes of the outside-cylinder engine would be about 25% lower. Another advantage was that with the space between the frames clear of cranks and valve gear, the axleboxes could be larger. The outside-cylinder version would need leading wheels but would also ride better at speed. Therefore, what emerged under Ivatt's supervision were simple, conventional, but thoroughly modern outside-cylindered 2-6-0s and 2-6-2 Tanks using as many interchangeable parts as possible,

including the same No.7 type boiler. Although this was of much the same size as the Class 6 used on the Stanier 2-6-2T, its design was entirely new, with less taper on the barrel than on the other Stanier-type boilers.

By 1944, the Stanier era on the LMS was over following his appointment as Scientific Adviser to the Ministry of Production in 1942, and Charles Fairburn, the Chief Electrical Engineer, became Acting and then Chief Mechanical Engineer. When Fairburn died suddenly in October 1945, George Ivatt was appointed as acting CME,

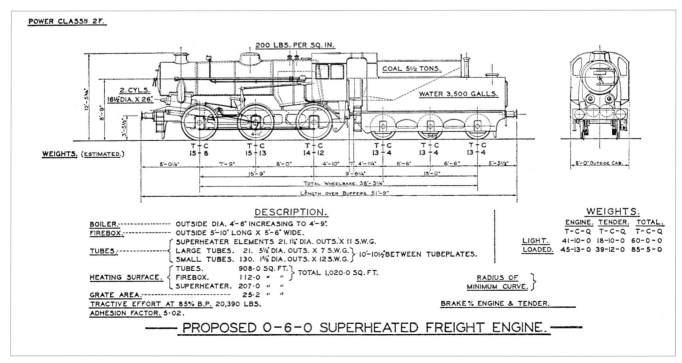

Proposed Superheated 0-6-0 diagram. From 1941 onwards the LMS Drawing Office draughtsmen schemed out an eclectic mix of outline diagrams for a modern secondary design. Amongst the ideas were bar frames, wide fireboxes, inside Walschaerts gear driven from outside return cranks, and stovepipe chimney with running plates, fall plates, splashers discarded. This example is for an 0-6-0 which incorporated a number of these ideas.

8

becoming CME on 1st February 1946. An out and out steam man, Ivatt had served his apprenticeship at Crewe and worked for the LMS or its constituents for most of his life becoming Principal Assistant, Locomotives to Stanier in 1937 and remained in the post when Fairburn became acting CME.

The Wooden Mock-up

One interesting by-product which appeared during the production design process arose through Fairburn's interest in what was being incorporated to make servicing easier in the depots. He was so concerned by the considerable amount of alteration work which always seemed to accompany each new design, that he ordered a full-size mock-up of the 2-6-2 tank to be produced in wood, complete down to the last detail, for inspection and comment by shed staffs. Cox commented, *This effort was a good deal jeered at by the old hands. Perhaps it did not cause anything of much moment to be discovered and corrected before the flesh and blood engines were turned out, but on the other hand it only cost £8 for each of the total number of Ivatt Class 2s, which were eventually produced.*

Detailed specification

The Locomotive magazine in February 1947 reproduced the detailed LMS press release for the new engines which provided a comprehensive description of their construction and principal features:

BOILER

The boiler is of normal construction and the shell is of carbon steel throughout. The barrel, which consists of two rings, is tapered equally at top and bottom, the outside diameter at the front end being 4 ft. 3in. and at the firebox end 4 ft. 8in. The front ring is of ½ in. thick plate and the back ring

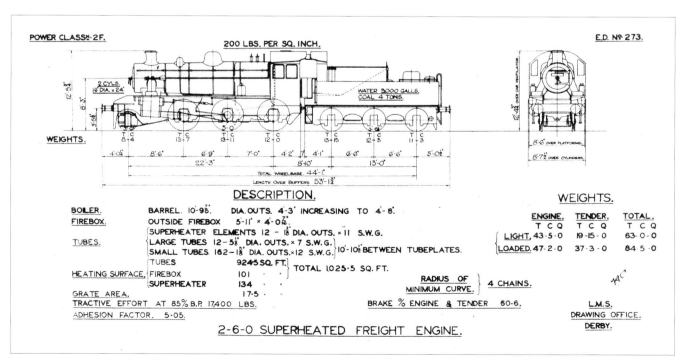

ED 273 was the final Engine Diagram covering the engines up to 46464, after which the diameter of the cylinders was increased by ½in. Note the low axle weights which allowed the class to operate over almost all of the former LMS system and on the ex-Great Western lines in mid-Wales.

6406 is lowered gently onto its driving wheels in the Crewe Erecting Shop with a Beyer-Garratt under repair immediately behind. The stencilled E462/7 on the front frames indicates this is the seventh engine of Order No. 462.

of $^{17}/_{32}$ in. thick material. The smokebox tubeplate is of the drumhead type and there are 12 flue tubes $5\frac{1}{8}$ in. diameter (outside) and 7 s.w.g. thick; the 162 small tubes are of $1\frac{5}{8}$ in. diameter outside and 12 s.w.g. thickness. The length between tubeplates is 10 ft. $10\frac{1}{2}$ in. A large steam dome is provided and contains a grid type regulator arranged vertically. Top feed clack-boxes are of the latest type in which the clack valves and settings are integral with the coverplate casting, so that only one joint is necessary to each feed pipe. Instead of perforated trays, a simple arrangement of sloping plates is secured to the longitudinal stays underneath the top feed outlet to deflect the incoming water round the barrel side clear of the tube nest.

FIREBOX

This is of the Belpaire type with a steel wrapper plate $^{17}/_{32}$ in. thick; the inner firebox is of copper $^9/_{16}$ in. thick. Monel metal side stays $^5/_8$ in. diameter are mainly employed with $^{11}/_{16}$ in. diameter stays in the breaking zones. All stays are nutted on the fireside. The firebox is 5 ft. 11 in. long outside and just over 4 ft. wide giving a grate area of 17.5 square feet. Heating surfaces are, tubes 924.5 sq. ft., firebox 101 sq. ft., and superheater 134 sq. ft., the total being 1,159.5 sq. ft. The working pressure is 200 lb. sq. in.

GRATE AND ASHPAN

A rocking grate and ashpan is provided consisting of six rocking sections divided into two groups of three fore and aft which may be rocked independently. The operating gear is so arranged that two different travels may be employed ie the full travel for fire dropping when the engine is over a pit, and a shorter travel for agitating the fire to eliminate ash and break up clinker whilst the engine is out on the road. The ashpan is of the self-emptying type having two bottom 'flap' doors; these are connected by a linkage and operated by means of a lever from the ground. One front damper door only is provided.

SMOKEBOX

This is of plain cylindrical type with a solid bottom resting on a saddle of conventional design. The blast pipe has a plain circular cap of $4\frac{3}{8}$ in. diameter which incorporates the blower ring. The smokebox is of the "self-cleaning" type having plates and wire mesh grid arranged in such a way as to eject all accumulations of char through the chimney when the engine is working. The blast pipe has a cap of $4\frac{3}{8}$ in. diameter.

CYLINDERS AND VALVE GEAR

The two cylinders of 16 in. diameter and 24 in. stroke are disposed outside the frames and take steam through piston valves of 8 in. diameter. Steam distribution is by Walschaerts gear. The combining lever and union links have case-hardened steel bushes and pins grease lubricated. The remaining joints of the gear have phosphor bronze bushes lubricated by oil. The piston head incorporate a bronze spring-loaded slipper which carries the head in the cylinder. For reasons of weight saving the crosshead is of a new built-up design.

MAIN FRAMES AND AXLEBOXES

The main frames are of carbon steel plates one inch thick. In order to maintain the frames at the correct distance apart, pin-jointed cross stays are attached across the engine from driving hornblock to hornblock. The driving horns have one-piece hornblocks of the "horseshoe" type whilst the leaders and trailers have separate guides. All are fitted with composite liners bolted to the horn guides. The liners consist of flanged plates of manganese steel riveted and welded to mild steel backing plates. The faces of the axlebox in contact with the horn guides are also provided with manganese steel liners welded to the body of the axlebox. The coupled wheel axleboxes are steel castings with pressed-in horseshoe brasses. A sliding underkeep of gunmetal containing a worsted-trimmed oil pad is provided and the oil from the mechanical lubricator is fed direct to the underkeep thus permitting an uninterrupted bearing surface of the crown. The journal diameter is $7\frac{1}{2}$ in. and the length of the bearing $8\frac{3}{4}$ in.

The stencilled E462/4 on the front frames indicates this is the fourth engine of Order No.462, 6403, nearing completion in the Crewe Works Erecting Shop on 16 October 1947. W.L. Good, M. Bentley.

The prototype, 6400, at Kings Norton on the Midland Railway line south of Birmingham with a local passenger train on 16 May 1947. It was allocated to Derby at this date. W.L. Good, M. Bentley.

One of the most significant allocations was to Kettering, beginning with 6404 in w/e 11 January. It was used mainly on passenger trains to Cambridge, Gretton and Northampton. Next came 6400 on loan at the end of February. The new 2-6-0s clearly fitted the bill because by the middle of the year 6401-6403 arrived to complete the set. They took over the service to Huntingdon and Cambridge from ex-Midland Railway Johnson 2F 0-6-0s. All five remained at the shed for many years, with 46403 and 46404 not leaving until 1963.

SPRINGING

All pairs of coupled wheels are provided with laminated springs with compression spring hangers and two types of spring are being applied for comparative purposes.

PONY TRUCK

The same design of truck is used for the leading wheel of both the tender and tank engines. It is of the bar framed type and side control is effected by swing links. A spring-loaded friction retarder is provided to supply the necessary damping. The bearing springs are of the coil type and the axleboxes of bronze have a journal size of 6¼ in. diameter and 10⅞ in. length.

TENDER

The tender is of a completely new design and is arranged to give good conditions for tender-first running. It has two large windows which give a clear view rearwards and avoids the necessity for the driver to lean out of the side of his cab when in reverse. A cab on the forepart of the tender gives complete protection to the crew. The tank which is practically rectangular, affords a good visibility from the cab provided on both engine and tender. The coal bunker which is also of rectangular section is narrower than the tank. Water pick-up gear is provided. The construction of the tender tanks is partly by welding and partly by riveting. An external feed sieve is provided on both classes to enable the water to be effectively strained before passing to the injectors. The sieve is easily withdrawable for cleaning. The tender carries 4 tons of coal and 3,000 gallons of water.

The tractive effort, calculated at 85%, is 17,400 lb.

EQUIPMENT

The following is a list of the principal items of equipment provided:-
"Monitor" injectors
Steam Brake on engine and tender, with vacuum brake fittings for working fitted trains, and the standard combination drivers' brake valve.
"Silvertown" Mechanical Lubricators to cylinders and axleboxes
Steam Sanding Gear
Grease lubrication of brake and water pick-up gear pins, and to the rocking grate and ashpan gear
Manually operated blowdown in addition to the standard continuous blow-down equipment
Carriage Warming Apparatus
Fire-iron tunnel placed on R.H. side platform in front of the cab

A number of other features which were not described in the press release are worth noting. The wheels, with the now standard Gibson ring tyre fastenings, had 15 spokes on the coupled and 9 spokes on the carrying wheels, and the coupled wheel axles were hollow to save weight. Only the coupled wheels were braked, the hangers with single brake blocks ahead of each one. Buffers were of the Turton & Platt 'no-weld' type with a footstep on top of the housing. All of the motion was fluted.

SPECIAL FEATURES

A booklet for staff was produced soon after the class was introduced to 'summarize and illustrate where necessary' the special features on Class 2, 2-6-0 tender and 2-6-2 tank types: *All engines of this class embody these features, and as others may be introduced from time to time further sheets will be Issued as becomes necessary for inclusion in this booklet. The features selected for description are those in which a departure has been made from what has previously been standard practice.*

Self-cleaning Smokebox

This type of smokebox arrangement incorporates deflector plates of the conventional pattern and a wire mesh screen at the front end of the smokebox. The deflector plates and the screen are readily removable when accessibility is required for boiler washing out and tube cleaning.

The function of the arrangement is entirely automatic and is as follows:-
The draught induced by the blast pipe causes the flue gases to be deflected downwards by the deflector plates and drawn through the restricted opening A.B. (see sketch page 18). This restriction imparts increased velocity to the gases and causes the smokebox char to be entrained and carried along and through the wire mesh screen and thence ejected from the chimney. Any large particles of char are broken up by impact with the screen.

The smokebox door only requires opening for cleaning out the box on washout days. At the same time, it is particularly important

Principal dimensions

The principal dimensions of the first 2-6-0s and 2-6-2Ts were:

Cylinders (2)	16in x 24 in
Heating surface total	1,159.5 sq. ft
Grate area	17.5 sq. ft
Boiler pressure	200 lb. per sq. in
Coupled wheels	5ft. 0in. diameter
Carrying wheels	3ft. 0in. diameter
Coupled wheelbase	6ft 9in + 7ft 0in
Tractive effort at 85% boiler pressure	17,400 lb
The diameter of the cylinders was increased to 16½in from 46465 and 41290 onwards with a consequent increase in tractive effort to 18,510 lbs per sq.in.	

Only in weight, coal and water capacities did they vary:

	2-6-0 (46400-46502) *	2-6-2T
Adhesion weight	38 tons 18cwt	39 tons 5 cwt
Engine weight (empty)	43 tons 5 cwt	50 tons 8 cwt
Engine weight (working)	47 tons 2 cwt	63 tons 5 cwt
Tender weight (loaded)	37 tons 3 cwt	-
Max axle load	13 tons 11 cwt	13 tons 5 cwt
Coal capacity	4 tons 0 cwt	3 tons 0 cwt
Water capacity	3,000 gallons	1,350 gallons
*The later, Swindon built, examples 46503-46527, differed in weight from those built at Crewe and Darlington with an empty weight of 45 tons 3 cwt and a working weight 48 tons 9 cwt.		

Newton Heath had the last two of the second Lot, 6418 and 6419. They spent much of their time as Manchester Victoria station pilots and Miles Platting bankers, a rather wasteful use of new engines although with their tender cabs they were undoubtedly welcomed by the crews. H.C. Casserley, courtesy M. Casserley.

46465 the first of the Darlington-built engines at Marks Tey on 22 August 1953. They incorporated a number of detail changes from the previous Crewe-built batches including enlarged cylinders, taller thinner chimney to improve the draughting and guard irons attached to the pony truck instead of the frames. 46465 has the lined black livery standardised for the class with the addition of a couple of Darlington touches, the 2MT power classification on the bufferbeam and large 10in size cab numbers.

that the wire mesh screen be examined and cleared of char that has become lodged in the mesh.

All engines fitted with self-cleaning smokebox have the letters "S.C." clearly shown on the smokebox door.

Rocking-grate and Self-emptying Ashpan

The object of this arrangement is principally to facilitate the disposal of engines at sheds, but the rocking grate also provides mechanical means for agitating the fire to eliminate ash and break up the formation of the clinker while running.

The grate is comprised of firebars that have end trunnions which can be rocked by means of connecting linkage to a lever above the footplate.

The front half of the grate is rocked independently of the back, the crank on the left-hand side in the cab operating the front half and the right-hand side operating the back.

Each crank is provided with a two way stop and locking clip as shown at page 19. With the stop in position A, the movement of the operating lever is limited by the bracket and the bars can be rocked through a wide angle (about 40° each way) for dropping the fire. In position B the movement is restricted by the stop and only a limited rocking movement is permitted for breaking up the clinker when running. The lever is locked in the normal mid-position by the "U" clip

shown in chain-dotted lines. It should be noted that position B is the normal running position of the "U" clip and the stop. To agitate the firebar sections it is only necessary to raise the "U" clip, which can be done by hand. Except in an emergency, the stop must only be released for full rocking of the grate when the engine is standing at a fire-cleaning or disposal point.

The self-emptying ashpan has two butterfly type doors which are opened by means of a lever on the left-hand side of the ashpan. A catch is provided for locking the doors in the closed position and care should be taken to ensure the catch is dropped back into position and the locking key inserted immediately after the doors have been operated.

The same detachable lever is used for operating either the rocking grate or the ashpan doors and means have been provided in the cabs of both types of engines for stowing the lever when not in use.

Top Feed

A new design of clackbox in which the clack valves are incorporated in the manhole casting. This has been introduced to eliminate the trouble experienced with the top feed pipe joints leaking.

Continuous Blowdown

When softened water is used, dissolved solids gradually concentrate in the boiler water and after a time a point is reached when

priming takes place. In order to reduce this concentration below priming point in the boiler, a certain amount of water is required to be discharged by means of the blowdown valve.

Since it is desirable that the quantity of water blown down should be a fixed proportion of the total that is used, a new arrangement is now being fitted by which the blowdown valve operates only when the injectors are in use.

An automatic throw-over valve is introduced so that the blowdown valve will function whichever side injector is used.

Manual Blowdown

While the automatic blowdown valve deals with the dissolved solids in the boiler water, it does not assist with the discharge of sludge which tends to accumulate at the bottom of the boiler barrel and around the water space at the bottom of firebox.

An additional manually operated blow-off valve is therefore fitted for the purpose at the front of the firebox just above the foundation ring. The valve is operated by a hand lever on the right side of the cab.

Its use should be confined to when the engine is standing over a suitable pit in the shed or shed yard.

Frame Cross Stays

Tee-section cross stays are fitted between the driving hornblocks to reduce lateral flexing of the frames. The cross stays are

14

secured to lugs cast on the hornblocks by pin joints with the pins horizontally placed, so that, whilst allowing a certain degree of freedom of movement to prevent fracture, they also maintain the frame plates at the correct distance apart and so keep the axle side play reasonably constant.

Frame Keep
This is the Horwich, or single bar type which is located to the frame by a tapered fit and is secured by four special countersunk hexagon headed bolts.

The purpose of this type of keep is to hold the frame rigidly across the horn gaps and thereby reduce the trouble experienced with fractured frames. Furthermore, it is not connected to the axlebox guides, so that flexing of the guides in service will not produce loosening of the frame keep.

Manganese Steel Liners
The driving horns have one-piece hornblocks of the "horseshoe" type whilst the leading and trailing have separate guides. All are fitted with composite liners bolted to the horn guides.

These liners are produced from flanged plates of manganese steel which are rivetted and welded to mild steel backing plates.

The faces of the axleboxes in contact with the horn guides are also provided with manganese steel liners welded to the body of the axlebox.

Axlebox Bearings and Lubrication
The coupled wheel axleboxes are steel castings with pressed-in brasses. A sliding underkeep of gunmetal which has ample oil capacity and contains a worsted oiling pad is provided and the oil feed from the

mechanical lubricator is fed direct to the underkeep, thus permitting an uninterrupted bearing surface of the crown of the box.

Crosshead
A built-up crosshead has been employed to effect a saving in weight and a modified arrangement of securing the gudgeon pin has been adopted. The split coned washer has been dispensed with and the pin is secured in position by means of a castellated nut with a good fitting flat split cotter.

A modified design of crosshead arm has also been adopted.

Cylinders and Cylinder Cocks
The cylinders are 16" diameter and 24" stroke, steam ports are 2" in width.

A redesigned cylinder drain cock which incorporates a vertical mushroom type valve. The valve is not spring loaded and is actuated by a short cranked lever which engages in a slot in the valve spindle.

Care should be taken to ensure that the valves close properly when the operating lever in the cab is in a full forward position.

A new form of automatic steam chest drain cock has been provided and is located under each cylinder between the two cylinder drain cocks.

Pistons
A reversion has been made to the two ring type of piston, with the rings and carrier quite separate.

Monitor Injector
The Monitor Injector has been designed to be as simple as possible in construction and operation combined with maximum efficiency

and is fitted with cones specially suitable for working with high pressure steam.

Construction
The injector is of gunmetal throughout, and consists of a casing containing the cones, overflow valve, and water regulating and shut off cock.

The inner and outer steam cones screw together to form one piece and are screwed into the upper part of the body, similarly the combining and delivery cones form one piece and are screwed into the lower part of the body.

The complete steam cone consists of the outer steam cone which screws on to the inner cone, so forming an annular space between the two cones. Steam is admitted to the injector in two jets, first the primary steam which is admitted through the annular space between the outer and inner cones, and then the secondary or forcing jet formed by the bore of the inner steam cone.

The combining cone is the usual converging cone with three gaps or slots in its length. These slots open into the overflow chamber and so allow water and steam to escape freely into the overflow until the jet is formed and the injector starts to work.

The delivery cone, which is provided with a renewable tip, consists of a short parallel bore followed by a diverging cone.

Overflow Valve
This consists of an ordinary drop valve resting on a seating formed in the injector casing and cuts off communication between the overflow chamber and the atmosphere.

When the injector is working a vacuum is formed in the overflow chamber, so that the overflow valve is held on its seating,

Two of the Ivatts under construction at Swindon Works in 1952, with gas turbine 18000 on the next road.

46504, the second of 25 engines built for the Western Region at Swindon. They did not differ in detail from the Darlington-built engines apart from the provision of AWS and an unexplained reversion to unlined black livery on the first few engines.

preventing any air from being drawn into the injector. Should the injector break off, steam and water from the cones pass into the overflow chamber and force the overflow valve off its seating so allowing a free flow into the overflow pipe and thence to the atmosphere, until the jet is reformed, when the overflow valve falls on to its seating again.

This sealing of the overflow chamber is important, as any air drawn in may affect the working of the injector.

Water Feed Valve

A new type combined water feed valve which incorporates a stop plug and sieve. These are located on each side and outside the tender or side tanks. The sieve is readily removable for inspection and cleaning without the necessity of emptying the tanks.

Pistons

Cast iron box type piston heads are employed which are fitted with spring loaded bronze carriers.

Engines 6400-6409 have three rings on each piston head and engines 6410-6419 have two rings only.

Motion Bushes

The valve gear comprising the "lap and lead" motion to the valve and also all reversing gear joints are fitted with case hardened steel bushes and pins which are lubricated by grease.

Coupled Wheel Bearing Springs and Suspension

Non-adjustable compression spring hangers are provided and two types of springs are being applied for comparative purposes.

Those of L.M.S. design have 8 plates 5" x 3/8" section working at a span of 3'-6" centres when loaded. These are of carbon

steel and the top plate has forged eye ends. The plates are secured in the buckle by means of a vertical rivet.

Engine numbers 6404-6406 are fitted with the second type of spring which is designed and manufactured by William Griffith and consists of six plates 5" x 11/16". A feature of these springs is that the top three plates have projections on each side at mid-span which fit into slots in the buckle. In addition, an elongated cotter rivet is fitted to hold all plates together.

A further speciality of the "Griffiths" spring is that the plates are ground and shot blasted in order to increase the fatigue resistance.

Top Feed Deflector Plates

A simple arrangement of sloping plates secured to the longitudinal stays underneath the top feed outlet to deflect the incoming water round the barrel side.

Washout plugs are provided on the first ring of boiler barrel in front of the top feed clackbox in order that effective use can be made of the standard washing out equipment for removing any dirt that tends to build up at the smokebox tubeplate and particularly between the large and small tubes.

Pony Truck

The same design of truck is used for the leading wheels of both the tender engine and the tank. It is of the bar frame type and side control is effected by means of swing links. A spring-loaded friction retarder is provided to effect the necessary damping. The bearing springs are round section coil type.

Modifications applied to engines built in 1949
Miscellaneous items

(1) Side Tanks

In an attempt to overcome the fracture of side tank plates, the tanks have been re-designed. The mid pocket which previously accommodated the supporting bracket has been eradicated.

(2) Smokebox Door

A non-slip type of handle is fitted for fastening the smokebox door.

(3) Platform Doors

The access doors in the platform immediately above the front steam chest covers are now bolted down at the front end to prevent them from blowing open in service.

(4) Weather Shields and Storm Sheets

The flanged plates behind the cab seats have been extended upwards to the roof to form weather shields, and the necessary hooks are fitted around the opening above the door to enable storm sheets to be fitted if required.

(5) Motion Plate Footstep

This item has been left off these engines. It was a source of trouble because of its tendency to become loose and was very seldom used.

(6) Water Feed Sieve Box

The operating wheel for the shut off valve on these sieve boxes has been removed and replaced with a square, which will require a spanner for operation. This has been done to minimise unauthorised interference with the position of the valve.

(7) Damper Gear Catch

To reduce the wear sustained, the damper rod is fitted with a hard steel insert which carries the notches, and the catch plate on the bracket is of hard steel. The catch plate can be moved sideways and also reversed, to give alternative positions for wear.

Rocking-grate and Self-emptying Ashpan

Some minor modifications of this gear have been applied to engines built in 1949. These are listed below:-

16

Lot	Quantity	Nos.	Built at	Authorised £	Each £	Region
182	10	6400-6409	Crewe	68,300	6,830	LMS
189	10	6410-6419	Crewe	65,750	6,575	LMS
194	15	46420-46434	Crewe	97,500	6,500	London Midland
201	15	46435-46449	Crewe	129,375	8,625	London Midland
207	10	46450-46459	Crewe	?	?	London Midland
208	5	46460-46464	Crewe	?	?	Scottish
NER 1309	18	46465-46482	Darlington	?	?	Eastern/NER
NER 1310	20	46483-46502	Darlington	?	?	North Eastern
WR 394	25	46503-46527	Swindon	?	?	Western
	128					

(1) The lever ends for both rocking grate and ashpan gear are now cylindrical in form and the removable handle has been re-designed to suit. This arrangement has been introduced to overcome the troubles due to excessive wear and occasional fracture of the original lever ends.

(2) The locking catch for the hopper ashpan gear has been simplified. The locking key is dispensed with and the catch held in position by its own weight.

(3) The attachment of levers to rods in the hopper ashpan gear has been improved by the adoption of either squares and locking bolts, or welded fastening, in place of the keys and taper pins originally fitted.

(k) The rocking grate sections have the air slots running down the firebox, instead of across, as formerly, and the front and back edges are correspondingly "toothed". This has been found to be beneficial in keeping the slots clear of slag, and in breaking up clinker on the grate.

Top Feed
The wing type of clack valve has proved unsatisfactory in service due to a tendency to stick open and has been replaced by a standard type of valve. Existing engines with wing type clack valves will be fitted with cage type valves in the near future.

Cylinder Cocks
Provision has now been made for individual adjustment of cylinder cocks.

AUTHORISATION, BUILDING AND COSTS
Ivatt, as Acting CME, presented the 1946 Locomotive Renewal Programme to the LMS Mechanical & Electrical Engineering Committee on 21 December 1944. This included ten Class 2 Freight Tender 2-6-0s at a cost of £68,300 and ten Class 2 Passenger Tank 2-6-2Ts costing £62,650 'to replace the large number of old non-standard types due for breaking up'. Another ten 2-6-0s were authorised on 19 December 1945 in the 1947 Locomotive Renewal Programme at the slightly lower cost of £65,750. The following year, 15 more were approved on 23 October 1946 in the 1948 Programme at an estimated cost of £97,500, and a further 15 were authorised in the last LMS Programme on 29 October 1947 at £107,500.

The first ten engines all emerged in December 1946 at the same time as the first ten 2-6-2Ts, with the next ten delivered over the next three months. No more were built until almost a year after nationalisation when another 15 went into service during the final two months of 1948. There was then a gap of a year before the final 15 engines from Crewe were built between January and June 1950.

British Railways ordered three more batches totalling 78 engines in their 1950, 1951 and 1952 Programmes; only ten of these were for the London Midland Region, the others going to the Scottish, Eastern, North Eastern and Western Regions. (table above).

British Railways had selected the LMS engine in preference to a new small 2-6-0 designed by A.H. Peppercorn at Doncaster to replace older classes on the Eastern and North Eastern Regions, and 38 were built at Darlington Works between June 1951 and April 1952. It was similarly chosen for the Western Region which built 25 engines at Swindon between November 1952 and April 1953. The latter were not the first LMS designed engines built there because Swindon had produced eighty 8F 2-8-0s during the Second World War; however, these 2-6-0s had the distinction of being the final LMS designed locomotives built.

At the same time as Swindon was building the final batch, the first ten of the new British Railways Standard Class 2 2-6-0 design (78000-78009) were delivered to the Western Region from Darlington. These were dimensionally almost identical with the Swindon-built Ivatt engines, although they naturally incorporated BR standard fittings together with a redesigned cab with sloping upper side sheets and sloping front footplate ahead of the cylinders. They had the BR No.8 boiler which was dimensionally almost the same as the LMS No.7 boiler used on the Ivatt 2-6-0s and 2-6-2Ts, but with a revised water delivery from a side clack valve arrangement rather than top feed, and the regulator was a vertical grid type operated by an external rod at the side of the firebox. The BR design weighed 2 tons 3 cwt more and had the same tractive effort as the later Ivatt engines.

The costs recorded on the Engine History Cards of the Crewe built engines increased by 12.6% between the first and last batches, reflecting the rise in material and labour costs over the four years, and were broadly comparable with the equivalent figures for the Black 5s over the same period. The figures for the Darlington and Swindon engines were significantly higher; how much of this can be attributed to differences in costing methods and price inflation is not known. The Swindon engines were fitted with AWS equipment which would explain a small amount of the increase, but it is probable that there was a considerable additional cost to start a completely new production line with 'foreign' components, new jigs, tools, etc at both works. The costs of the first batch of the BR Standard Class 2 2-6-0s were £14,377 each. A total of 275 No.7 boilers were made to cover the 258

Nos.	Built at	Into traffic	Engine £	Tender £	Total £
			£	£	£
6400-6409	Crewe	December 1946	6,382	1,515	7,897
6410-6419	Crewe	January-March 1947	6,296	1,512	7,808
46420-46434	Crewe	November-December 1948	6,952	1,684	8,636
46435-46449	Crewe	January-March 1950	7,025	1,709	8,734
46450-46464	Crewe	April-June 1950	7,198	1,734	8,932
46465-46502	Darlington	June 1951-April 1952	9,583	2,214	11,797
46503-46527	Swindon	November 1952-April 1953	n/a	n/a	13,756

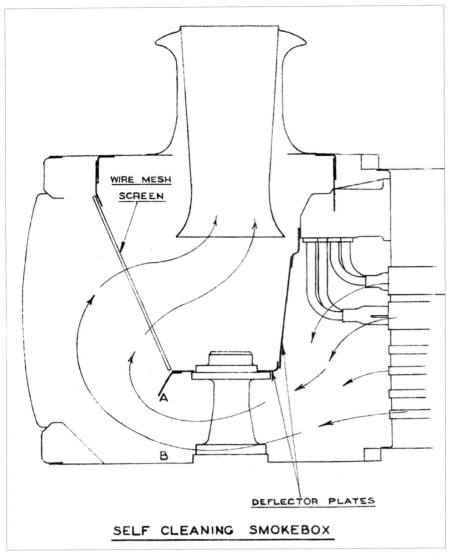

WIRE MESH SCREEN

A

B

DEFLECTOR PLATES

SELF CLEANING SMOKEBOX

In the self-cleaning smokebox the draught induced by the blast pipe caused the flue gases to be deflected downwards by the deflector plates and drawn through the restricted opening A-B. This restriction increased the velocity of the gases and caused the smokebox char to be carried along and through the wire mesh screen and thence ejected through the chimney. Any large particles of char would break up on impact with the screen. The smokebox door would only need to be opened for cleaning out the smokebox on washout days.

problems such as poor steaming, as was the case with the Jubilees. When the Ivatt designs emerged after the war it was natural that they went through the same procedures and so the Class 2 2-6-0 was put through its paces in April 1947.

The objective was 'to ascertain the coal and water consumption and the general performance ...... when working a heavy train to a fast schedule'. A special train of empty carriage stock was worked non-stop from Crewe to Holyhead and return on April 15/16 and 17/18. The 270 tons train had a schedule requiring an average speed of 46.2 mph for the 105.5 miles.

The engine used was 6419 which had entered traffic on 15 March 1947 and was loaned to Crewe North from Newton Heath for the duration of the tests. Its recorded mileage from new was 1,116 and several modifications were made prior to the tests:

The blastpipe was fitted with a 4⅛in cap. The 9mm cones in the two Monitor injectors were replaced with 8mm cones. The Ash Deflector plates riveted to the table plates in the smokebox were cut back from 4½in deep to 3½in deep. Two firedoors with reduced area air passages were fitted.

The Official Report concluded that *The stringent test schedule was well within the capabilities of the engine. Running times were maintained without difficulty, and the engine was extremely free steaming. The boiler pressure was maintained at 195-200 lbs. per square inch practically throughout the test. The ability of the engine to run at satisfactorily at high speeds was demonstrated during the tests with periods of running at 70 to 75mph. The riding of the engine was very good and at the highest speeds there was no undue vibration or discomfort in the cab.*

The same driver and fireman worked the engine throughout the tests, and a

moguls and 2-6-2Ts, 206 at Crewe, 44 at Darlington (13823-60 and 14093-7, 14181) and 25 at Swindon (13861-85). This gave 17 spares, the last one of which (14436) was not completed until December 1959. The boilers from new were not all fitted in numerical order to the engines, and many were inter-changed between the two classes during works visits.

Testing Times

The LMS had, since before the war, carried out extensive tests on its newest engines, sometimes related to specific

The same design of truck was used for the leading wheelset of both the tender and tank engines. It was a bar-framed type with side control effected by swing links. A spring-loaded friction retarder was provided to supply the necessary damping. The bearing springs were of the coil type.

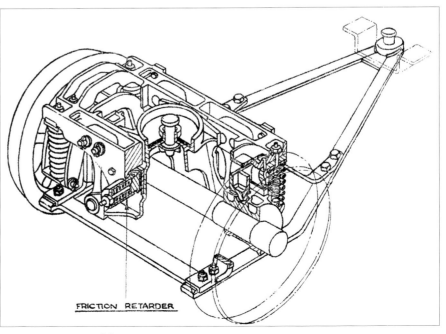

FRICTION RETARDER

ROCKING GRATE AND SELF-EMPTYING ASHPAN.

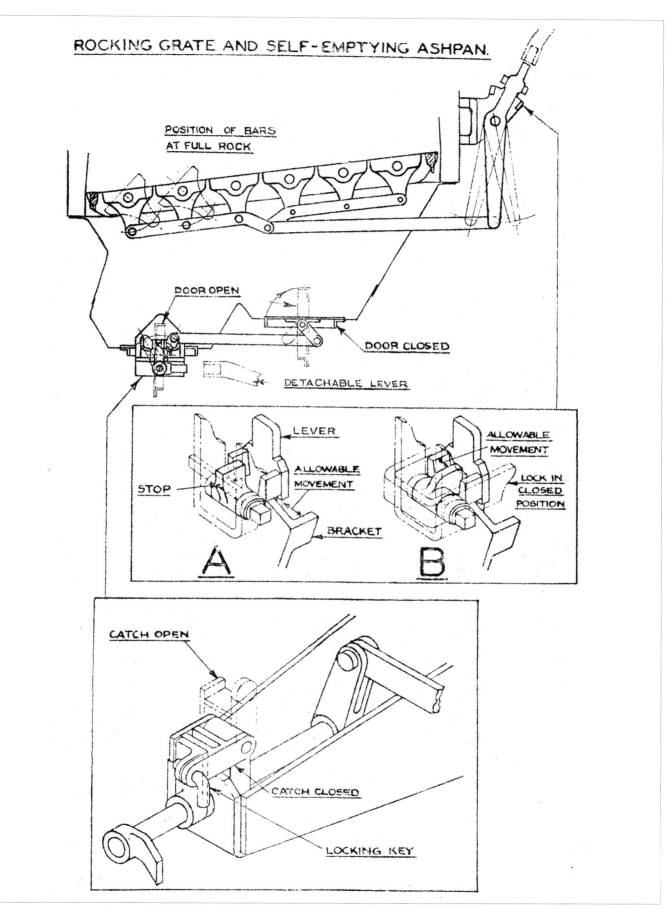

The rocking grate and self-emptying ashpan was intended to facilitate the disposal of engines at sheds. It also provided a mechanical means of agitating the fire to eliminate ash and break up clinker while running. The grate had firebars with end trunnions which could be rocked by means of connecting linkage to a lever above the footplate. The front half of the grate could be rocked independently of the back, the crank on the left-hand side in the cab operating the front half and the right-hand side operating the back. The self-emptying ashpan had two butterfly type doors which were opened through a lever on the left-hand side of the ashpan.

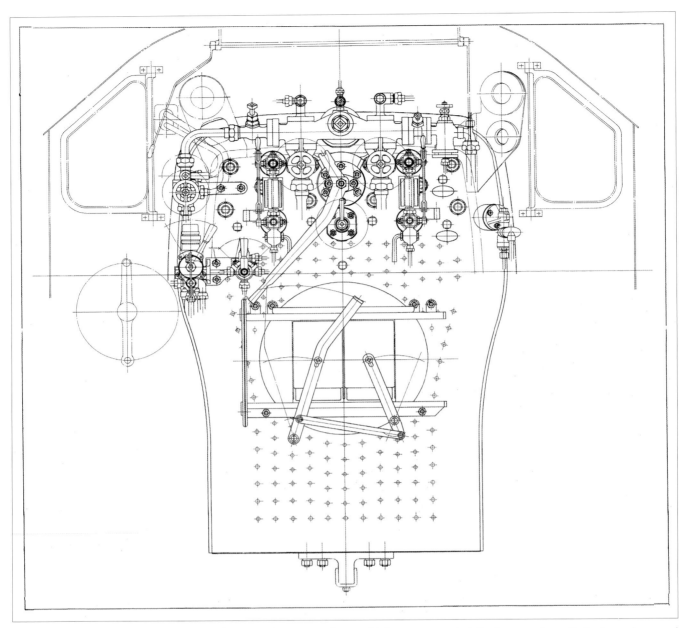

Immediately in front of the driver was the reversing screw above which were mounted the large and small ejector valves, and a standard LMS vacuum controlled steam brake valve was located within easy reach of his right hand. The steam manifold which was above the boiler inside the cab supplied all the auxiliary equipment other than the blower. On the fireman's side were the boiler pressure and carriage warming apparatus pressure gauges while the driver only had the vacuum gauge. There were two standard LMS water gauges with combined shut-off cocks and hollow sliding firedoors with a small flip-up combustion plate below.

C.M.E. footplate observer together with a Motive Power Inspector rode on the engine. The engine was mainly worked with full regulator or with the second valve well open, and with a cut off of 17-22% on the easier sections and 27-35% on the severest sections of the run.

A thin fire, slightly built up at the back corners of the firebox, was consistently maintained throughout the test. The engine was fired very lightly, with an average of four shovelsful of coal at each application. The damper door was fully opened and the firehole doors were shut with the firehole flap down between firing, and a hot incandescent fire was maintained. On several sections where the demand on the engine was considerable the injector, set in

the maximum feed position would just maintain the level of water in the boiler.

After working 420 miles there was only 48lbs of ash in front of the smokebox deflector plates, vindicating the ability of the self-cleaning smokebox. The average power developed by the engine on the level and easier sections of the route was approximately 400 D.B.H.P. with a maximum of approximately 600 D.B.H.P. on the severest gradients.

Having regard to the comparatively heavy demand upon the engine in maintaining the special test timings, the coal and water consumption figures can be considered most satisfactory. Also, in view of the high combustion rate, the boiler efficiency was well maintained as indicated by the average

evaporation rate of 7.94 lbs. of water per lb. of coal burnt.

46419 was followed by its bigger brother on the Crewe-Holyhead route when Class 4 2-6-0 43027 was tested in April 1949, surprisingly almost 18 months after the first of the class entered traffic and despite frequent reports of steaming troubles. This time the outcome was disappointing, the somewhat understated conclusion of the tests was that 'some modification to the draughting arrangement will be necessary, and further trials will be carried out with one of these engines fitted with a single blastpipe and chimney'. Less than a month later 43027 was fitted with a single blast pipe and the tests were re-run over the same

46413 wired up to the GWR Dynamometer Car at Swindon in 1950 ready for testing on the road. Note the LMS on the tender and the cage containing the pre-weighed and selected coal above the bunker.

route with the same load. It was tested with three different chimney and blast pipe arrangements between 17 and 25 May. The results were still not conclusive, because the variable quality of the coal used 'made it difficult to assess the comparative efficiency of the various blast pipe and chimney modifications'. Ironically, this was a foretaste of what would happen with the Class 2 only a few weeks later after Blackpool Central's 46413 was loaned to the Western Region in July 1949, ostensibly to assess the suitability of the class as replacements for the ageing Dean Goods 0-6-0s. It had covered 64,924 miles from new and completed a Light Intermediate repair in June, and initially operated from Didcot shed on Reading, Oxford and Swindon local trains. The outcome was not good and 'It was found that the locomotive was less suitable than the obsolescent W.R.2301 Class on certain duties demanding relatively high efforts at low speeds and high rates of evaporation at higher speeds from locomotives of limited axle loads'. 46413 was summoned to Swindon to be scrutinised by Sam Ell and his team under the auspices of the BR Locomotive Testing Committee. 'Tests on the L.M. Class 2 were initiated to find what alterations to this Class were necessary to enable them to work to best advantage under conditions of Welsh coal, and the firing technique most suitable to this coal. This arose from the experience gained from the loan to the Western Region of Engine 46413, in which Region it was assigned to the duties of the "A" Group locomotives of the Region'. Ell's team put 46413 through

their standard regime, firstly on the stationary testing plant followed by tests on the road using the Controlled Road Testing System.

46413 arrived at Swindon on 17th October 1949 for trials on the testing plant after which it was planned to undergo dynamometer car tests on the Newport-Brecon line. It was to be tested against a 50-year old 'Dean Goods' 0-6-0 2579 which was specially lined out as part of the preparations; 46413 had L.M.S. on its tender. 'It was decided to investigate the relative efficiencies and upper limits of the combustion-steam-air cycles of the two classes of locomotives on the Swindon Testing Plant, and to follow this with tests of the L.M. Class 2 on the track to confirm the efficacy of such modifications in the draughting system which might result from the Testing Plant Trials'.

46413 received some minor mechanical alterations, which included the closing of the blast pipe orifice to 4 inches, and then ran trials over the next few weeks. These took place between Swindon and Bristol rather than on the intended Neath to Brecon line because there were no suitable freight turns over the latter route. On 16 November the engine left Swindon at 7.0am light engine to Lydney (via Gloucester). From Lydney it made a trial trip over the Severn Bridge and back, at a speed restriction of 15 mph and afterwards returned light to Swindon. On 21, 22 and 23 November, 46413 hauled the 9.25am Swindon-Bristol (via Bath) stopping train due in at Bristol (Temple Meads) at 11.2am; it returned with the 1.24pm Lawrence Hill (Bristol)-Swindon

(via Badminton) stopping train. The load on the downward journey consisted of Dynamometer car W7, the booked 5-coach corridor set, and one through Paddington to Weston-super-Mare parcels van, a total of around 216 tons. On 24 November 46413 hauled the 12.5pm Stoke-Gifford Moreton Cutting freight train with 39 loaded wagons and the Dynamometer car.

Following further sessions on the Swindon testing plant by the 'Dean Goods', 46413 was again on the plant on 16 December having previously run further freight trials between Swindon and Gloucester on 10 and 11 December 1949. Up to the end of the year, it had covered 6,447 miles while on loan to the Western Region.

In its original condition with self-cleaning plates 46413 achieved an evaporation rate of 9,050 lb/hour compared with the 'Dean Goods' 13,700 lb/hour on both Bedwas (South Wales) and Blidworth coal. Reducing the blast pipe orifice by ¼in and removing the self-cleaning plates increased this to 11,600 lb/hour. 'The original blastpipe was restored and the chimney remodelled on the obviously superior proportions of the W.R. engine'. This produced a slightly better output – 12,300 lb/hour with Bedwas coal and 14,000 lb/hour with Blidworth, without the self-cleaning plates, and 10,600 lb/hour and 11,200 lb/hour with them. The report noted 'the most economical working range of the Class 2 corresponds to steaming rates between 8,000 and 11,000 lb/hour' so that while keeping the self-cleaning plates 'the improved chimney proportions make it

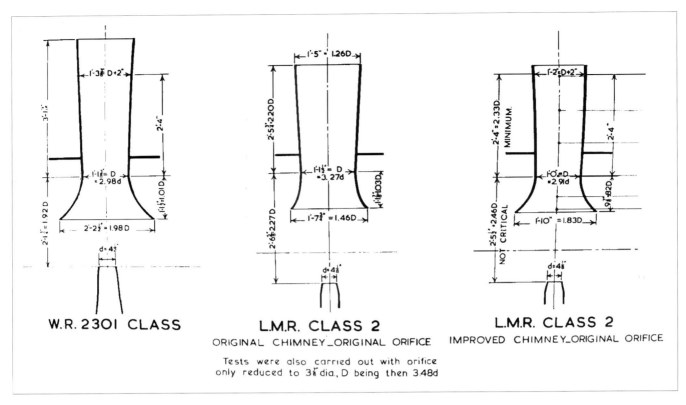

W.R. 2301 CLASS

L.M.R. CLASS 2
ORIGINAL CHIMNEY–ORIGINAL ORIFICE

L.M.R. CLASS 2
IMPROVED CHIMNEY–ORIGINAL ORIFICE

Tests were also carried out with orifice
only reduced to 3⅞in dia, D being then 3.48d

In its original condition with self-cleaning plates 46413 achieved an evaporation rate of 9,050 lb/hour compared with the Dean Goods' 13,700 lb/hour. Reducing the blast pipe orifice by ¼in and removing the self-cleaning plates increased this to 11,600 lb/hour. The original blastpipe was then restored and the chimney remodelled on the proportions of the Dean Goods which further improved the output.

Swindon's boffins watch 46413 on the Testing Plant in 1950 after its draughting had been improved by changing the chimney proportions.

After tests on the stationary plant 46413 worked test trains out on the line with the WR Dynamometer Car in August 1950. On the first day with a train of 15 coaches (455 tons) it attained a speed of 40mph on 1 in 300 rising gradients between Little Somerford and Badminton and 70mph on 1 in 300 falling gradients with a continuous steaming rate of nearly 14,000lb/hour.

possible to work freely to the upper limit of this range'.

There were no reports in the contemporary press while this was going at the plant and the next reference to the tests was not until August 1950. 46413 emerged from Swindon to work test trains on 23, 24, and 25. On the first day, 'The efficacy of the improved draught arrangements was confirmed by practical demonstration when, without difficulty, a train of 15 coaches [455 tons] attained a speed of 40 m.p.h. on 1 in 300 rising gradients [between Little Somerford and Badminton] and 70 m.p.h. on 1 in 300 falling gradients with a continuous steaming rate of nearly 14,000lb/hour'. The loads were reduced on the second and third day.

The final verdict from Swindon was that *The existing chimney should be modified…so that, by improvement in draughting efficiency, a high proportion of the potential capacity of the boiler is made available and rates of evaporation are made possible that will cover the whole of the useful and efficient operating range of the locomotive, especially in view of the draught*

requirements of South Wales coals and restrictions imposed by self cleaning plates in the smokebox of a small boiler. The locomotive will then meet the requirements specified for the Western Region 'A' Group locomotives as regards available evaporative capacity'. The second recommendation was 'For maximum load on the steepest gradients to conform to those specified for the Group 'A' locomotives, the diameter of the cylinders needs increasing by ½" to 16½". The increase in available evaporative capacity made possible by the improved draught arrangements enables the boiler to serve the larger cylinders.

46413 finally returned to Blackpool Central in w/e 9/9/50. The recommended changes were incorporated in the 2-6-0s built in 1951/2 at Darlington (46465-46502) and 1952/3 at Swindon (46503-46527), so it can only be assumed that Swindon was happy with the modified design. The 2-6-2Ts built from September 1951 onwards incorporated the same changes, and the tractive effort of both classes was increased from 17,400 to 18,510lbs per sq.in as a result.

The chimneys of the 2-6-0s 46400-46464 were subsequently modified at a cost of £36 each under Job 5599 with financial authority WO/R1340, but those on the 2-6-2Ts, 41200-41289, were not altered. Although the Job was opened on 12 February 1951 and recorded as complete on 3 April 1959, the Engine History Cards show 46424 as the first engine dealt with, in May 1952, and 46451 the last in February 1957. A possible explanation comes from the fitting of a stovepipe chimney to 46424 as photographed at Widnes on 24 April 1951; it was in Crewe Works from 25 October until 18 November 1950 and it seems likely that it was modified then which was subsequently changed to the more aesthetically pleasing version in 1952.

46522 at Banbury in 1966. Note the prominent springs and guard irons on the pony truck, the elongated slot for the coupling, painted 2D Banbury shed code; also Swindon pattern of lamp irons which were angled rather than straight like the LMS type. www.rail-online.co.uk

2. The Devil in the Detail

The Class 2 2-6-0s had a relatively short life, lasting an average of 15½ years, and although no radical alterations were made, unlike their Fowler and Stanier predecessors with their frequent changes of boiler and tender, there were a number of minor detail differences and subtle livery variations for the engine picker to while away those long winter evenings.

Boiler and smokebox

Apart from the stovepipe chimney on 46424, three chimney styles were eventually used on the class. The second type was taller and thinner than the original type on 6400-46464 and was used on the first 25 Darlington built engines from new, 46465 to 46490. The third chimney was basically a taller version of the original with a resultant improvement in appearance and was fitted, at building, to all those from 46491 onwards and as a modification on those up to 46464; this last variant also appeared later, on some of the engines built with tall thin chimneys. The height from rail level as built was 12ft 5⅜in for 46400-46464 and 12ft 9½in for 46491 onwards; the Engine Record Cards show the height for 46465-46490 as unchanged from 46400-46464 but clearly this is incorrect.

The wing type of clack valve in the top feed of the LMS built engines proved unsatisfactory in service due to a tendency to stick open and was replaced from 46420 onwards by a standard type of valve and cage which was distinguishable by its raised cover. These were subsequently fitted to most of the earlier engines.

The Swindon-built engines, 46503-46527, had ejectors with GWR pattern control valves fitted to the tops of the ejector bodies and an additional short exhaust pipe to the smokebox, probably to reduce back-pressure in the exhaust.

Cab

Despite the relatively small size of the engines, the tender cab gave good protection from the elements when running tender-first or when standing waiting in an exposed location.

The crew accessed the cab via steps on the tender frame and then through spring-loaded folding doors leading on to the footplate; there was a conventional fall plate covering the gap between the engine and tender.

The cab layout followed current LMS practice and was similar to the contemporary Black 5s. Immediately in front of the driver was the reversing screw above which were mounted the large and small ejector valves, and a standard LMS vacuum controlled steam brake valve was located within easy reach of his right hand. The steam manifold which was above the boiler inside the cab supplied all the auxiliary equipment other than the blower. On the fireman's side were the boiler pressure and carriage warming apparatus pressure gauges while the driver only had the vacuum gauge. There were two standard LMS water gauges with combined shut-off cocks and hollow sliding firedoors with a small flip-up combustion plate below.

A large box section tunnel was provided on the fireman's side platform at the front of the cab alongside the firebox to house the fire-irons, avoiding the need to swing them outside the cab when used.

There were two windows on each side, the rear one sliding forward to open. Draught screens were fitted between the two windows from 46420 onwards, but they were not retro-fitted to 46400-19.

Injectors

The injectors on the first twenty engines were horizontally mounted under the cab but from 46420 onwards they were positioned vertically; 46400-46419 were not modified. The 2-6-0 Drawings List shows that Davies & Metcalfe No.9 injectors were fitted to 6400-6419 and the 8mm version thereafter; 8mm cones soon replaced the 9mm cones on 6400-6419. A number of Engine Record Cards show the D&M type replaced with Gresham & Craven 8mm injectors.

The wire mesh screen which filtered the smokebox char is visible inside the smokebox. The easy access for staff at the front end both to reach the smokebox and to get at the pistons shows up well in this picture.

especially compared to some other classes. Sand was delivered at the front ahead of the leading coupled wheels, and at the rear, behind the intermediate coupled wheels.

Guard irons
6400-46464 had prominent life guards (guard irons) attached to the front frames. On 46465 onwards, smaller guard irons were instead fixed to the pony truck. This kept them at a more constant height and position above the rail at all times. Some of the early engines were modified to this pattern during overhaul at Darlington; those confirmed are 46400, 46409, 46413, 46438, 46450, 46451, 46453, 46460, 46461 and 46463.

Snowploughs
A number of the 2-6-0s which took over from the LNWR 18in Goods 'Cauliflower' 0-6-0s working on the Cockermouth Keswick & Penrith line were fitted in the winter with No. 3A type snowploughs. These were designed to clear drifts between 5ft and 8ft deep and the engines involved were given strengthened pony truck springs to carry the 1½ ton weight of these large steel ploughs; they also had two 4in diameter holes bored in the bufferbeam behind the buffers and two thrust strips welded on top of the buffer beam with the platform plate cut away to accommodate them. Five engines were called in specially to Crewe Works and modified to take these ploughs in January and February 1954: 46449, 46455, 46488, 46489 and 46491.

Some of the class working from Darlington across to Penrith also had smaller nose type ploughs, eg 46475, which were fitted to the underside of the bufferbeam. With these, the engines could run through small drifts whilst hauling normal trains, or as patrolling light engines, preventing the build-up of snow drifts which would otherwise cause a complete blockage if traffic ceased; they were not intended to tackle snow deeper than 18 to 24 inches., but the type of plough was not specified.

Cow catcher
A cow catcher was fitted to 46460 at Inverurie in January 1952 for use on the Fraserburgh to St. Combs Light Railway in Scotland which was unfenced and required the locomotives to be equipped with catchers. It was attached via three unequal sized steel plates fixed to the front bufferbeam; there was a similar catcher on the tender.

Lamp brackets
The engines built at Swindon for the Western Region had GWR pattern lamp brackets instead of the LMS type on the earlier engines. The angle iron over which the lamp dropped was turned at 90° compared with the LM version.

Also, from late-1963 the upper lamp bracket was, for safety reasons when

The front end of 46406 at Huddersfield on 11 September 1964 illustrating a number of details on the 2-6-0s. From left to right, the 'Turplat' no-weld buffers with footsteps on the top, frame-mounted guard irons, open footsteps, Stanier pattern pony truck wheel, cylinder drain pipes and concave type sandbox lid. R.J. Essery.

Crossheads
The most significant modification applied to the class was the replacement of fabricated crossheads by cast steel crossheads on all the Crewe and Darlington built engines under Job 5746 at a net cost of £76 per each; those from Swindon had the cast steel pattern from new. The first engine dealt with was 46414 in May 1953 and the last was 46497 in August 1958.

Lubrication
There was a 'Silvertown' mechanical lubricator on the footplate on each side of the engine, over the leading coupled wheels. The one on the right hand-side fed the axleboxes and that on the left-hand side the cylinders and motion.

Sanding
There were only two sandboxes on either side; those at the front fitted between the frames and, were filled by the usual tube extension with a concave pattern lid while those at the rear were very noticeable, standing proud of the platform, which made filling easy,

Left. The wing type of clack valve in the top feed of the earlier LMS built engines proved unsatisfactory in service due to a tendency to stick open and was replaced from 46420 onwards by a standard type of valve and cage which was distinguishable by its raised cover as shown by 46458 at Upperby on 9 July 1966. The 'Silvertown' mechanical lubricator on the left-hand side lubricated the cylinders and motion. D.P. Rowland.

6402 has the wing type of clack valve in the top feed which had rounded covers as on all of the LMS-built engines. The injectors on the first twenty were horizontally mounted under the cab.

There is no record of the fitting of this stovepipe chimney to 46424 pictured at Widnes on 27 April 1951 but is seems likely that it was connected with the revised draughting arrangements applied to the class after the trials of 46413 at Swindon in 1950. According to the Engine History Cards, 46424 was the first engine to be fitted with the new pattern of chimney and it may be a plain trial version of that chimney. H.C. Casserley, courtesy M. Casserley.

Motion bracket, slidebars and crosshead of 46404 on 9 July 1961 at Kettering. Compare this to the inside motion of the 0-6-0 classes which the Ivatt engines replaced and it is easy to see why they were welcomed enthusiastically by both footplate and maintenance staff. www.rail-online.co.uk

Detail on the right-hand side of the engine and tender. On the footplate is the long box section fire-iron tunnel which avoided the need to swing the irons outside the cab when used. There were two sandboxes on either side; those at the front fitted between the frames and were filled by the usual tube extension with a concave pattern lid while those at the rear were very noticeable, standing proud of the platform, which made filling easy, especially compared to some other classes. Sand was delivered at the front ahead of the leading coupled wheels, and at the rear, behind the intermediate coupled wheels. The tender cab was another feature which made life better for crews when working tender first or waiting around on local freight or station pilot work. 46520 was one of the engines painted in lined green by Swindon complete with an 'A' below the number to indicate the power group. www.rail-online.co.uk

Still gleaming after from a Heavy General overhaul at Crewe completed on 27 June, 46404 is back at its Kettering home on 9 July 1961. It arrived in January 1947, a few weeks after it was built, and remained there until transferred to Nottingham in March 1963. Crewe Works had not bothered with straightening the rather bent bars protecting the rear tender cab window. The pipework under the cab leads from the horizontally mounted injector, a feature of the first twenty engines. www.rail-online.co.uk

46504 at Swindon Works, probably during a HI 12/5-17/7/56 since it was built in unlined black and there is no sign of lining on the cab side. It has the later pattern of vertically mounted injector. Also visible are the draught screen between the two side windows, the front one fixed and the rear one sliding, the fallplate and the side doors, the intermediate buffing plates, tender coupling and the simple footsteps at each side. www.rail-online.co.uk

working under overhead live wires, moved down to the right of the central door fastening. The central lamp bracket above the bufferbeam was also moved to the right to remain directly underneath it. This only applied to a few engines; examples confirmed are 46412, 46517 and 46520.

Overhead line warning flashes
With the onset of electrification from around 1960 'electric overhead' warning flashes, white enamel plates with the symbolic warning sign of forked lightning (in red), were fixed to those parts nearest to where footplate crews could come into contact with overhead wires.

Generally, these were on the front framing, firebox shoulders with two at the top of the tender backplate; 46467 and 46468 also had them on the sides of the tender cab and 46468 had them on cab front too. 46451 and 46469 managed to sport just single plates on their steam pipe covers. A number of engines, including 46420, 46426, 46440, 46449, 46452, 46488, 46492, 46504 and 46508, had an extra set near the top feed.

ATC and AWS
The engines from Swindon, 46503-46527, were built with GWR pattern ATC – the only visible external evidence of this was the rectangular battery box below the left-hand platform immediately in front of the cab.

The BR version, titled more accurately as AWS (Automatic Warning System rather than Automatic Train Control), was fitted to at least 17 North Eastern Region engines at Darlington in early 1961; another eight were dealt with at Crewe for LMR based engines, but not until 1963. It used a magnetic induction system whereas the GWR system operated by physical contact between the engine and a ramp between the tracks.

The receiver was mounted between the pony truck frames and therefore did not have a protection guard attached to the buffer beam. The cylindrical vacuum and timing reservoirs were on the left-hand platform immediately in front of the cab and the rectangular battery box was in the corresponding position on the left-hand side. The recorded cost was £302 per engine.

Tenders
The tenders had a 13ft wheelbase, equally divided, a bunker carrying 4tons of coal and a rectangular 3,000 gallon water tank with straight sides. They weighed 37tons 3cwt in running order and had an axle loading of 13tons 15cwt on the front, 12tons 5cwt on the intermediate and 11tons 3cwt on the rear axle. The most distinctive feature, and one that was referred to in the LMS publicity material issued to the trade press, were the almost rectangular-shaped tanks and narrow, inset, rectangular bunkers which gave good visibility when working tender-first. Protection for the crew from inclement weather when running backwards was provided by tender cabs, producing almost a tank engine-like enclosure.

The tender fronts had equipment lockers, water feed and brake handles, water feed cock handles and steam brake cylinder lubrication. The rectangular-shaped side air vents faced outward, to ensure that any overflow went down the tender side. All had sieve boxes on each side of the frames, Carriage Warming Apparatus and water pick-up gear. The first eighteen tenders of the Darlington built engines, 46465-82, were fitted with water scoop uptakes but this was blanked off because no external water scoop fittings were carried. However, the last twenty tenders from the same works did have the full arrangement of water-scoop gear.

The tenders were numbered 7000-7127 and were attached in numerical

The cab layout followed current LMS practice and was similar to the contemporary Black 5s. Immediately in front of the driver was the reversing screw above which were mounted the large and small ejector valves, and a standard LMS vacuum controlled steam brake valve was located within easy reach of his right hand. The steam manifold which was above the boiler inside the cab supplied all the auxiliary equipment other than the blower. On the fireman's side were the boiler pressure and carriage warming apparatus pressure gauges while the driver only had the vacuum gauge. There were two standard LMS water gauges with combined shut-off cocks and hollow sliding firedoors with a small flip-up combustion plate below. Note the large box section tunnel on the fireman's side to house the fire-irons, avoiding the need to swing them outside the cab when used.

Below. After 46460 was transferred to Kittybrewster in January 1952 to replace former GER Class F4 2-4-2Ts on the St. Combs branch. It was equipped at Inverurie Works with a cow catcher attached via three unequal sized steel plates fixed to the front bufferbeam. For some reason, the one on the left was around a third of the width of the bufferbeam and the one on the right was only a few inches wide. 46460, at Fraserburgh soon after its transfer, still has a Haymarket 64A shedplate. www.rail-online.co.uk

Left. Tender No. 7060 paired with 46460 also had a cow catcher for working the Fraserburgh to St Combs Light Railway. Unlike the one at the front of the engine, this catcher was attached to the bufferbeam by two equal sized plates. This was one of the last tenders built with a long ladder and without vertical handrails at the rear of the tank sides. www.rail-online.co.uk

Some working from Darlington to Penrith were fitted with small nose ploughs mounted beneath the bufferbeam, including 46475 at its home shed on 23 April 1961. These allowed them to run through small drifts, or when patrolling light engine, preventing the build-up of snow drifts which would otherwise cause a complete blockage if traffic ceased; they were not intended to tackle snow deeper than about two feet.

Five were modified in 1954 with strengthened pony truck springs and thrust strips on top of the bufferbeam so they could work with the 1½ ton No.3A snowploughs used on the Cockermouth Keswick & Penrith line. These were still in use during the 1960s as shown by 46455 at Tebay, some time after it had been fitted with AWS in February 1963. M. Bentley.

The tender of 6400 when new, showing the part-welded construction of the tanks and the long ladder stretching down to the bottom edge of the frames. The rectangular maker's plate shows this was tender No.7000 built in 1946. The oval plate below shows the water capacity, at 3,000 gallons.

The tender from 46400 in Crewe Works on 5 October 1952, illustrating the earlier type of tender floor mounting with the flat vertical ends on the first twenty tenders. This picture shows clearly the tender cab, the sieve box mounted on the frames between the front and intermediate axles, the shovelling plate and toolboxes. The operating handles for the hand brake, on the left of the picture, and for the water scoop on the right, were mounted on cast iron columns. W. Potter.

order of the engines; most kept their original tenders, but some were changed during Heavy General or Intermediate overhauls, and latterly at withdrawal; over 20 changes were recorded.

Over the course of the various batches there were a number of minor variations. The tender cab floor mounting was changed, probably for safety reasons, from a vertical edge inset above the top footstep on the first twenty tenders, built with 6400-6419, to a 'waisted-in' shape on all subsequent engines.

The tenders built at Crewe (Nos.7000-64) had a long ladder on the rear of the tank which reached to the bottom of the frames, and no vertical grab rail. The ladders were shortened to platform level on the Darlington and Swindon built tenders (from No.7065 onwards, paired with engines 46465-46527) and a vertical handrail was added to the rear end of the tank sides with footsteps on the frame below it.

The step at the front end of the frames was a rather lightweight fabricated construction. The London Midland Region replaced these with a more substantial wider and deeper type under

Job 5699 WO/R3672 (16/12/53-29/11/62) but this was not done on the tenders operated by other Regions. Extension plates were fitted to the coal bunker access doors under Job 5793 WO/R7331 (11/7/57-1/4/63).

The tenders built by the LMS had 'LMS' on the top line of the rectangular tender number plates and those built after nationalisation 'M' in the same position. The capacity plates below were oval.

A cow catcher was fitted to tender No.7060 running with 46460 for use on the Fraserburgh to St. Combs Light Railway in Scotland.

Liveries

When built, all of the class was painted black, with a variety of different embellishments of insignia and lining, which varied both between batches and

then over time. The first twenty were in LMS livery but later engines carried a mix of styles as British Railways decided on their standard liveries; Swindon added its own variants and Darlington naturally added a few LNER touches to their engines.

6400-6419 emerged in plain black LMS 1946 livery which had pale straw-coloured sans serif 12½in letters and 10in numbers with inset maroon lining and maroon edging and a scroll and serif smokebox numberplate. Since they had been ordered as freight locomotives they were given the 2F power classification, which was positioned immediately below the cab windows and above the cab number. Most, if not all, ran for a time with LMS lettering on the tender after receiving their BR 40000 numbers.

The first ten of the BR built engines, 46420-46429, were unlined and had cab numerals in the final BR pattern, cream Gill Sans 8in high, and the tenders were adorned with 'BRITISH RAILWAYS' in 8in Gill Sans letters. Also appearing for the first time on this batch were the standard Gill Sans smokebox number

Nos.		Built by	Lining	Cab no.	Power classification	Smokebox plate	Tender insignia
6400	6419	Crewe	No	LMS 1946	2F- below window	Scroll & serif	LMS
46420	46429	Crewe	No	8in Gill Sans	2F - above number	Gill Sans	BRITISH RAILWAYS
46430	46434	Crewe	Yes	8in Gill Sans	2 - above number	Gill Sans	BRITISH RAILWAYS
46435	46464	Crewe	Yes	8in Gill Sans	2 - above number	Gill Sans	Small BR emblem
46465	46502	Darlington	Yes	10in Gill Sans	2MT on bufferbeam	Gill Sans	Small BR emblem
46503	46506	Swindon	No	8in Gill Sans	2 - above number	Gill Sans	Small BR emblem
46509	46527	Swindon	Yes	8in Gill Sans	2 - above number	Gill Sans	Small BR emblem

Tender Nos.		Date		Built	Engine Nos.		Cab floorplate	Ladder	Rear steps and vertical handrail
7000	7019	Dec-46	Mar-47	Crewe	6400	6419	Rectangular foothold	Long	No
7020	7064	Nov-48	Jun-50	Crewe	46420	46464			
7065	7102	Jun-51	Mar-52	Darlington	46465	46502	Curved foothold	Short	Yes
7103	7127	Nov-52	Mar-53	Swindon	46503	46527			

The tender cab gave complete protection to the crew while, unlike the earlier Fowler and Stanier tenders with their full width bunkers, the narrow bunker afforded good rearward visibility through the two large windows and avoided the driver having to lean out of the side of his cab when running tender-first. The layout followed existing LMS practice with toolboxes above the shovelling plate and the operating handles for the hand brake, on the left, and for the water scoop on the right; these were mounted on cast iron columns. Note the intermediate buffers between tender and engine on the front dragbox.

Below. Tender No.7002 at Bescot in the early 1960s coupled to 46429. It had been built with 6402 and still has the long ladder at the rear end but has been modified with the more substantial front footstep. The shed cat seems unconcerned. www.rail-online.co.uk

46500 is paired with tender No.7107 at Derby on 27 May 1961. The later type of tender introduced with the Darlington-built engines in 1951 had a short rear ladder with a vertical handrail on the rear of the tank sides and front footsteps.

plates. The final five engines of the batch, 46430-46434, were lined out in the new British Railways mixed traffic livery of black, lined grey, cream and red in LNWR style as the 2-6-0s were now officially recognised as mixed traffic engines. The power classification was changed from 2F to a plain '2', placed immediately above the number. The lining on the cab sides and tender was, from the outside, grey $^5/_8$ in wide, cream $^1/_8$in, a gap of 1 $^5/_8$in and then a $^1/_4$in red line. Boiler bands were $^1/_4$in on each side and there were pairs of twin vertical lines of the same size on the outer edges of the cylinder casings; however, the footplate angle was too narrow to be lined.

The 8in cab numerals and tender lettering continued on 46430 and 46431, but there was a change to 6in lettering with 46432-46434. By the time the next batch entered traffic, starting with 46435 in January 1950, the smaller version of the new BR 'lion on a wheel' emblem replaced the lettering on the tender; all other details remained the same. The remaining Crewe-built engines up to 46464 were outshopped in this style, and the emblem was applied to 46400-46434 during subsequent repaints.

When Darlington started building the class in mid-1951 there were two noticeable changes. Firstly, the size of the cab numbers increased to 10in and secondly the '2' power classification was omitted from the cab side and replaced by 2MT on the bufferbeam, LNER style.

There was an unexpected reversion to unlined black when the first engines emerged from Swindon, for at least 46503-46506. 46509 onwards were lined but it is uncertain whether 46507 and 46508 were originally lined.

every engine repaired in green if it could be considered as mixed traffic or above. The table shows those known to have received green livery, the tender emblem or crest used and the date and works where it was applied.

No.	Unlined green	Lined green	Works	Tender
46504		31/7/59	Caerphilly	Small crest
* 46505		29/1/60	Wolverhampton	Small crest
46509		28/3/57	Swindon	Emblem
46515		22/1/60	Caerphilly	Small crest
46517		3/1/58	Swindon	Small crest
46518		2/12/59	Swindon	Small crest
46519	14/3/60		Caerphilly	Large crest
46520		28/9/59	Swindon	Small crest
46521		20/4/56	Swindon	Emblem
46521		25/9/59	Caerphilly	Small crest
46522		12/5/59	Swindon	Small crest
46523		27/11/59	Wolverhampton	Small crest
46525		11/10/57	Swindon	Small crest
46526		28/11/56	Swindon	Small crest
46527		18/11/60	Wolverhampton	Small crest
* 46505 is assumed to have been painted in green but photographs in the 1960s are not sufficiently clear to confirm this, and it may have remained in unlined black.				

From late 1956 when regional identities were allowed to flourish, the Western Region began repainting almost

When the green was lined, the bands on the cab side and tender were, working from the outside, $^1/_8$in orange,

½in green gap, 1in black, ½in green gap, ⅛in orange. Boiler bands were ⅛in orange on each side and there were pairs of twin vertical lines of the same size on the outer edges of the cylinder casings; the footplate angle was not lined.

The 'lion on a wheel' emblem used from 1950 was replaced from mid-1956 with crests approved by the College of Arms, at first with forward facing lions on each side, but after complaints from the College all lions faced left. The smaller version of the crest was used on tenders with lining and the larger size if the tender was not lined, although inevitably there were exceptions to this rule.

Engines repaired and repainted at the former LNER works exhibited further variations from the as-built condition. Darlington outshopped some engines with 8in cab numbers although for the most part continued to use its 10in cab numbers. Lining was omitted from mid-1955 on 46478 while the later unlined examples all had the large version of the post-1956 crest on the tender. Gateshead, on the other hand, used 8in numbers while retaining the lining, but with large crests.

Several lined engines also received 8in numbers in place of the 10in type when repainted at other works, and 46400 reverted to a small crest at Crewe in January 1963. From the end of 1963 when Crewe stopped lining repainted engines, these had the small version of the crest and 8in numbers. The table below shows known examples of variants of black livery detail.

Insignia and lining variations on engines painted in black					
No.	Date	Works		Cab Nos.	Tender
46400	2/5/58	Gateshead	Lined	8in	Large crest
46407	14/6/57	Darlington	Unlined	8in	Large crest
46409	14/8/59	Darlington	Unlined	10in	Large crest
46438	20/1/61	Darlington	Unlined	10in	Large crest
46450	4/4/62	Darlington	Unlined	10in	Large crest
46461	1/9/59	Darlington	Unlined	10in	Large crest
46463	29/1/60	Darlington	Unlined	10in	Large crest
46464	22/3/60	Darlington	Unlined	8in	Large crest
46465	5/6/59	Darlington	Unlined	10in	Large crest
46467	17/6/58	Darlington	Unlined	10in	Large crest
46468	24/8/57	Darlington	Unlined	10in	Large crest
46469	7/3/58	Gateshead	Lined	8in	Large crest
46473	31/8/57	Darlington	Unlined	8in	Large crest
46478	28/5/55	Darlington	Unlined	10in	Emblem
46479	10/7/58	Darlington	Unlined	10in	Large crest
46480	15/11/57	Darlington	Unlined	8in	Large crest
46482	25/9/58	Darlington	Unlined	10in	Large crest
46483	1/8/58	Darlington	Unlined	10in	Large crest
46492	14/4/64	Crewe	Unlined	8in	Small crest
46493	By 17/6/61	Darlington	Unlined	10in	?
46503	22/1/64	Crewe	Unlined	8in	Small crest

In LNER style, Cowlairs painted the allocation NEWTON HEATH on the bufferbeam of 46485 instead of a cast shedplate in August 1964. At least three other examples, albeit with no surviving record of a Cowlairs works visit, were SALTLEY on 46448, OBAN on 46468 and BOLTON on 46506.

Power Classification
From 31 October 1948 the engines were reclassified as a 'Mixed Traffic' class and

Although the first few engines built at Swindon emerged in unlined black, most of them entered traffic in what had become the standard lined black livery, as on brand new 46522 in March 1953. www.rail-online.co.uk

designated by the simple '2' power classification above the cab number; 46423-9 were changed from 2F before they left the Crewe Paint Shop by painting out the 'F'; the earlier engines were brought into line during subsequent works visits.

The engines built at Darlington, 46465-46502, had in LNER fashion, '2MT' on the front bufferbeam and nothing on the cabside. This was perpetuated by Cowlairs on a few London Midland engines repainted there and on at least one, 46485, the '2MT' appeared above the cab number.

Some of the Western Region engines had an 'A' below the cab number during the late 1950s - signifying a Group A engine – as did 46413 while on trial in 1949/50. Examples confirmed include 46509, 46517, 46519, 46520 and 46522 – all when in green livery.

Number plates
As built, 6400-6419 had LMS scroll and serif pattern smokebox number plates. When renumbered between May 1949 and June 1951, these were replaced by the BR standard Gill Sans pattern used on the remainder of the class. The

spacing of the numbers on the Darlington-built engines was slightly closer than on those from Crewe or Swindon.

Works plates
The works plates were attached to the front framing; Crewe and Derby/Swindon used standard LMS style cast iron oval plates with white letters and figures on a black background; Darlington fitted LNER pattern oval brass plates with black lettering and works numbers. 46465-46502 had works numbers 2157-2194; those up to and including 46494 were dated 1951 and 46495 onwards 1952.

Capacity plates
Oval capacity plates were fitted to the rear of the tender tank.

'SC' plates
'SC' plates to signify the Self-Cleaning equipment in the smokebox were fixed below the shedplates on the smokebox doors from new. The plates seem to have disappeared from many of the class by the 1960s, even when the equipment was not removed.

Left. 46522 at Swindon in lined green with a small crest acquired during a works visit completed in May 1959. Note also the 'A' classification code below the number and the Western Region ATC battery box under the cab; this equipment was fitted to all of the Swindon-built engines as was a GWR pattern ejector with a control valve fitted to the top of the ejector body and an additional exhaust pipe into the smokebox. www.rail-online.co.uk

Bottom left. Swindon liberally interpreted British Railways slackening of the corporate colours in the mid-1950s by repainting as many engines as possible in green. This included the Ivatt 2-6-0s, like 46521 repainted at Swindon in April 1956 in lined green but still with the early BR emblem.

46465 at Ely on 11 March 1961 had been repainted in unlined black with large 10in cab numbers during a Darlington overhaul completed in June 1959. Darlington outshopped some engines with 8in cab numbers although for the most part continued to use its 10in versions. Lining was omitted from mid-1955 on 46478 while the later unlined examples all had the large version of the post-1956 crest on the tender. H.C. Casserley, courtesy M. Casserley.

6414 in Swansea Paxton Street shed on 27 August 1948. 6414 and 6415 from Bank Hall were loaned to Swansea in December 1947 for trials, working up to Craven Arms and Shrewsbury. 6414 stayed for twelve months and 6415 for six months, but none of the class was ever allocated there again. H.C. Casserley, courtesy M. Casserley.

6417 at Bank Hall, where it had gone new, on 9 June 1949. Together with 6416 it was loaned to the Eastern Region in June and July 1948, based at Stratford.

3. Here, there and (almost) everywhere

During their relatively short lives, the class worked on all BR Regions except the Southern although the majority were naturally allocated to London Midland Region sheds. Those built for the other Regions stayed on their original territories for most of their days, but those which were not withdrawn there after they were displaced by line closures or dieselisation ended their days on the LMR. Examples of the class were allocated to more than 120 different sheds during their lifetime. Their workings did not attract the attention from enthusiasts that the more glamorous express classes received but it is possible to put together a reasonable picture of their operations over the years.

Early days - up to nationalisation

The original twenty engines were transferred around during their first few months in service, on loan to various sheds, to try them out on different duties and types of work. They were sent to places such as Bank Hall, Coventry, Low Moor, Stafford and Stockport during the early months of 1947. Almost without exception, once these loans had completed, all twenty remained at their permanent allocations for many years thereafter.

The first five went to the Midland Division and the other fifteen to the Central Division. 6400 had two spells at Derby before moving to Kettering in August 1947 having been there on loan during March and April. The only mentions of it in the contemporary press were when it piloted Black 5 5280 out of Birmingham New Street with a Bradford-Bristol express on 31 January 1947, and on 19 April it was noted taking seven coaches and a van up the Lickey Incline, banked by a single Jinty 0-6-0T.

More attention was paid to the other Midland Division engines. 6401 and 6402 were at Kentish Town for their first six weeks in service and worked between St. Pancras and Southend on duties normally handled by Stanier 2-6-2Ts. 6401 was first noted on 2 January 1947 on the 2.55 pm from St. Pancras, returning on the 6.2 pm from Southend, and it worked this turn for the rest of the week. The next week 6402 was on this duty, while 6401 worked the 9.27 am St. Pancras-Southend returning tender first on the 11.50 a.m. from Southend. Trials were carried out on 5 January with 6401 on a 3F 0-6-0 freight working but they were not conclusive. 6401 and 6402 filled in their time on empty coaching duties at St. Pancras. They were transferred to Sheffield Millhouses in w/e 18 January where they were employed mainly on local freight and trip work.

One of the most significant allocations was to Kettering, beginning with 6404 in w/e 11 January. It was used mainly on passenger trains to Cambridge, Gretton and Northampton. Next came 6400 on loan at the end of February. The new 2-6-0s clearly fitted the bill because by the middle of the year 6401-6403 arrived to complete the set of five. They took over the service to Huntingdon and Cambridge from ex-Midland Railway Johnson 2F 0-6-0s. All five remained at the shed for many years, with 46403 and 46404 not leaving until 1963.

On the Central Division, 6405-6407 were first allocated to Goole and were joined by 6408 in June 1947 which moved from Wakefield where it had gone from new with 6409. 6405 and 6406 were soon transferred away to Farnley Junction in March, but 6407 and 6408 were to stay there until the 1960s, the former never being allocated to any other shed. 6410-6413 went to Blackpool, 6414-6417 to Bank Hall and Newton Heath had the last two, 6418 and 6419. 6414 and 6415 were loaned to Swansea Paxton Street in December 1947 for trials, working up to Craven Arms and Shrewsbury, and were reported 'most satisfactory'; 6414 stayed for twelve months and 6415 for six months, but no members of the class were ever allocated there again.

Several of these engines were observed south of Crewe on loan before they moved to the Central Division sheds. 6405 was at Coventry on 17

An impressively clean 46406 with a parcels train at Leeds City on 25 June 1949. It had been renumbered the previous month during a Light Intermediate repair at Crewe, although it retained LMS lettering on the tender. 46406 was originally allocated to Goole, moving to Farnley Junction in March 1947; it was transferred to Bank Hall at the end of the year. G.H. Hunt, ColourRail

46495 at Kettering on 30 March 1959. It had been allocated there from new in 1952 and stayed for nine years before moving to Derby. Its train is the usual three-coach set used for the Cambridge service.

December 1946 heading the 4.35 pm Coventry-Nuneaton and was reported to be working from Stafford. 6413 was seen in Coventry carriage sidings on 15 February 1947, also working the 4.35 pm to Nuneaton. It had a 5C (Stafford) shed-plate although it was never formally allocated there.

6405, 6407 and 6408 worked from Mirfield during week ending 21 December 1946. 6408 then went to Wakefield, its permanent allocation, from where it was used on the Barnsley branch. On 18 December 6409 was on shunting duties at Holmes Chapel, and on 20 December it worked into Manchester (London Road) on a local from Crewe. 6405, 6408 and 6409 were then noted on trial trips with passenger workings in and out of Bradford (Exchange). 6405 was in Stockport (Edgeley) on 18 February 1947, and was understood to be on loan there, but this was not formally recorded.

6406 was at Southport on 2 January 1947 working Preston and Wigan trains, and on 4 January it took the 7.35 am Southport-Rochdale train, returning with the 12.30 pm Rochdale-Southport express. 6407 worked into Southport on the 1.2 pm Padiham-Southport train, a Rose Grove duty, on 11 and 18 January. On 13 January 6406 and 6407 were both seen at Manchester Victoria, 6406 shunting coaches in the local platforms and 6407 passing through light towards Exchange.

6413, allocated to Blackpool, worked the 8.42 am Halifax-Blackpool express from Accrington on several occasions, although the Blackpool engines were normally confined to Blackpool-

Fleetwood, Lytham and Kirkham trains. 6414/5/7 were noted in the Liverpool (Exchange) area working local goods turns and on station pilot and empty carriage stock duties.

The authorities were naturally keeping a close watch over their new 2-6-0s and 2-6-2Ts and an internal LMS memorandum dated 19 June 1947 stated: *The new 2-6-0 and 2-6-2 engines have now become established at the sheds to which they are allocated and below are observations of a general nature on the class of work these engines are now being utilised for.*

The performance at all depots has been highly satisfactory, and during my visits to the sheds I have received no adverse comments that the engines were unable to fully meet the demands of the Operating Department.

At certain sheds however, owing to the nature of traffic requirements and the booked power diagrammed to work these trains, the turns available for the new engines are sharply limited. It cannot therefore be regarded that full advantage is being obtained from these engines.

I find at Sheffield the two 2-6-0 engines are being relegated to unimportant work such as ballast trains and local trips, and in many cases are only running 40 miles per day. These jobs could be worked by any engine that is in a run-down condition, or engines that require a period of breaking in under light and easy conditions of running after attention on the wheel drop, etc.

At Derby shed the two 2-6-2 engines are almost confined daily to station shunting and trip work, and I am of the opinion that much better use could be made of these two engines at Tredegar, Abergavenny or Bangor where the 2-6-2 engines which are

allocated are giving such excellent service.

The one 2-6-0 engine working at Kettering is a good example of the class of work where these engines are being satisfactorily utilised. In this instance the engine is working daily passenger trains and is running two double trips between Kettering and Cambridge and return. The reduced time required for shed duties between trips for these engines has enabled an improved working to be arranged locally, for the booked workings provide for two Class 2 0-6-0 freight engines to work three single trips only.

Considerable benefit would be obtained if the complete passenger service between Kettering and Cambridge was worked by the new 2-6-0 engines and to enable this to be done one more engine is required. Heated bearings on the 0-6-0 Class 2 engines working these trains is a very frequent trouble, and during the dry summer season line-side fires are frequently started due to the emission of sparks thrown out by these engines on the heavy up-hill gradients on this section of the line.

I find that full availability is being obtained from the new engines at certain sheds, for 'X' repairs and washing out is arranged to be done on Sundays.

Certain defects have developed on the new engines which have influenced availability. The major trouble has been due to leakage and steam blows from rivets in the dome base, dome cover joint, safety valve joints, and top feed casting joint. These defects are common to all 30 engines, and in order to correct these defects the engines require to be taken out of service for two or more days. The leaking rivets in the dome base appear to be the most serious trouble for on several instances repeated caulking has been carried out but without permanent results.

Minor troubles have also been experienced, these are twin type top feed clacks sticking and blowing through. Broken air valves, and rocking grate operating levers becoming defective. All these matters are in hand and have received attention.

The modifications that require to be carried out at the sheds on M. P. Order No. 214 have now been completed on all the 30 engines other than the fitting of 8 m/m injector cones. Six engines only have been fitted and we are now waiting further supplies from the Makers. Particulars are attached giving the approximate mileage these engines are running weekly, and the total miles run since new to present date. The Farnley Junction example below shows the type of work that the class was typically employed on at this time:

Workings after Nationalisation

45 engines (46420-46464) were built at Crewe after nationalisation. Of the first forty, 25 went new to the Western Division, the first permanently allocated there, five to the Central and fifteen to the Midland (left). The final five of the 45 from Crewe, 46460-46464, were built for the Scottish Region. The LMR received a further twenty, 46483-46502, in 1951/2 from the Darlington batch (below).

Western Division	
Widnes	46420-46424
Bescot	46425-46427
Preston	46428-46430
Willesden	46431-46434
Workington	46447-46448 *, 46456-46458 *
Penrith	46449, 46455, 46459 *
Coventry	46445, 46446 *
Central Division	
Blackpool Central	46435
Fleetwood	46436-46439
Midland Division	
Skipton	46440, 46442
Lancaster Green Ayre	46441
Derby	46443-46444, 46454
Sheffield Grimesthorpe	46450-46451
Manningham	46452-46453

* Initially allocated to Crewe North for a few weeks

LONDON MIDLAND REGION
West Midlands

Although *The Railway Observer* of December 1946 quoted a 'tentative allocation' of five engines to Bournville in place of the Kirtley double-framed 0-6-0s on the Halesowen branch, these never arrived and the only engine allocated

Engine No.	Depot	Approx. weekly mileage	Approx. miles to date
6400	Derby	800	13,000
6401	Sheffield	500	11,000
6402	Sheffield	500	9,000
6403	Derby	850	13,500
6404	Kettering	1,200	23,948
6405	Farnley Jct	800	16,000
6406	Farnley Jct	800	15,600
6407	Goole	1,000	14,500
6408	Goole	700	13,500
6409	Wakefield	750	13,700
6410	Blackpool	700	12,000
6411	Blackpool	700	12,000
6412	Blackpool	700	12,000
6413	Blackpool	700	12,000
6414	Bank Hall	600	11,000
6415	Bank Hall	600	11,000
6416	Bank Hall	600	11,000
6417	Bank Hall	600	11,000
6418	Newton Heath	650	10,000
6419	Newton Heath	650	10,000

Central Division	
Blackpool Central	46483
Newton Heath	46484-46487
Western Division	
Workington	46488, 46491
Preston	46489
Bescot	46490
Aston	46492
Midland Division	
Burton	46493, 46494
Kettering	46495, 46496
Holbeck	46497, 46498
Toton	46499, 46500
Nottingham	46501, 46502

there was 46400, for a few weeks in summer 1953. Instead, Bescot was the first West Midlands shed to have any of the 2-6-0s on its books when 46425-46427 went there from new in December 1948; they were joined by another new engine, 46490 in November 1951. 46445 and 46446 were delivered to Coventry in early 1950, and Aston acquired 46427 from Bescot together with newly built 46492 in 1951.

The Bescot engines replaced ex-L&NWR Webb 0-6-0s, but there were few contemporary reports of their activities. In early 1950 46425 was noted as a fairly frequent replacement for the usual Walsall 2-6-4T on the 1.20pm Birmingham-Rugeley (Trent Valley), and 46426 and 46427 similarly deputised on the 11.4am Lichfield-Birmingham. On 8 August, 46425 was noted on the 5.15pm 'Sutton Express' from New Street to Lichfield, first stop at Wylde Green, working the train tender-first; three minutes were lost by signal checks (including two dead stands) as far as Aston, but although 'working easily and quietly' the engine lost no time after that point, at least as far as Four Oaks. The 7.54am from Worcester to York was worked as far as

2-6-0 ENGINE WORKINGS - FARNLEY JUNCTION			
14 TURN			
Light engine	5.45 a.m.	Shed - Leeds City South	5.50 a.m.
Passenger	6.20 a.m.	Leeds City South – Lockwood	7.19 a.m.
Empty Carriage	8.05 a.m.	Lockwood - Huddersfield	8.10 a.m.
Passenger	8.30 a.m.	Huddersfield - Leeds City South	9.16 a.m.
Light engine	9.45 a.m.	Leeds City South - Copley Hill	9.53 a.m.
Freight	10.15 a.m.	Copley Hill - Leeds Goods	10.20 a.m.
		Test Vacuum Stock	
Light engine	11.05 a.m.	Leeds Goods - Copley Hill	11.10 a.m.
Freight	11.25 a.m.	Copley Hill - Leeds Goods	11.30 a.m.
Light engine	12.00 noon	Leeds Goods – Shed	12.10 p.m.
		Relief	
Light engine	1.15 p.m.	Shed - Leeds City South	1.20 p.m.
Empty vans	1.47 p.m.	Leeds City South – Mirfield	2.50 p.m.
		Shunt at Mirfield	
Empty Carriage	4.41 p.m.	Mirfield – Huddersfield	4.53 p.m.
Passenger	5.20 p.m.	Huddersfield - Leeds City South	6.09 p.m.
		Shunt Leeds City South	
Light engine	7.30 p.m.	Leeds City South – Shed	7.50 p.m.
		Total Daily Mileage: 150	

46495 on 9 April 1959 climbing from Thrapston with the early afternoon Kettering-Cambridge train; an additional non-corridor coach has been added to the rear of the train. Peter Groom.

46403 with the 2.10pm to Cambridge at Barton Seagrave on 18 May 1959; it was allocated to Kettering from mid-1947 until March 1963. www.rail-online.co.uk

One of two 2-6-0s on the books of Coventry shed from 1950 until November 1958, 46446 crosses the River Nene at Wellingborough on 30 May 1960. It moved to Nuneaton for a few weeks before going to Rugby in January 1959.

Coventry's 46445 at Leamington Spa Avenue in 1950. It was at Coventry from new in February of that year and stayed until 1956 when replaced by 46420. The tank version of the Ivatt design was much more often seen at this station, working the push-pull services.

46488 at Penrith. It was planned to allocate ten of the first twenty engines to Penrith and Tebay to replace the ex-L&NWR 'Cauliflower' 0-6-0s on the Cockermouth, Keswick & Penrith Railway. None appeared in the area until May 1950 yet by 1952 all these 0-6-0s at Workington had been replaced by the new 2-6-0s after two, 46488 and 46491 of the Darlington batch, arrived in November 1951.

Derby on 23 October 1950 by Derby's 46444 in place of the usual Compound from that shed. The engine had a load of seven coaches and was assisted by two bankers up the Lickey incline.

The first 2-6-0 allocated to Bescot, 46425, remained there until it was withdrawn in September 1965 apart from a month away on loan to Rhyl in summer 1953; 46490 stayed until March 1966. 46426 was there until May 1956 and 46427 until September 1950, and altogether 17 different members of the class were on its allocation during the 1950s and 1960s. Four others which arrived in 1962/3 and transferred away with 46490 in March 1966 to nearby sheds also had long spells there: 46421, 46429, 46445 and 46522.

The engines at Aston performed a range of light work including a local passenger turn that survived the onslaught of DMUs. This was from Brownhills and terminated at New Street, though it did not appear on timetables because it was a workman's train. They were used on transfer workings in and out of Curzon Street and Windsor Street goods depots and were regular bankers on the line from Perry Barr through Handsworth Park to Soho. 46423 arrived in January 1959 and stayed until September 1962 but 46427 and 46492 did not leave until October 1965.

Coventry had two 2-6-0s on its books from 1950 until November 1958, 46445 and 46446 although the former was

replaced by 46420 in April 1956. All three went to Rugby in 1958/9 along with 46472; 46420 was the first of the class to be permanently allocated there but left again in June 1960. Rugby gained 46442 at the end of 1962 but lost 46442, 46445 and 46446 in 1963 to be replaced by 46430 and 46459 which stayed until December 1964 before seeing out their final year at Nuneaton. There they went largely unnoticed with the only references to them being to their work on local pick-up freight in the Coventry area.

In October 1964 five engines 46428, 46442, 46457, 46470 and 46505, were transferred to Leamington for local goods and trip work and to replace 41xx and other GWR engines due for withdrawal; 46505 had been working the evening Leamington-Nuneaton parcels since 21 August instead of a 2-6-2T. All five left in June 1965 when the former GWR shed closed to steam, four to Tyseley and one to Saltley. The last members of the class at work in the West Midlands were withdrawn from Saltley and Tyseley between July and October 1966.

The ex-Midland Railway shed at Gloucester Barnwood had 46401 from July 1956 until November 1959; it worked up to Ashchurch and Tewkesbury on local passenger trains. Two of the former Western Region engines, 46526 and 46527, arrived in March 1962 but only stayed until October. They took over the twice-daily

goods from Ashchurch to Upton-on-Severn and a passenger turn from Ashchurch to Redditch. They were also used on the Dursley branch, replacing the 16xx pannier tanks for the last few months until the passenger service ended on 10 September.

North West
The Railway Observer reported that 'although Newton Heath have had [6418 and 6419] for nearly a year, they spend all their time on station-pilot duty. In contrast, Bank Hall used 6416 on the 6.55 a.m. and 12.56 p.m. ex-Liverpool to Rochdale, and on 14 February 1948 it was on the 3.50 p.m. Rochdale to Liverpool'. 6416 was seen working a No. 3 Goods from Wigan to Godley and return on 13 and 14 July, and later worked Manchester (Central) to Chester passenger services and on Gorton local passenger duties before returning to Newton Heath on 20 July. On 26 November 1948 new 46421 and 46422 were seen shunting in the works' yards adjoining Widnes shed, duties formerly in the hands of ex-LNWR 0-6-0s.

Within four months of entering service at the end of 1948, 46428 and 46434 spent around a year on loan to several former Cheshire Lines Committee sheds, although officially only allocated to Wigan CLC. Owing to a shortage of tank engines at the end of January 1949 the two engines were commandeered by Trafford Park and used on South District trains. The pair were seen in April working Wigan and St. Helen's trains into Manchester Central and in February 1950, working from Walton-on-the-Hill, often tender-first, while the Southport turntable was under repair. Among the duties of the Preston allocation (46428-46430) were freight workings on the Longridge branch and on the Knott End line where they replaced ex-L&YR 2F 0-6-0s.

Unlike their predecessors, the new Darlington-built engines delivered to Newton Heath at the end of 1951 did not appear on pilot duties at Manchester Victoria as was expected, and initially were confined to shunting at Oldham Road goods station and Collyhurst Street (Miles Platting), with occasional trip workings. These duties were mainly performed previously by L&YR 0-6-0STs.

Agecroft acquired two 2-6-0s in November 1953, 46412 and 46485, with 46486 joining them in February 1954. *The Railway Observer* reported in March that they were being used for shunting duties at Oldfield Road and Hope Street in place of L&YR 0-6-0STs. The coal stages at these points were due for renewal, and it was decided to provide engines with an increased coal supply rather than build new coal stages. 46412 left after less than a year but 46485 and 46486 would both remain at Agecroft until June 1962. In November 1961 it was noted that 'pilot duties at Windsor Bridge yard have for some years been

by Ivatt 2-6-0s from Agecroft but the work had recently become harder and so has been taken over by Crabs'.

The five engines which went new to Widnes in 1948, 46420-46424, all stayed together until April 1956, apart from several short loans, when they were replaced by BR Standard 2-6-0s 78032-78035 and 78059. Two of them, 46423 and 46424 returned to the shed in May 1963 along with 46410 in November; all three left for Speke Junction in April 1964 when the shed closed.

Aintree used its three engines, 46405, 46412 and 46439, mainly on transfer freights between the extensive sorting sidings near the depot and North Mersey. They all left in September 1962 but another six arrived between 1964 and 1966, four them working until 1967.

One of the sheds which received an allocation of the 2-6-0s late in the day was Northwich; 46472, 46503 and 46517 arrived in early 1963 but all left in August 1964. It was not until 1966 that any more appeared with five of these lasting into 1967 (46440, 46487, 46503 (again), 46516 and 46520).

The last shed to operate the class was the former L&NWR establishment at Buxton. On 15 May 1962 46429 on loan from Stoke worked the Buxton to Friden freight on a Buxton 3F diagram which involved working over part of the Cromford & High Peak line between Parsley Hay and Friden. The next month

46430, 46465 and 46480 arrived at Buxton although 46430 was only on loan and left in November. The widely travelled 46401 joined them the following May and 46402 and 46484 in November 1965; the last to arrive were 46485 and 46492 in 1966. 46485 was noted on the 9.39am all stations from Sheffield-Buxton in July 1966. Five of these were the last to remain in service when they were withdrawn in w/e 1 July 1967 (46402, 46484, 46485, 46492 and 46505).

Cockermouth, Keswick and Penrith line

The December 1946 *Railway Observer* quoted a 'tentative allocation' of ten of the first twenty engines to Penrith and Tebay to replace ex-L&NWR 'Cauliflower' 0-6-0s on the Cockermouth, Keswick & Penrith Railway (CK&P) line but none appeared in the area until May 1950 when 46447-46449 arrived after spending a couple of months operating from Crewe North. 46455-46459 followed within a few weeks, also after a short time at Crewe North.

On 3rd June 1950 46447 worked the 10.20am Penrith-Workington, followed by 46448 on a train of empty stock, both engines running tender-first because the 2-6-0s could not turn at Penrith as the scheme to install a 60ft. turntable there was deferred in 1939. On the same day

A well-groomed 46449 waits at Keswick. It was allocated to Penrith from May 1950 until April 1955, moving to Carlisle Upperby.

Two youngsters watch the tablet exchanging process at Braithwaite on 29 June 1965. 46432 had only arrived at Workington shed from Rhyl in January 1957 but remained there until the CK&P closed as a through route on 18 April 1966. It returned at the end of the month to its first shed, Springs Branch, for its final year in service. www.rail-online.co.uk

Despite the headlamp code, 46405 is on a freight working at Goole on 6 May 1956. It is heading south east towards Goole shed and has just passed under the line to Thorne. 46405 had gone to Goole from new in but moved to Farnley Junction and Bank Hall before returning in January 1950.

46465, the first of the class built at Darlington, at Sheffield Midland on 9 June 1964. It had been transferred from the Eastern Region to Buxton in August 1962. 46465 was working one of the Sheffield-Manchester Central 'stoppers'. M. Bentley.

46401 at Tewkesbury in the late 1950s was allocated to the former Midland Railway shed of Gloucester Barnwood which lost its 22B code in January 1958. It had arrived there in July 1956 after nine years at Kettering and stayed for just over two years and worked up to Ashchurch and Tewkesbury on local passenger trains. www.rail-online.co.uk

46527 at Coaley Junction with the 6.30pm to Dursley on 8 September 1962 during the last week of operation. It had arrived at Gloucester Barnwood along with another former WR engine, 46526, in March 1962 but only stayed until October. They took over the twice-daily goods from Ashchurch to Upton-on-Severn and a passenger turn from Ashchurch to Redditch. www.rail-online.co.uk

Left. A poster for the 1953 'Land Cruise' from Llandudno retitled appropriately for the Queen's Coronation. In 1951 as The 'Festival Train Cruise' it ran from Rhyl to Barmouth via Corwen and Dolgelley, returning via Harlech and Afonwen. The following year, it was retitled the 'North Wales Land Cruise' and increased to two trains. One for Prestatyn (changing at Rhyl) and Rhyl which ran Mondays to Fridays and the other, running Tuesdays to Thursdays, ran from Llandudno back to Llandudno, following the same route and taking up the previous year's timings from Rhyl, where reversal was necessary (as again at Llandudno Junction on the return). In 1953 the train ran every weekday from 29 June until 18 September for the bargain price of 13/-, about £17.50 in today's money, the passengers could enjoy 'the most magnificent scenery in North Wales'.

46434 was transferred from Widnes to Rhyl in June 1953 for the summer season where it worked the North Wales Land Cruise. It left at the end of October, moving to Springs Branch. It still has a tender lettered BRITISH RAILWAYS, the last of the class to be built with this before the first BR emblem was used. Note the ex-Coronation Scot brake freshly repainted in 'blood and custard' livery. transporttreasury

One of five engines transferred to North Wales in summer 1954, 46428 heads the Land Cruise near Portmadoc on 15 July 1954. A.G. Ellis.

46422 adorned with the North Wales Land Cruise headboard at Denbigh on 16 August 1956, the last year that the 2-6-0s worked the train, after which BR Standard Class 4s took over following the raising of the route restriction from Dovey Junction to Barmouth and along the coast from 'Yellow' to 'Blue'. The passengers can enjoy the delights of the local gas works rather than the 'most magnificent scenery'! On close examination the tour guide with her paperwork is organising the tour participants. www.rail-online.co.uk

A former Goole engine, 46437 was transferred to Newton Heath in March 1956 and remained there until withdrawn in May 1967. On 27 August 1964 it was having an easy day, as it arrives at Manchester Victoria with an Inspection Saloon. www.rail-online.co.uk

46480 at Dowlow Halt working a Friden to Buxton freight on 17 June 1965. It had moved from York to Buxton in August 1962. It was working back from the Cromford & High Peak line with the consist including at the rear two of the 3,500 gallon tenders used to take water up there after replenishment at Buxton. M. Bentley.

the 6.14pm from Workington was worked by 46449.

The 2-6-0s were subject to severe speed restrictions over seven bridges between Cockermouth and Workington. The Penrith engines worked a goods and a passenger turn to Carlisle every day and were turned there, thus avoiding some tender-first running over the CK&P. In other cases, engines were turned at Keswick and worked the remaining eighteen miles to Penrith tender-first, or vice versa. According to *The Railway Observer*, 'The drivers speak very highly of their new engines which take the heavy grades between Penrith and Keswick without any effort. On 1st August, the down 'Lakes Express' left Penrith behind 46447 (12D) eight minutes late and picked up two minutes to Keswick with a load of four bogies. Keswick was left on time and in spite of a 15 m.p.h. P.W. slack in parts, Braithwaite was reached three minutes early'. During a week's observation on the Penrith-Workington line no 'Cauliflowers' were seen on passenger work.

By 1952 all the 'Cauliflowers' at Workington had been replaced by the new 2-6-0s, after two arrived in November 1951 from the Darlington batch, 46488 and 46491. *With the introduction of the 1953 summer service and consequent additional trains on the Penrith-Workington line, some workings have been combined with those on the Maryport & Carlisle section. As a result, the 7.15 a.m. Workington-Carlisle, previously a Workington Class 2P 4-4-0 turn, was taken*

over by a Class 2 2-6-0 from the same shed, which then worked the 9.45 a.m. Carlisle-Workington via Penrith. The 11.7 a.m. Carlisle-Whitehaven, previously the next turn for this engine, was worked instead by a Workington 2-6-0, which took the 6.52 a.m. ex. Workington to Penrith, and thence went light to Carlisle. This engine then worked the 1.15 p.m. Whitehaven-Carlisle and 5.8 p.m. Carlisle-Whitehaven, which duties were previously performed by the 4-4-0.

The Ivatt engines continued to work on the CK&P into the 1960s despite the early use of DMUs in the area from 1955 onwards. On 3 August 1963 the 8.20am Workington-Manchester Victoria and Crewe was worked by 46491; it was followed by 42299 and 46488 on the Workington portion of the Up 'Lakes Express'. Later 46488 returned on the 10.15am Manchester Victoria-Workington. On the same day, the morning Carlisle-Keswick goods and return working were hauled by 46455. 46455 and 46489, which had both moved to Carlisle Upperby, were seen working the Saturday passenger service on the Silloth branch with Class 4 2-6-0s 43004 and 43103.

A year later 46491 was on the Workington portion of the Down 'Lakes Express' on 11 July 1964 and the 8.20am Workington-Manchester Victoria and Crewe was worked to Penrith by 46488 on 25 July and 46432 on 20 August. However, the daily freights from Workington and Carlisle to Keswick had ceased on 1 June 1964. During summer 1965 the 'Lakes Express' was still being

worked forward from Penrith by the 2-6-0s before they finally succumbed in 1967 after several had been in store for much of the previous two years.

The Workington allocation was stable for many years with 46447, 46456 and 46488 spending around ten years there from new; 46448, 46457 and 46458 also put in lengthy spells from new. The last to go off the books were 46452 and 46491 which were withdrawn in w/e 6 May 1967; the latter went to Workington from new and had only left during 1954 to Penrith on loan and to Upperby for three weeks in early 1955.

East Midlands

As recommended in the 1947 memorandum referred to earlier, the 2-6-0s took over the Kettering to Cambridge service, but they also worked westwards to Oxford. 46401, which was first noted at Oxford on 24 April 1953, replaced 2P 4-4-0 40551 as the regular engine on the Bedford-Oxford passenger turn. On 26 August of that year, three of the class were observed to arrive simultaneously at Kettering just before 7pm; 46403 came from Bedford, 46404 from Cambridge and 46402 from Leicester. At the same time, 46401 was outside the shed and 46495 was shunting in the Down yard; to complete the set 46400 had been noted earlier in the day at Leicester.

After the initial to-ing and fro-ing, the Kettering allocation remained virtually unchanged until the late-1950s with newly built 46495 and 46496 joining 46400-46404 and 46444 in 1952. 46400

46401 26-4-66 Higher Buxton on 12-05 ex Hindlow-M BentleyOne of the first ten engines built at the end of 1946, 46401 at Higher Buxton, about a mile outside Buxton on the Ashbourne line, on 26 April 1966. It was working the 12.5pm freight from Hindlow which was conveying Tarma Mexafelt tanks from Cromford to Ellesmere Port and sugar beet to Downham Market. M. Bentley.

Northgate was the Chester terminus of the CLC line from Manchester Central. Although 6416 had first been used on the service in 1948, the 2-6-2Ts were more common at the station on the push-pull trains to Shotton and Wrexham. 46516 from Speke Junction was on a special working, indicated by the crude 1T51 headcode on 2 July 1966.

One of the final five, together with 46402, 46484, 46485 and 46492, 46505 was withdrawn from Buxton at the end of June 1967. At Buxton shed the former Western Region engine has clearly already run its last revenue-earning duty. www.rail-online.co.uk

stayed there for six years and the others for nine or more years. The last three to go were 46403, 46404 and 46496 in March 1963.

On the last day of working on the Kettering-Cambridge line, 13 June 1959, 46496 hauled four coaches forming the 2.10pm from Kettering and was inscribed with numerous chalked comments. 46444 worked the 11.25am from Cambridge, delayed by the antics of the camera-carrying enthusiasts making their farewell journeys. In addition to their passenger work, one of their regular duties was on the daily Loddington iron ore train.

Although 6400 went there for its first three months in service, Derby had only a few of the class for local passenger and freight work for brief periods in 1946/7 and the early 1950s. Only 46440, 46443 and 46454 were there for any length of time up until January 1959 when the allocation increased with the arrival of 46402, 46497, 46499, 46500, 46502 and the return of 46440. Two of these stayed until late 1963 and the other four until May 1964. Their main duties were on the passenger shunts at Park Sidings and as Midland station north and south end pilots.

Further north, the two engines allocated from new to Nottingham were both seen at Northampton; 46502 was first noted on 26 May 1952 and 46501 on 3 June. 46502 appeared each day until 30th May, when it failed with injector trouble at Lamport, and was brought in together with its passenger train by an 8F 2-8-0. It left Northampton on 3 June with a freight towards Market Harborough. When the time came for 46501 to depart for Castle Station to take the 6.23pm to Nottingham, it too failed and Northampton's Class 2P 40657 took its place. By the following day, the 2-6-0 was able to return with the 6.23pm.

Hasland shed near Chesterfield had 46499 and 46500 from May 1953 until January 1959, and 46497 for almost two years between November 1956 and January 1959; all three were transferred to Derby. They worked on local freight and passenger services to Derby and north to Sheffield. 46499 was seen on the 4.30pm Barnsley Court House-Sheffield in June 1958, a working normally associated with the Ivatt 2-6-2Ts.

Yorkshire

The LMR lost four 2-6-0s in February 1958 when the Sheffield area sheds were transferred to the Eastern Region, Grimesthorpe's 46450 and 46451, and 46400 and 46494 which had both been at

PASSENGER ENGINE WORKINGS COMMENCING 2 NOVEMBER 1959				
MILLHOUSES TURN 42 ONE CLASS 2MT (EX LMS 2-6-0)				
ECS Trip Engine				
	Loco	5.10am	L	
5.13am	Heeley CS.	5.30	E	
5.37	Sheffield			
5.40	Shunt (passr) and work ECS trips as required			
	Sheffield	4.59pm	E	
5.12pm	Nunnery CS.		L	
MILLHOUSES TURN 44 ONE CLASS 2MT (BR 2-6-0)				SX
	Shed	5.23am	L	
5.30am	Sheffield Midland	6.5		
7.11	Chinley	7.40		
8.35	Sheffield Midland	9.50	E	
10.3	Nunnery CS.		L	
	Loco	4.58pm	L	
5.5	Sheffield Midland	5.30		
7.45	Manchester Central	9.30		
11.26	Sheffield Midland	Shunt	L	
12.15am	Loco			
Although this duty was allocated to a BR Class 2, it is typical of those for the Ivatt engines based at Millhouses during the 1950s, and which were termed 'Chinley stoppers' by the locals.				

The Ivatts were not well represented at the London end of the LMR although four went new to Willesden in December 1948. They were used on Empty Coaching Stock duties between Euston and Wembley, on cross-London freights, Permanent Way trains and for shed and yard pilot work. 46458 arrived in September 1955 and stayed until April 1960. It was on ECS duty at Willesden Junction in the late 1950s. The High Level station is visible at the far right of the picture. www.rail-online.co.uk

Millhouses since 1956 where they were employed on local passenger, shunting and pilot work. Typical passenger duties for the Ivatts at Millhouses during the 1950s were the 'Chinley stoppers' as the locals termed them. Grimesthorpe closed to steam on 11 September 1959

and its engines were transferred to Canklow.

Five of the first ten engines built in 1946 were at Goole at various times between then and 1950; of these 46407 and 46408 were both there for about fifteen years. Amongst their other

duties, they were used on the Isle of Axholme Joint line which had severe weight restrictions. *The Railway Observer* reported in 1955: *The daily goods train from Goole to to Haxey Junction was being worked by Cl. 2 2-6-0 46408. The engine of this train also works the five-mile Epworth-*

46460 arriving at Dalmeny having crossed the Forth Bridge with a stopping service to Edinburgh during the time it was allocated to St. Margarets from new in May 1950 until January 1952, when it was transferred to Kittybrewster. J. Robertson, transporttreasury

Hatfield Moor Peat Works branch. During the day several unconventional methods of operating were noticed in this somewhat remote part of Lincolnshire. The Hatfield Moor train, consisting of four wagons and a brake, was propelled up the branch by 46408. Shunting at Eastoft Depot added a further three wagons which were attached in front of the brake van!

Goole shed was transferred to the North Eastern Region at the end of 1956 with three 2-6-0s on its books: 46407-46409. 46408 moved to Malton in March 1962 but 46407 had been withdrawn at the end of 1961, the first of the class to be taken out of service. 46409 had three spells at the shed totalling over ten years, the last of which ended in November 1963; 46413 was also there during 1963 and when they both left in November 46473 arrived for the six weeks up to Christmas.

South East
The class was not well represented at the London end of the LMR although four engines, 46431-46434, went new to Willesden in December 1948. 46434 left in April 1949 and 46432 in July 1952 but 46433 stayed until May 1956 and 46431 until November 1958 when it moved to Watford. 46458 arrived in September 1955 and was replaced by 46472 in April 1960 which stayed until May 1963 along with 46424 which had been there since April 1956. They were used on Empty Coaching Stock duties between Euston and Wembley, on cross-London freights, Permanent Way trains and for shed and yard pilot work.

Watford acquired two more engines in 1962 using them on local passenger and freight and yard shunting, and a fourth in March 1963 when five of the class were also transferred to Willesden after the LMR had taken control over several former Western Region sheds. However, their stay was brief, and in May 1963 the Ivatts at both sheds were replaced by BR Standard Class 2s because engines in the London area needed to have AWS gear. There was a final flurry in early 1965 when Willesden had four engines on loan for a few months for Euston ECS work prior to electrification.

North Wales
Unlike the Ivatt 2-6-2Ts, the 2-6-0s were only transferred to North Wales for the summer timetable, the first being 46430, sent from Springs Branch shed to Rhyl in June 1951. 46420 and 46430 went in 1952, 46424-46425 and 46434 in 1953, 46422, 46428 and 46448 in 1954, with 46421 and 46430 going to Llandudno Junction. For some reason there were none in 1955, but in 1956 Rhyl received 46423, 46426, 46432, 46433 and 46445; this time they stayed longer with only 46426 leaving at the end of the summer. 46423 and 46433 stayed until 1958, and 46445 until June 1959. 46423 and 46445 were noted on the Denbigh-Chester service.

One of their regular duties, and the most well-known and glamorous, was on the 'Cruise' trains each summer. In 1951 The 'Festival Train Cruise' from

Rhyl to Barmouth via Corwen and Dolgelley, returning via Harlech and Afonwen, was worked throughout the summer by 46430, with the exception of one trip by 41287.

The following year, it was retitled as the 'North Wales Land Cruise' and increased to two trains. One starting from and returning to Rhyl and the other from Llandudno back to Llandudno. On 17 July 1952, the six-coach Rhyl train was worked by 46420 adorned with a special decorative headboard. The train included four armchair saloon coaches, all in LMS crimson livery. The Llandudno train worked by 46430 was in the new BR crimson and cream colours and used stock which formed part of the pre-war Llandudno-Manchester 'Club train'. The 2-6-0s worked the train each year until 1956, after which BR Standard Class 4s took over following the raising of the route restriction from 'Yellow' to 'Blue' from Dovey Junction to Barmouth and along the coast.

Scottish Region
The final five engines built at Crewe were sent to former LNER sheds in Scotland. The first to arrive was 46460, allocated to St. Margaret's at Edinburgh in May 1950, followed the next month by 46461 and 46462. 46463 and 46464 went to Dundee Tay Bridge in June and July respectively.

After running-in, 46460 made its first appearance on 14 June, working the Haddington Goods from South Leith. In July 46460 was noted at Galashiels,

46460, running round its train at St. Combs, was transferred to Kittybrewster in January 1952 to replace former GER Class F4 2-4-2Ts on the branch. The line, which ran for five miles down the coast from Fraserburgh, was built under the Light Railways Act of 1896 which reduced construction costs by not requiring the track to be enclosed with fencing. This meant that all engines that worked the line had to be fitted with cowcatchers as shown on 46460. R. Butterfield, Initial Photographics.

46463 was at Dundee Tay Bridge from June 1950 until May 1963. In its early days there, 46463 is departing from Wormit, on the south side of the Tay Bridge, and is about to enter the single line to Tayport.

Of the five engines which went new to Scotland 46462 was the longest to remain at a single shed, St. Margarets from June 1950 until the end of 1965. On 7 May 1955 it was passing through Craigleith on the former Caledonian North Leith line. M. Bentley.

46450 at Dumfries on 18 August 1962 had been a Sheffield engine until April of that year when it moved on loan to Dumfries becoming a permanent transfer the following month. It was soon noted on the Gretna Green pick-up goods where its tender cab was welcomed by crews when running tender-first.

46461 with the 1.38pm from North Berwick to Corstorphine arriving at Balgreen Halt on 12 October 1957.

The branch from The Mound to Dornoch was normally associated with tank engines of the Caledonian 0-4-4T variety and later two Western Region 16xx pannier tanks, but on 12 August 1959 46460 was arriving there from Dornoch with the usual mixed train. M. Bentley.

46460 was transferred from Aberdeen Ferryhill to Oban in August 1961 where it was used on the Ballachulish branch as pictured at Creagan on 9 September 1961.

46461 spent over 13 years working from St. Margarets shed before moving to Bathgate in January 1964. It was withdrawn at the end of July and stored there until around November when it was despatched to McLellans at Coatbridge for scrap. www.rail-online.co.uk

46461 was seen on a freight at Drem and 46462 was observed on a Dunbar-Edinburgh passenger train. After being tried on various types of trains in the district, they settled down to regular local passenger work, including turns to Galashiels via Peebles and Hawick and on the Edinburgh South Side Suburban line.

The St. Margaret's engines also worked on the two freight-only branches from Dalkeith to Gifford and the Lauder branch, both of which had been built under the Light Railways Act. 46462 became the regular engine for the Gifford Light Railway on the south-east side of Edinburgh, which started at Ormiston Junction and itself was on a branch from Monktonhall Junction to Macmerry. The 9¼ miles long line had previously been the preserve of LNER Class J24 0-6-0Ts.

In July 1952, 46461 was used on the Lauder Light Railway which ran from Fountainhall Junction on the Waverley route between Edinburgh and Carlisle for 10½ miles to Lauder. Because of the line's severe weight restriction and line speed of 25mph, two former Great Eastern Railway Class J67 0-6-0Ts had been used, running with empty side tanks, the water being supplied to the engine from a separate tender to spread the axle loading. This was well before until the maximum axle load on the line was raised to 14 tons in 15 June 1956, by 'The British Transport Commission (Dornoch and Lauder Branches) Light Railways (Amendment) Order, 1956', allowing the 2-6-0s to take over regular

working; the branch was closed to all traffic from 1 October 1958.

46460 was transferred to Kittybrewster in January 1952 to replace former GER Class F4 2-4-2Ts on the St. Combs branch. The line, which ran for five miles down the coast from Fraserburgh, was built under the Light Railways Act of 1896 which reduced construction costs by not requiring the track to be enclosed with fencing. This meant that all engines that worked the line had to be fitted with cowcatchers and 46460 was therefore equipped with catchers attached via two large steel plates fixed to both the front bufferbeam and to the tender bufferbeam. 46461 was loaned to Kittybrewster three times, in late 1954, early 1955 and again in 1960, as temporary cover for 46460 although it was not fitted with cowcatchers.

The two Dundee engines were first observed at Arbroath, 46463 was on Dundee-Arbroath locals during week ending 1 July 1950 and 46464 arrived light engine on 8 July. 46463 regularly worked the Tayport and St. Andrews branch services and occasionally the Carmyllie branch, although 46464 was the regular engine on that line until its closure in May 1965 and was christened 'The Carmyllie Pilot' by the locals. The Carmyllie line was five miles long and ran from Eillot Junction (near Arbroath) to the village of Redford, about a mile away from the tiny hamlet of Carmyllie. It was freight-only from December 1929 and the motive power until the arrival of the 2-6-0s was provided by ex-NBR Class J31 0-6-0s and later ex-NER Class

J24s. There were few recorded observations of the two engines but on 2 January 1954 46464 was seen on the 12.30 pm Forfar to Arbroath. The following year, it was noted at Aberdeen working the 5.55 am to Keith on 30 April, and on 2 May was on GNSR section freight work. 46463 was working the Carmyllie branch on 28 February 1959 and 46461 was working the Saltoun branch on 26 August 1960.

In 1961, three 2-6-0s were transferred from the Eastern Region, followed by another in 1962; in 1963 eight moved from the North Eastern Region and 46403 from the London Midland Region. The first to arrive was 46468 from Cambridge which arrived at Oban in March 1961 and was apparently earmarked for the summer 9.42am Oban-Ballachulish and 12.26pm return. It spent a few weeks at Perth before returning to Oban, although it would move back to Perth in July 1962. Its final shed was Grangemouth from November 1963 until withdrawal in October 1965.

46451 moved from Sheffield Millhouses to Hurlford on loan in p/e 7 October 1961 and permanently a few weeks later. It was followed by 46467 from Cambridge which was officially transferred in the same month but according to the *Observer* did not actually arrive until May 1962 following a two-month long General overhaul at Darlington; it stayed until 1963, moving on to Stranraer and later Dumfries up to withdrawal in July 1964. In 1962, 46450 was transferred to Dumfries from

61

46479 with a Permanent Way train on the Dumfries-Stranraer line collecting materials on the penultimate day of service, 11 June 1965. The former North Eastern Region engine was withdrawn from Dumfries three weeks later. W.J. Verden Anderson, Rail Archive Stephenson.

Canklow and stayed until withdrawn in January 1966. It was soon noted on the Gretna Green pick-up goods where its tender cab was welcomed by crews due to the tender-first running involved.

In June 1962 passenger trains on the Ballachulish branch were being worked by Oban's 46460 and 46468 but the arrival of BR Standard 2-6-4T 80093 which was cleared for working the line meant that this would soon replace the 2-6-0s. At the same date, the Saltoun-Ormiston branch, all that remained of the Gifford & Garvald Light Railway, was normally operated by 46461 from St. Margarets.

In January 1963, 46482 was loaned to Polmadie from Darlington and 46498 from Holbeck, the allocations becoming permanent later in the year. 46467 went to Stranraer in February and was used on the Whithorn goods branch, running three times a week. 46403 moved from Kettering to Motherwell on loan in March and permanently in the Autumn after returning on paper, at least, to Kettering for three weeks in the summer. 46468 was yard pilot at Forfar shed, a sub-shed of Perth, on 16 August and was noted there again the next month as station pilot.

When the North Eastern Region cleared out the last of its allocation in November 1963 seven engines were transferred to Scotland allowing the

withdrawal of a number of pre-grouping 0-6-0s. Hurlford received 46409 and 46413 from Goole and 46435 from Low Moor, while Tweedmouth sent 46474 and 46475 to Dumfries and 46479 to Stranraer which stayed until March 1964 when it also moved to Dumfries. Withdrawals of the Scottish Region engines began in mid-1964 with 46403 at Stirling but several survived until 1966, with 46451 at Hurlford the last to go in December.

Eastern Region

In June and July 1948, 6416 and 6417 from Bank Hall were loaned to the Eastern Region. 6416 went to Colwick shed at Nottingham and was first noted running light on the Leen Valley line on 15 June. On 18 June it was working passenger trains between Nottingham Victoria and Grantham. After three weeks 6416 moved to New England for a week, and finally to Gorton for three weeks where it was used on local passenger turns, on Cheshire Lines services from Manchester Central to Chester Northgate, and on goods workings between Wigan (GC) and Godley Junction.

6417 went with 4F 2-6-0s 43011 and 43013 to Stratford for trials. It stayed for five weeks, but the only contemporary report of it was on 6 July

when it was working on the Colchester (St. Botolph's) to Brightlingsea branch.

It would be three years before any more of the class came to the Eastern Region. After British Railways put a stop to work on a lightweight 2-6-0 design from Doncaster, the Region received five of the Ivatt design in June and July 1951. These were built at the former LNER works at Darlington; 46465-46467 went to Cambridge and 46468-46469 to Colchester.

They replaced Holden GER J15 0-6-0s on the Colne Valley line and as well as the ordinary weekday trains they comfortably handled excursions between Clacton or Walton and Cambridge or St. Ives loading up to ten coaches. *The Railway Observer* reported 'Much of the traffic on this route is now handled by Cl. 2 2-6-0s from Colchester and Cambridge sheds. There are four passenger trains each way daily between Marks Tey and Haverhill. On 20/12/52 the 11.50 a.m. train from Marks Tey to Cambridge via Long Melford was worked by 46466 with four coaches. The 11.59 a.m. Marks Tey-Haverhill train, consisting of two modern semi-corridor carriages, was hauled by 46469'.

The Cambridge engines also worked through to Oxford, with 46465 and 46466 both noted there on the 1.18 pm from Cambridge in May 1952, and they took over the Brightlingsea branch.

Kettering's 46402 crosses Godmanchester viaduct near Huntingdon on 19 July 1952. 46400-46404 were based at Kettering from mid-1947 and they took over the service to Huntingdon and Cambridge from ex-Midland Railway Johnson 2F 0-6-0s. All remained at the shed for many years, with 46402 staying until November 1956. L.R. Peters.

46495 at Huntingdon East on 19 July 1952 with a Cambridge-Kettering train, strengthened to four coaches with a non-corridor coach at the front. As with the other engines at Kettering, 46495 was there for almost a decade, leaving for Derby in February 1961. L.R. Peters.

The engines allocated to Cambridge worked through to Oxford in their early years there as shown by 46466 in May 1952. It has the Darlington style of power classification, 2MT on the bufferbeam and the tall chimney shows up well in this photograph. www.rail-online.co.uk

46400 at St Ives with a Kettering-Cambridge service on 27 May 1953. The train comprises four LMS Stanier coaches with a horsebox tacked on at the rear. 46400 went on loan to Bournville a few months later but left for Bristol Barrow Road in February 1954. E. Sawford.

46404 departs from Huntingdon East with an afternoon Kettering-Cambridge train on 16 July 1954. The usual three-coach corridor set has been strengthened by a non-corridor coach at the front. E. Sawford.

46465 stands at Mildenhall on 19 August 1958.

46466 departs from Cambridge with the 9.35am excursion train to Clacton on 22 June 1958. K.L. Cook, Rail Archive Stephenson.

46467 in 1951 at Marks Tey on a Colne Valley train to Haverhill. There were four passenger trains each way daily between Marks Tey and Haverhill. www.rail-online.co.uk

46468 in the east end bay platform at Colchester North during the early 1950s. It was one of two engines allocated to Colchester, both remaining there until November 1959.

46469 departing in 1954 from the south end of Cambridge station, probably with a Bletchley/Oxford train. www.rail-online.co.uk

46496 after arrival at Cambridge with the 2.10pm from Kettering on 13 June 1959. This was the last day of services over the Kettering to Cambridge Varsity line, hence the numerous chalked inscriptions on 46496. www.rail-online.co.uk

However, no more of the class appeared on the Great Eastern branch lines, presumably because many of the services still used Westinghouse-braked stock. The *Observer* even reported the appearance of one at Liverpool Street, when 46467 arrived with the 2.15pm parcels from Cambridge on 6 March 1959. 46468 and 46469 worked regularly over the Walton-on-the-Naze branch taking trains as far as Thorpe-le-Soken.

The five engines all remained at their original sheds for several years; 46465 and 46466 staying at Cambridge until the shed closed in June 1962 when both moved, on paper at least, to March. They were there for only a couple of months before 46466 was withdrawn and 46465 went to Buxton where it survived until March 1967. 46467 had already departed to Scotland in October 1961.

The two Colchester engines were transferred as a pair, to Parkeston Quay in November 1959, and then both moved to Cambridge in January 1961. After a few weeks 46468 was sent to Scotland but 46469 stayed on Great Eastern lines until withdrawn in August 1962, spending its final weeks (nominally) allocated to March.

North Eastern Region
In June and July 1948, 6418 and 6419 from Newton Heath were loaned to the North Eastern Region at Darlington. 6418 spent most of its time at West Auckland on goods duties while 6419

worked mainly on passenger duties over the Darlington-Kirkby Stephen-Penrith line with a view to replacing the veteran NER Worsdell J25 and J21 0-6-0s.

Three years later, after British Railways put a stop to work on a lightweight 2-6-0 design from Doncaster, the former LNER works at Darlington began to turn out a batch of the LMS Ivatt 2-6-0s, which eventually numbered 38 engines (46470-46502). The first five went to the Eastern Region and the next thirteen to the North Eastern Region, divided between West Auckland, Kirkby Stephen and Darlington, with the remainder going

West Auckland	46470, 46473, 46479, 46482
Kirkby Stephen	46471, 46474, 46476, 46478, 46481
Darlington	46472, 46475, 46477, 46480

to London Midland Region sheds. The new engines ran their first thousand miles from Darlington Bank Top, mainly on the Darlington-Tebay line (above).

They quickly established themselves on the Darlington-Penrith route over Stainmore summit and Belah viaduct, with *The Railway Observer* reporting in 1954, 'This section is now almost entirely in the hands of Cl. 2 2-6-0s on both passenger and goods'. They worked both passenger and goods trains and often completed two return trips each day, covering around 260 route miles.

The class then virtually disappeared from view in the North Eastern Region as far as the contemporary press was concerned, with only a handful of mentions over the next decade. The North Eastern gained more of the class on 1 January 1957 after several sheds were transferred from the LMR in late 1956; 46407-46409 at Goole, 46413, 46415, 46435, 46438 and 46483 at Wakefield, 46453, 46493 and 46498 at Holbeck - see table page 70.

In the other direction, Kirkby Stephen was transferred to the London Midland on 1 February 1958 and with it went 46470 and 46472, the 1951 quintet all having left in 1955 when they were displaced by BR Standards. Although 46470 departed in September 1960 the shed acquired several other Ivatt 2-6-0s in that year, replacing their BR Standard cousins, but all had gone before the end of 1961. Although DMUs had been working on the Darlington-Penrith services since 6 January 1958, steam returned for the 1958 and 1959 Whitsun and August Bank Holiday Monday services. A visitor to Kirkby Stephen shed on 26 September 1960 found 46458 in sole occupation. It was rostered for

The Darlington-Penrith line was virtually taken over by the class within a short time of their introduction on the North Eastern Region. They worked both passenger and goods trains and often completed two return trips each day, covering around 260 route miles. 46472, allocated to Darlington from July 1951 until November 1954, makes an energetic start from Barnard Castle passing NER G5 0-4-4T 67256.

46476 passes under the second of two impressive signal gantries at Barnard Castle East Junction with a freight on 25 October 1952. It was allocated to Kirkby Stephen shed from new in September 1951 until April 1955.

PASSENGER ENGINE WORKINGS COMMENCING 2 NOVEMBER 1959			
HOLBECK TURN 77 ONE CLASS 2MT			
	Shed	7.0am	LE
	Leeds C. No.	7.30	Pcls
8.2am	Bradford F.S.	10.15	
10.39	Leeds C. No.	12.6pm	
12.39pm	Knottingley	1.13	
1.50	Leeds C. No.	-	LE
2.12	Shed	4.50	LE
-	Leeds C. No.	10.55	LE
11.5	Shed		

two freight trips each day to Warcop and Merrygill.

There were several other changes in the North Eastern allocation during 1958: 46471 went to Northallerton in March – the only LMS designed engine permanently allocated there although 46473-46477 and 46479 from Darlington went there when the shed's 78xxx 2-6-0s were away for works visits. 46476 moved to Tweedmouth in January and was followed in October 1959 by 46482 and in 1962 by 46471, 46473-46475 and 46479 where one of their duties was freight traffic on the line from Coldstream to Wooller. In August 1958, West Auckland's 46480 and 46481 were transferred to York where both stayed for almost four years. On 17 September 1958, 46480 visited Ripon in the morning with the weedkiller train, and 46481 brought down official saloon 900269 in the afternoon.

In January 1961 Heaton took over the freight workings to Morpeth, Rothbury and Reedsmouth acquiring 46473, 46474, a J21 and a J25 from South

Left. **46473 from West Auckland shed leaves Darlington with a tea time train for Bishop's Auckland on 2 June 1953. W. Rogerson, Rail Archive Stephenson.**

Below. **46422, banked by a Class 4 2-6-0, heads a mixed freight across Belah Viaduct. The 347 yard-long viaduct which was between the summit at Stanmore and Kirkby Stephen and when it was completed in 1860 was the highest bridge in England, at 196ft high. This picture was taken in around 1960 after 46422 arrived at Kirkby Stephen in April; it left in June the following year.**

In between spells at Goole, 46409 was allocated to Scarborough from January until October 1962 and was heading towards Scarborough with a mineral train made up of a wonderful variety of wagon types on 9 June at Scarborough Mere, to the south of the town. There are still greenhouses on the site in the background, which is now a garden centre.

Blyth in exchange for J27s; 46473 was replaced by 46479 in April and the two Ivatt engines remained at Heaton until February 1962.

Malton acquired 46408 and 46413 in March 1962 and 46473 and 46481 in August to replace its three J27s. 46408 was withdrawn in October and 46481 in December; when Malton shed closed in April 1963 46473 went to York and 46413 to Goole.

After Goole withdrew 46407 in December 1961, several others went during 1962 leaving a dozen or so to work on the Region into 1963. The last to remain on the NER books was Goole's 46473 which was withdrawn in December. The remainder of the NER allocation was transferred to the Scottish

for use over the mid-Wales lines, thereby enabling the withdrawal of most of the Cambrian Railway Class 15 and Dean Goods 0-6-0s operating there. The first of the 25 to enter traffic was 46503 early in November 1952 and the final one was 46527 in April 1953.

All except the last three Ivatt engines were initially allocated to Oswestry, 46525-46527 going to Bristol St. Philips Marsh. At the same time, the first ten of the new BR Standard Class 2 2-6-0s were also delivered to Oswestry between December 1952 and April 1953 – an example of the seemingly strange decisions taken in the early days of British Railways. Within a few months, the Standards were transferred away, eight to the Cambrian section at

and Moat Lane. Their novelty soon attracted the immediate attention of the enthusiast press. *The Railway Observer* reported several sightings on the 7.35 a.m. Brecon to Newport returning with the 11.0 a.m. Newport to Brecon. 'The following engines have been noted so far: 46510 on 29/1/53, 46507 on 31/1/53, and 46513 on 12/2/53'. At Builth Wells on 17 March, the 2.33pm to Moat Lane was hauled by 46516 and 46510 arrived from the south on a goods. '*The driver of one of the new Class 2 2-6-0s spoke well of his engine. He was enjoying the comforts of the modern cab after many years endurance of weather among the Welsh mountains savoured from the footplates of Dean and Cambrian 0-6-0s which have for long monopolised these bye-ways. He said (with obvious pride and sincerity): The old Great Western was a good company to work for .... but, they thought all their enginemen liked to have plenty of fresh air.'*

The Ivatt engines took over most of the duties from the elderly 0-6-0s and could be seen everywhere west of Oswestry, as far as Newport in the south, and across to Aberystwyth, Ruabon and Barmouth. They worked the Brecon to Moat Lane trains, and some of the trains between Newport and Brecon although these were mainly handled by GWR 2251 0-6-0s and Pannier tanks, and they ousted the Dean Goods and ex-MR 0-6-0s over the

Oswestry	46503-46524
St. Philips Marsh	46525-46527

46516-46518 and 46521-46524 were transferred to Brecon within a few weeks of entering service.

Region in November 1963: 46409, 46413, 46435, 46474, 46475, 46479 and 46483.

Western Region

After 46413 had been "improved" at Swindon in 1950, it was perhaps inevitable that a batch of the LMS-designed moguls should be built there

Machynlleth and two to Worcester. 46516-46518 and 46521-46524 were reallocated to Brecon within a few weeks of entering service, and that shed always had half a dozen or so of the class on its books until late 1959. The Oswestry engines were sub-shedded at Aberystwyth, Builth Road, Llanidloes

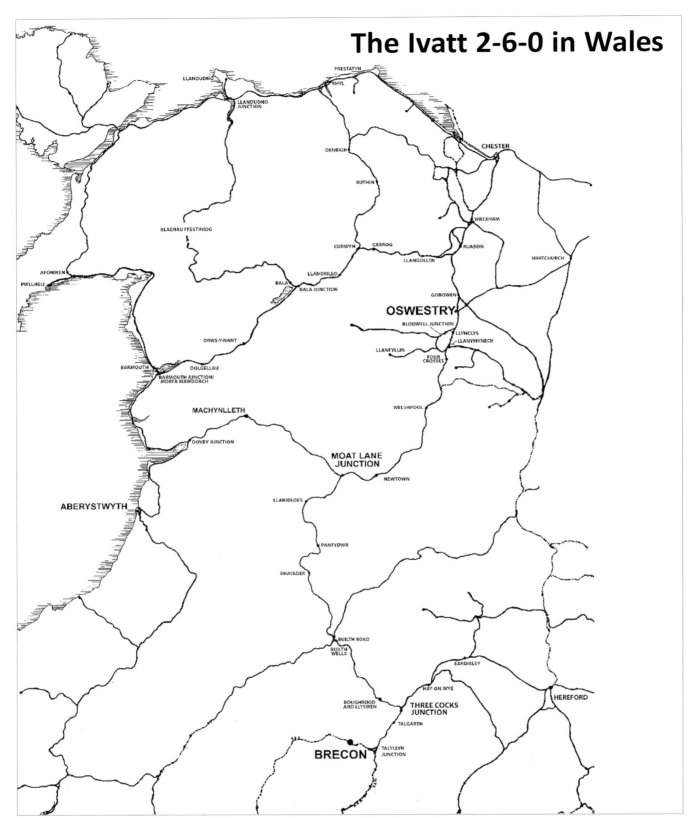

The Ivatt 2-6-0 in Wales

All except the last three Western Region 2-6-0s were initially allocated to Oswestry, 46525-46527 going to Bristol St. Philips Marsh. 46516-46518 and 46521-46524 were reallocated to Brecon within a few weeks of entering service and it always had half a dozen or so on its books until late 1959. Two of the Brecon allocation were sub-shedded at Builth Wells (the former Cambrian Railways shed) and exchanged fortnightly. The Oswestry engines were sub-shedded at Aberystwyth, Builth Road (the former L&NWR shed), Llanidloes and Moat Lane. They could be seen almost everywhere west of Oswestry, as far as Newport in the south, and across to Aberystwyth, Ruabon and Barmouth. They worked the Brecon to Moat Lane trains, and some of the trains between Newport and Brecon and ousted the Dean Goods and ex-MR 0-6-0s over the former Midland Railway line from Hereford to Three Cocks, and thence to Brecon. Further north they worked the Oswestry to Llanfyllin branch and trains between Gobowen, Oswestry and Welshpool and in later years they were used on the Barmouth-Ruabon line running through to Wrexham. They also appeared on the Cambrian Coast lines north of Dovey Junction up to Pwllheli. In the early 1950s a number were transferred to North Wales sheds for the summer timetable and were noted on the Denbigh-Chester service. Their most glamorous duty was on the 'Cruise' trains, initially from Rhyl to Barmouth via Corwen and Dolgelley, returning via Harlech and Afonwen, and later with a second train starting from Llandudno.

The Ivatt 2-6-0s took over most of the workings on the former Midland Railway line from Hereford to Three Cocks Junction and thence to Brecon, which had been transferred to the Western Region in 1950. The line had been worked by L&Y 0-6-0s, MR 3F 0-6-0s and latterly Deans Goods. 46509 is ready to depart from Hereford in either 1961 or 1962. M. Brown, www.rail-online.co.uk

46518 at Eardisley, mid-way between Hereford and Three Cocks, on 31 July 1962 waiting to depart with 4pm train to Brecon. M. Brown, www.rail-online.co.uk

46518 takes on water at Hay-on-Wye before it sets off for Brecon. There is no shed plate which suggests the picture probably dates from when Oswestry changed from 89A to 89D in January 1961. Note the Midland Railway bridge plate number 60 in the foreground. www.rail-online.co.uk

The classic view of Three Cocks Junction at the western end. On the line curving away to the left, 46523 had arrived from Moat Lane over the former Cambrian Railways route via Llanidloes and Builth Wells. In the platform on the right, 46518 had come from Hereford over the Hereford, Hay and Brecon Railway line. The name Three Cocks came from that of a nearby inn rather than the adjacent but tiny village of Aberllynfi. M. Brown, www.rail-online.co.uk

46518 on 9 June 1961 at Three Cocks Junction with the 10.25am from Brecon to Hereford. M. Brown, www.rail-online.co.uk

On the same day, 46503 is ready to depart from Three Cocks Junction with the 9.2am from Hereford to Brecon. M. Brown, www.rail-online.co.uk

The enclosed tender cabs of the 2-6-0s must have been very welcome for the engine crews who had previously braved the elements when working on this line tender-first with a Dean Goods or other engines. The design of the tender with the narrow tank also gave easy access to the coal space where the fireman of 46514 has a rather large lump of coal, rather as if holding a specimen fish. He would certainly appear to be in need of a hammer. 46514 was at Three Cocks on 9 June 1961 working the 11.15am to Builth Wells and Moat Lane Junction. M. Brown, www.rail-online.co.uk

46513 runs through the passenger loop at Three Cocks Junction with a northbound freight for the Mid Wales Line up to Moat Lane on 9 June 1961. The 2-6-0s worked not only on the passenger trains which passed through Three Cocks Junction but also on most of the freight. M. Brown, www.rail-online.co.uk

46511 arrives at Talyllyn Junction with 9.55am Moat Lane to Brecon on 16 June 1961. It is crossing the junction with the Brecon & Merthyr line. The triangular junction, which took its name from the adjacent tiny hamlet, was four miles east of Brecon and had north, east and west chords. The Brecon and Merthyr Railway from the south met the Mid-Wales Railway from the north-east, which had running powers over the B&M from Talyllyn into Brecon. The eastern spur of the triangle allowed through running from South Wales to mid-Wales and also to Hereford. M. Brown, www.rail-online.co.uk

former Midland Railway line from Hereford to Three Cocks, and thence to Brecon, which had been transferred to the Western Region in April 1950. 46508 replaced 46523 at Brecon in January 1955, maintaining the seven engines on the strength; 46517 left in mid-1957 but the others stayed on until 1959. Two of the Brecon allocation were sub-shedded at Builth Wells and exchanged fortnightly; the shed was closed in September 1957 and the engines transferred to the ex-LNWR shed at Builth Road.

On 15 August 1959 a *Railway Observer* correspondent toured the four lines which met at Brecon. *'In the morning at Three Cocks Junction the 11.15am to Moat Lane consisting of two coaches worked by 46511 (89A) left late owing to the late arrival of 46522 (89B) on the 11.6am Brecon-Hereford. The 12.15pm from Brecon to Newport was worked by 0-6-0 2218 and made a connection [at Talyllyn Junction] with the 10.55am from Moat Lane which left behind 46518 (89B) to Brecon'.*

The June 1962 *Observer* contained a detailed account of operations of the 2-6-0s on the Hereford-Brecon and the Mid-Wales line in April 1962, before the withdrawal of passenger services on the line to Hereford at the end of that year.

Over the Easter weekend observation of passenger traffic on the branches serving Brecon found trains lightly loaded, many passengers being camera laden enthusiasts taking the opportunity of a trip over the lines before it is too late.

On Easter Monday, 23 April, several early morning trains on the Mid-Wales line did not run. The first through train from Moat Lane to Brecon was the 9.55 a.m. consisting of two coaches hauled by 46515 (89D). The early morning 5.45 a.m. from Moat Lane which is something of a mail train was actually the first train of the day as far as Builth Wells, through passengers changing there, but on this date the connecting train was not running. The 5.45 a.m. had been worked by 46505 (89D) which was noted at Builth Wells preparing to work stock to Builth Road for the 12.30 p.m. to Brecon.

The 1.20 p.m. Brecon to Moat Lane (the return working of the 9.55 a.m. from Moat Lane) makes good connections at Three Cocks from Hereford and is shown at Brecon as having connections to Crewe and the North, passengers travelling via the Central Wales Line from Builth Road (High Level). On Easter Monday about six people boarded this train at Three Cocks Junction behind 46515 and no passengers were picked up or set down until Builth Wells was reached. At Builth Road (Low Level) connections are made with the 12.20 p.m. Swansea (Victoria) to Shrewsbury, unfortunately on this occasion this train arrived at the High

Level station some thirty minutes late behind 48732, several people alighted and changed trains.

Normally the 1.20 p.m. crosses the 2.50 p.m. from Moat Lane at Pantydwr but due to the delay at Builth Road it was crossed at Rhayader behind 46508 (89D); this train is the return working of the 12.45 p.m. from Builth.

At Llanidloes, due to there being no freight workings and the curtailment of early morning passenger trains, two of the three engines allocated here were on the small two road shed; these were 46504/22 both 89D. Apart from turns over the Mid-Wales line, Llanidloes has one long-distance turn, the 6.15 a.m. to Whitchurch, returning to Llanidloes with the 6.50 p.m. from Whitchurch. On Easter Monday this train was worked by 46401 (89D).

At Moat Lane the down "Cambrian Coast Express" hauled by 7800 (89D) and the 2.30 Aberystwyth to Oswestry had been held to make connections. 46515 retired to Moat Lane shed to be prepared for the 3.2 p.m. to Llanidloes returning light engine to Moat Lane. The Moat Lane freight engine 46518 (89D) was dead on the shed.

Freight over the Mid-Wales lines consists mainly of farm produce, basic slag, and the like, and comprises one daily working over the whole length, leaving Moat Lane at 8.55 a.m. and reaching Brecon at 6.45 p.m. The opposite working leaves Brecon at 9.0 a.m.

46505 on an Up freight in August 1963 alongside the River Dee near Carrog, between Ruabon and Corwen on what is now the heritage Llangollen Railway. I. Travers.

Brecon had three through platforms and a fourth bay platform at the east end. 46513 is probably leaving on a service to Moat Lane over the Mid Wales line, with the stock for a Hereford train in the bay. www.rail-online.co.uk

An unidentified 2-6-0 is ready to depart from Brecon in 1961 with what appears to be a train to Moat Lane Junction. 46513 is in the bay platform waiting to leave with a Hereford service. M. Brown, www.rail-online.co.uk

46508 at Llandrillo, the largest station between Corwen and Bala, on 28 May 1963 with a train to Bala.

Bala Junction was purely an interchange station with no road access. 46507 has arrived there from Ruabon on 28 May 1963.

The class continued to work on the Ruabon to Barmouth line until the end. 46509 is approaching Drws-y-nant station with a train to Barmouth in October 1964. www.rail-online.co.uk

46446 at Morfa Mawddach, working a Barmouth-Dolgellau local in the 1960s. Formerly Barmouth Junction, the station was renamed Morfa Mawddach on 13 June 1960. www.rail-online.co.uk

46511 takes the Engineer's Inspection saloon towards Barmouth from Morfa Mawddach on 22 May 1962, adorned with a home-made headboard containing the three Prince of Wales plumes with the words 'Engineer's Inspection' below. The Engineers used the saloon to travel from their headquarters at Oswestry when inspecting their District. www.rail-online.co.uk

46521 arriving at Barmouth on 7 August 1964 with the 5.5pm SX from Dolgellau. The train has crossed the 113 spans of the timber main section of the viaduct and the steel bridge which incorporated an opening 'swing' section over the deep water channel. 46521 is running on what had originally been the Borthwen viaduct but which had been filled in. www.rail-online.co.uk

46508 at Oswestry on 15 August 1957, probably after arriving from Llanfyllin. B.K.B. Green, Norman Preedy Collection.

Two 2-6-0s tender-first on a freight at Oswestry in August 1965. 46510 and 46511 are bringing in a heavy train including stone in 'Mermaid' ballast wagons, from Llynclys to Gobowen. www.rail-online.co.uk

46513 on a freight working at Blodwell Junction (for the Tanat Valley) in the mid-1950s. Oswestry's 2-6-0s worked over a number of different branch lines including the Tanat Valley Light Railway. This was fifteen miles long and ran westwards from Llanyblodwel in Shropshire, about five miles south-west of Oswestry over the Wales-England border up the Tanat valley, terminating at Llangynog in Denbigh.

and arrives Moat Lane at 4.40 p.m. There are also two shorter workings from Brecon to Builth Road.

On Easter Monday no fewer than twenty-five people joined the 5.27 p.m. from Moat Lane to Builth Wells which makes good connections from the Oswestry direction. The train was headed by 46519 (89D) and at Llanidiloes the majority of the passengers alighted. The 5.27 p.m. terminates at Builth Wells, and due to the level crossing there, 46519 caused quite a congestion of road traffic when running round the train to work back to Builth Road with the 7.40 p.m. It returns to Builth Wells with the 7.55 p.m. and then retires to Builth Road shed adjacent to the High Level station.

On the former Midland Line to Hereford traffic is very thin, the first train on Easter Monday was the 9.50 a.m. from Brecon, a three-coach train headed by 46509 (89D), returning from Hereford at 12.42 p.m. making connections at Three Cocks for both Brecon and Moat Lane. All Hereford line trains are handled from the Brecon end with the exception of the 9.35 a.m. pick-up goods from Hereford (Moorfields) to Three Cocks which is diagrammed to Hereford's Standard Cl. 2 2-6-0, 78004.

A normal service was provided on Tuesday, 24th April, and the writers boarded the 9.2 a.m. from Hereford consisting of three coaches and 46508 (89D). Permanent way work was in progress near Eardisley and a speed restriction of 15 m.p.h. was in force over the bridge spanning the River Wye at Whitney, a flagman is also provided here. At Talgarth 46519 (89D) was passed

with the pick-up goods from Brecon. Brecon was reached in good time at 10.44 a.m.

Owing to the peculiar service provided over the Neath line, this was not visited and attention was turned to the lines of the former Brecon and Merthyr Railway. The first train over this line was the 8.3 a.m. from Newport which was formed of two coaches behind 0-6-0PT 3747 (86A). 3747 worked the 12.10 p.m. return to Newport with few people aboard. At Talyllyn 46515 was crossed with the 9.55 a.m. from Moat Lane and at the next station, Talybont-on-Usk 2243 (86A) was passed with the morning freight to Brecon. Down trains (Brecon to Newport) take water at Pentir Rhiw, to enable them to tackle the 1-in-38 climb to Torpantau summit. Up trains take water at Torpantau after the climb to this place from the other side. On 24th April 3691 (86A) was passed here with the 11.15 a.m. ex-Newport. This is the return working of the 7.35 a.m. from Brecon, one of the two Brecon turns over this line, the other being the 2.5 p.m. from Brecon returning from Newport at 6.55 p.m.

Power for most of the Brecon lines is supplied by Brecon shed which is officially in the Cardiff Valleys District and coded 88K. Despite this, no allocation has been made or 88K plates used and the depot relies on Oswestry (89D) and Ebbw Junction (Newport) (86A) to supply engines for the workings. L.M.S. Cl. 2 2-6-0s are used for the Hereford and Mid-Wales lines, a G.W.R. 0-6-0PT works over the Neath line, while the Newport line and local shunts are worked by Collett 0-6-0s and four 0-6-0PTs. On

22nd April the shed contained 2218/40/7, 3691, 3706/14 (all 86A) and 46507/ 9/10/ 21/3 (all 89D). Nominally two Brecon engines are stationed at Builth Road but these are also supplied by Oswestry, on 22nd April they were 46508/19 (both 89D).

On 29 December 1962 the last passenger services ran from Brecon. 46518 took the last train to Moat Lane at 5.5pm with three coaches, and the final train to leave was the 9.35pm to Builth Wells headed by 46526. All engines and coaches were cleared out from Brecon that night.

In contrast, there were very few reports of the St. Philips Marsh trio. At Wells on 15 April 1953 the afternoon goods from Bristol was hauled by 46527, the first visit of this class to the Cheddar Valley line. This train was normally a Collett 2251 working from St. Phillips Marsh; both 46527 and 46526 were seen subsequently on this working. Two years later the Observer reported 'They are frequent visitors to the Cheddar Valley Branch, on passenger as well as freight trains. One is invariably provided for the 5.20 p.m. Bristol-Frome passenger on the North Somerset line'. Following a shortage of power in the Oswestry district in late 1956, 46526 was sent there straight from overhaul at Swindon Works in December 1956; 46506 replaced it at Bristol after repair later in the month. 46527 spent two years away at Bath Road shed from January 1955 until March 1957, returning to St. Philips Marsh only until January

46518 at Whitchurch, northern limit of the Cambrian Railways, with a local train from Welshpool in August 1959.

An Ivatt 2-6-0 sets off from Four Crosses with the 4.30pm from Whitchurch to Welshpool on 30 March 1964. www.rail-online.co.uk

46401 arrives at Welshpool in February 1962 with a train from Oswestry. After almost a decade at Kettering, 46401 had moved to Gloucester Barnwood for three years and then to Oswestry in late 1959. www.rail-online.co.uk

46446 at Newtown in Montgomeryshire, with a train to Welshpool from Moat Lane Junction. It was transferred to Machynlleth in May 1963 from Rugby which dates this picture to 1963 or 1964. www.rail-online.co.uk

46518 at Moat Lane Junction where the line from Whitchurch and Oswestry to Machynlleth and Aberystwyth met the Mid Wales line from Llanidloes and Three Cocks Junction. 46518 waits there in 1961/62 with a train to Llanidloes, Builth Wells, Three Cocks Junction and Brecon. This picture was taken between October 1959 when 46518 was transferred from Brecon to Oswestry and January 1961 when Oswestry shed became 89D. The line stretching into the distance is to Newtown and Welshpool. www.rail-online.co.uk

Shortly after Machynlleth the Cambrian main line divided at Dovey Junction going south to Aberystwyth and north along the Cambrian Coast Line to Barmouth and Pwllheli. 46518 is approaching the station with a seven coach train to the coast, probably a summer Saturday working, in the early 1960s. www.rail-online.co.uk

46521 at Builth Wells with a service to Three Cocks Junction and Brecon on 29 July 1961. The view is towards Builth Road with a train on the Central Wales line just visible in the right distance. www.rail-online.co.uk

The now preserved 46521 at Builth Road Low Level on 15 August 1962, taken from the platform of the High Level station on the former LNWR Central Wales line. It is on a Brecon to Moat Lane service. www.rail-online.co.uk

Two trains cross at Pantydwr, south of Llanidloes, with 46518 on a train to Brecon. www.rail-online.co.uk

A rarely photographed station, Boughrood and Llyswern was between Builth Wells and Three Cocks Junction. Green liveried 46518 waits there before departing for Brecon in April 1960. Boughrood was in Radnorshire and Llyswern was in Breconshire. www.rail-online.co.uk

The strawberries are flowering on the trackside allotment as 46518 approaches Llansantffraid on the Llanfyllin branch with a train from Oswestry on 30 May 1963. Some of the branch trains ran beyond Oswestry to Gobowen and apparently the clearance between the buffer stops and the end of the bay platform there was insufficient if the engine was arriving tender-first and hence the engines would face north when running the branch service. www.rail-online.co.uk

At Llanmynech, there was a junction where the Llanyfyllin branch left the Whitchurch to Welshpool line. 46509 was there in January 1965, the final month of operation, working the 12.55pm to Llanyfyllin. www.rail-online.co.uk

46512 approaching Llynclys on the double track Cambrian main line with the usual two coach train from Llanfyllin to Oswestry on 2 November 1964. www.rail-online.co.uk

46512 arriving at Llynclys on 2 November 1964 with a train to Oswestry. When the axe fell on the lines worked by the Oswestry engines and the shed closed in January 1965, 46512 was transferred on loan to Shrewsbury before moving on to Willesden two weeks later. www.rail-online.co.uk

46508 runs past Morfa-Mawddach signal box with a train from the Barmouth line on 17 October 1964. It was allocated to Croes Newydd shed at this date and the train is probably a Barmouth-Wrexham service. L. Rowe, ColourRail

1958 before moving to Oswestry while 46517 had arrived from Brecon in July 1957; 46506, 46517 and 46525 left St. Philips Marsh in late 1962.

The workings of the class further north went almost unreported in the *Observer*. There was an early mention in 1954 when 46515 was seen on the 3.35 pm train from Oswestry to Llanfyllin on 4 December; the 2-6-0s worked tender-first in this direction. It was not until July 1961 that they were next commented on. 'Class 2 moguls

Long Term Storage

No.		From	To	Weeks	At
46403	S	10/9/62	28/2/63	24.4	Kettering
46461	U	9/4/61	1/10/61	25.0	St Margarets
46467	U	6/11/61	10/3/62	17.7	Hurlford
46469	U	10/6/62	12/8/62	9.0	March

work passenger trains between Gobowen and Oswestry in conjunction with other workings. On 22/7/61 46509 worked the 3.32pm from Gobowen as far as Llanfyllin and a few days later 46512 hauled the 1.20pm Gobowen-Welshpool'. A two-day tour in summer 1962 around most of the former Cambrian Railway lines, saw GWR Manors working most of the passenger services while the Ivatt 2-6-0s 'monopolised local goods traffic'.

All of the Western Region engines were transferred to the London Midland on 1 January 1963 (46503-46527 plus 46401 which had arrived in late 1959). Of these, 46506 and 46517 were the only ones not at Oswestry, having been transferred to Bristol in 1957 and 1960 respectively, firstly to St. Phillips Marsh and then to Barrow Road, before moving to Stourbridge Junction in December 1962.

Eight engines remained at Oswestry (46510-46516, 46518) until the shed closed in January 1965 and five were transferred to Machynlleth (46519-46523). 46401, 46503-46505 went to Willesden, 46507-46509 to Croes Newydd and 46524 and 46525 to Shrewsbury; 46526 and 46527 joined 46506 and 46517 at Stourbridge. The four engines acquired by Stourbridge Junction in late 1962/early 1963, 46506/17/26/27, were used on banking and light shunting duties and a daily parcels to Wolverhampton. They were also intended as replacements for the 74xx pannier tanks on the Longbridge branch but were found to be less suitable and they were all transferred away in March 1963.

46515 was observed on the 12.40pm Oswestry-Llanfyllin on 25 June 1963, returning with the 1.30pm from Llanfyllin, almost ten years since it was last reported on the 8½ mile long branch. 46512 was working the branch on 15 August 1964 and on 16 January 1965, the final day of the Llanfyllin branch, trains were hauled by 46514 and 46516.

46470 from Chester shed, 46508 and 46521 were noted working on Barmouth-Wrexham trains during 1963. The workings of the class were also recorded several times on the Cambrian Coast lines: in June/July nearly all traffic north of

Dovey Junction was in the hands of BR Standard 82xxx, 75xxx, 78004 together with 46510, 46519 and 46521. Steam operation continued between Dovey Junction and Pwllheli through 1964.

On 31 December 1964, 46521 and 2268 worked the 2.45pm Aberystwyth-Oswestry and 46519 was also seen on a passenger train. On the last day of the Ruabon-Barmouth line, 16 January 1965, 46446 worked the final Barmouth-Dolgellau, 46509 the Llangollen-Chester and 46521 the Bala-Barmouth. Oswestry shed closed on 18 January and its 2-6-0 allocation was moved to Croes Newydd or Shrewsbury.

Storage and Withdrawals

Unlike their 2-6-2T contemporaries which were displaced by DMUs or branch line closures, few of the 2-6-0s went into long-term store. Only four instances were recorded up to mid-1963: 46526, which arrived at Watford on 9 April 1963, had only a brief spell of activity before going into store on 19 May after the arrival of three BR Standard 78xxx which were fitted with the AWS equipment needed for operation in the London area by that date; it then stood in a siding next to the coaler for 6 months before being

Withdrawals by Year

Year	No.	ER/NER	ScR	LMR
1961	1	1		
1962	11	11		
1963	5	4		1
1964	8		7	1
1965	21		5	16
1966	40		6	34
1967	42			42
	128	16	18	94

Note – all Western Region engines were transferred to LMR control before any were withdrawn.

moved into the shed and finally left for Saltley in December.

The only others of note were 46424 which was stored at Workington from November 1965 until December 1966 and withdrawal. 46508 was stored at Croes Newydd between August 1965 and July 1966 and then from August 1966 until November 1966 at Machynlleth before withdrawal the following month at Shrewsbury.

Note – all Western Region engines were transferred to LMR control before any were withdrawn.

The first to be withdrawn was 46407 in December 1961; it had spent its entire 15 year working life at Goole. Eleven more Eastern Region and North Eastern Region engines went in 1962 and then came a slowdown with just five in 1963, four more from the ER/NER and eight in 1964, of which seven were in Scotland. After that, 21 went in 1965, 40 in 1966, and 42 in 1967, including 24 in w/e 6 May. The final five, 46402, 46484, 46485, 46492 and 46505 were withdrawn from Buxton at the end of June 1967, bringing to an end a class life spanning just over twenty years. The average working life was 15.5 years; ten were in service for less than 12 years, with 46478 the lowest at 10.6 years. 13 lasted for 19 years or longer – all of them from the first 20 engines – with 46402 just pipping 46400 at around 20½ years.

Preservation
Seven of the class escaped the cutter's torch, two direct from British Railways and five via Woodham Brothers scrapyard at Barry, and all except one have steamed during the preservation era.

Shortest working life			
No.	Built	Withdrawn	Years
46466	22/6/51	1/9/62	11.2
46469	10/7/51	1/9/62	11.2
46471	18/7/51	20/10/62	11.3
46476	8/9/51	5/1/63	11.3
46477	15/9/51	22/12/62	11.3
46478	22/9/51	5/5/62	10.6
46481	6/10/51	15/12/62	11.2
46493	21/12/51	20/10/62	10.8
46494	27/12/51	15/9/62	10.7
46525	17/3/53	12/12/64	11.7
Longest working life			
No.	Built	Withdrawn	Years
46400	11/12/46	6/5/67	20.4
46401	10/12/46	7/5/66	19.4
46402	10/12/46	1/7/67	20.6
46405	11/12/46	12/11/66	19.9
46406	12/12/46	21/1/67	20.1
46410	18/1/47	19/3/66	19.2
46411	25/1/47	14/1/67	20.0
46412	31/1/47	6/8/66	19.5
46414	13/2/47	11/6/66	19.3
46416	22/2/47	23/4/66	19.2
46417	4/3/47	18/2/67	20.0
46418	13/3/47	21/1/67	19.9
46419	15/3/47	27/8/66	19.5

46464
46464, the first to be preserved, was bought in 1966 by Ian Fraser, a Scottish railway engineer. The initial intention had been to put it on display in a museum at Dundee, and it was stored for several years before being loaned to the Strathspey Railway where it hauled the first scheduled passenger train in July 1978. 46464 remained in service there until 1980 when it suffered accidental firebox damage and it left the Strathspey Railway in November 1989 for the Caledonian Railway at Brechin. After Mr. Fraser's death in 1992, preliminary investigation work took place to determine the overall condition of the engine and to give the railway some idea of the eventual cost of restoration. The Caledonian Railway decided it did not have the necessary finances or resources and a group, The Carmyllie Pilot Company, was formed to restore and subsequently operate 46464. In March 2002 it was dismantled and moved to a private site nearby with better facilities and improved access, but the work is still not complete.

46441
46441 was withdrawn from service at Carnforth in April 1967 and purchased by Dr Peter Beet's wife. It remained there when the Carnforth steam depot became Steamtown and worked regularly on preserved railways and the main line until 2002. It was taken out of service because of the condition of its firebox and moved to the Ribble Steam Railway where it was put on static display. In April 2018 46441 was transferred to the Lakeside & Haverthwaite Railway where it will be returned to steam over the next few years.

46443
46443 was purchased privately from BR immediately after withdrawal and moved in steam to the Severn Valley Railway on 22 April 1967. It was used in the early gala events before the official opening of the line and was operational until early 1973. After repairs it returned to service until the end of 1979. It had been purchased by the railway's holding company in 1972 but was sold to the SVR 46443 Fund in 1984. It has since worked on the main line and on other preserved lines but has been out of use since its boiler ticket expired in 2011 and is currently on static display at the Highley Engine House, pending its next overhaul.

46447
46447 was purchased from Woodhams scrapyard by the Ivatt Locomotive Trust and moved to Quainton Road in June 1972. Although missing a great many parts and with its boiler in poor condition, some limited restoration was carried out there before it was moved to The Isle of Wight Steam Railway in late 2008. The following year the Ivatt

Locomotive Trust transferred ownership of 46447 and their two Ivatt 2-6-2Ts, 41298 and 41313, to The Isle of Wight Steam Railway. After limited initial conservation work was completed, it was stored pending restoration as a static exhibit but in 2012 a deal was agreed with the East Somerset Railway whereby the Isle of Wight Steam Railway acquired the former London Brighton and South Coast Railway E1 0-6-0T 110 BURGUNDY from an East Somerset Railway based private owner. 46447 moved to the East Somerset Railway's Cranmore base in October 2012 with an agreement that it would be restored to running order. The restoration was completed within two years and 46447 hauled its first passenger trains on the East Somerset Railway in October 2014. It will remain at Cranmore on a ten year loan.

46512
46512 was withdrawn in November 1966 and sold for scrap to Woodham Brothers at Barry. It stayed there until 1973 when it was purchased by the embryonic Strathspey Railway for its Aviemore to Boat of Garten line. It was stored on the Severn Valley Railway before moving on to the Strathspey Railway in 1982 to begin restoration, which was completed in 2000. It worked until 2005 and then underwent a major overhaul which took around six years. Its boiler was re-tubed and cylinders re-bored in late 2017 and 46512 returned to traffic in early 2018.

46521
46521 was withdrawn in October 1966 and also sold to Woodham Brothers at Barry where it remained until March 1971 after it was purchased by a Severn Valley Railway member. It was the first ex-Barry restoration on that railway and entered service in July 1974, working until 1977 when it was withdrawn for major boiler repairs. Following completion of the overhaul, it worked until 1985 and returned to service again from 1991 until 2000. It was moved to the Great Central Railway for overhaul in November 2001 which involved extensive repairs to the boiler and firebox and did not steam again until the end of 2011. It has worked on several preserved lines since then and is currently operational.

46428
46428 was purchased by the Strathspey Railway from Barry scrapyard in 1979, with the intention of using the boiler as a replacement for the damaged boiler on 46464, but this did not happen. In May 1988 the Bury Standard 4 Group purchased 46428 and it was moved to the East Lancs Railway in August 1988. However, the Group had other priorities and restoration did not begin in anger until 2016 and is ongoing.

46420 in Crewe Works on 10 June 1956 at the end of a Light Casual which lasted from 26 May to 12 June 1956. R. Broughton, ColourRail

The first five of the British Railways-built engines went to Widnes. 46422 was there on 27 August 1949. It transferred to Rhyl in May 1954. K.C.H. Fairey, ColourRail

5. On the Record

Health Warning

As pointed out previously, the LMS/ LMR Engine History Cards and the Engine Record Cards, while containing much useful and even fascinating information, should be regarded as a guide to what happened to the engines, not an unimpeachable document to be afforded the status of gospel. It seems to be stating the obvious that the Cards only show what was written on them at the time, and the temptation to read and interpret too much should be resisted. Nevertheless, the Cards are a marvellous, fascinating, invaluable record of what happened, but they are often infuriatingly silent on events that we enthusiasts half a century or more later consider of vital interest and importance. They were filled in, by hand, by clerks and naturally enough contain errors of omission (quite a few) and commission (a few).

Dates of leaving and entry to works were of course to some extent nominal and a day or two either side should always be assumed. Worse, the works were not above 'fiddling' dates slightly at the beginning or the end of a month to enhance the monthly figures, either of engines 'in' or engines 'out'. It was thus not entirely unknown for a locomotive to be out on the road with the figures showing it still in works and vice versa - for a few days at least.

Although the History Cards for the engines which were built at Crewe and withdrawn from the London Midland Region survive at the National Railway Museum, the picture is much less complete for the remainder. Unfortunately, the History Cards which still exist for the Darlington and Swindon built engines, except for those allocated to the LMR, contain very little information other than withdrawal dates. The gaps were partially filled for the locomotives allocated to the Western, Scottish, Eastern and North Eastern Regions from the Engine Record Cards and Western Region Engine History sheets held by the National Archives at Kew.

Sheds...

Many shed moves at the end did not find their way onto the History Cards but the Chief Accountant's Statistics Office at Derby kept going to the bitter end of BR steam and beyond, and so the LMR shed allocations from 1963 onwards were taken from the weekly Locomotive Stock Book Alteration Lists produced there. The Engine Record Cards were used for the locomotives allocated to the other Regions supplemented by the Stephenson Locomotive Society *Journal*. Transfer dates are for the week ending, unless otherwise stated.

Over half of the class, 68 engines, remained at a single shed for more than eight years continuously, and 45 of these for ten years or more. The longest continuous allocations were:

No.	MPD	From	To	First shed	Years
46404	Kettering	11/1/47	30/3/63		16.3
46407	Goole	11/12/46	23/12/61	Goole	15.1
46408	Goole	21/6/47	3/3/62		14.8
46411	Newton Heath	21/11/53	14/1/67		13.2
46418	Newton Heath	24/7/48	21/1/67	Newton Heath	*19.8
46419	Newton Heath	24/7/48	15/9/62	Newton Heath	*15.4
46425	Bescot	25/7/53	11/9/65		12.2
46427	Aston	17/3/51	16/10/65		14.6
46441	Lancaster Green Ayre	9/2/50	23/4/66	Lancaster Green Ayre	16.3
46462	St Margarets	10/6/50	1/1/66	St Margarets	15.6
46463	Dundee Tay Bridge	24/6/50	11/5/63	Dundee Tay Bridge	12.9
46490	Bescot	28/11/51	26/3/66	Bescot	14.4
46491	Workington	23/4/55	6/5/67		12.1
46492	Aston	19/12/51	16/10/65	Aston	13.9
46510	Oswestry	9/12/52	23/1/65	Oswestry	12.2
46511	Oswestry	12/12/52	23/1/65	Oswestry	12.2
46512	Oswestry	16/12/52	23/1/65	Oswestry	12.1
46513	Oswestry	19/12/52	23/1/65	Oswestry	12.1
46514	Oswestry	23/12/52	30/1/65	Oswestry	12.1
46515	Oswestry	6/1/53	23/1/65	Oswestry	12.1

*ignoring the five weeks on loan to the North Eastern Region in mid-1948.

46433 outside the Crewe Paint Shop on 5 February 1950 after a Light Casual involving a partial repaint at the front end. R. J. Buckley, Initial Photographics.

46485 was transferred to Buxton from Oldham Lees in w/e 18 June 1966. Pictured at its home shed in June 1966 and with its 9L shedplate already in place, it would remain there until withdrawn in w/e 1 May 1967, one of the final five in service. M. Bentley.

Three sheds had twenty or more different engines on their books: Oswestry (26) had the most followed by Newton Heath (25) and Springs Branch (21).

Repairs and Maintenance
Under the LMS motive power organisation subsequently adopted by British Railways, most sheds carried out minor running repairs and adjustments, including boiler wash-outs etc. Jobs which required the engine to return to Works or to one of the larger sheds, were usually designated under one of the 'Classified Repair' codes. These were either 'Heavy, (H) or 'Light' (L), further sub-divided into 'Casual' (C), 'Intermediate' (I). 'Overhaul' (O), 'Service' (S) or 'General' (G). Occasionally engines were sent to Main Works for other reasons, such as modifications (e.g. fitting of AWS equipment) if this did not coincide with a normally programmed visit) and in these cases the code 'NC' (Non-Classified) was used. The other code which appears from time to time on the Engine Repair cards is 'TRO', which stands for 'Tender Repair Only'. Suffixes, usually after 'NC' were (EO)', which signified 'Engine Only' and 'Rect.', or 'Rect. (EO)' which was used when an engine had to be returned to Works soon after a works visit for 'rectification', ie tightening-up bits that had come loose and loosening bits that were too tight. The terminology was not consistent between the regions with Darlington and Gateshead using GEN without the 'H' prefix, ADJ rather than 'Rect.' and variations on LI, LC, HI; Swindon used

'U' rather than 'NC'.
According to the classification prescribed by the Board of Trade, a Heavy repair was any one during which an engine was reboilered or had its boiler removed from the frames. It was also when any two of the following were carried out:
Fitting new tyres to four or more wheels.
Fitting new cylinders.
Fitting new axles.
Re-tubing or otherwise repairing the boiler whilst still in the frames with not less than fifty firebox stays renewed.
Both turning wheels and refitting axleboxes.
Stripping and renewing both motion and brake gear.

Intriguingly, Light repairs often involved major work such as fitting new axles, replacing cylinders, partially re-tubing or patching the boiler in situ, or refurbishing the motion, axleboxes, frames, etc. As long as only one of these items was involved, however, the repair was still regarded as Light.
Most Heavy repairs were 'Generals' whilst most Light repairs were 'Intermediates'. General repairs were carried out either at set time intervals or at predetermined mileages beyond which it was deemed that an engine could not safely remain in service and were designed to return it virtually to 'as new' condition. Intermediate repairs were normally undertaken when some major component reached the stage where it had to be attended to before the engine was due for general repair, but the aim was to carry out as few intermediate repairs as possible.

Therefore, Heavy General repairs were usually done at approximately 3 to 4-yearly intervals, with in the case of the Ivatt engines, typically one Intermediate repair (either Light or Heavy) between. A Heavy General repair usually took between 25 and 40 weekdays: this was insufficient time to do the necessary work on the boiler, so engines undergoing HG Repairs invariably left Works with a different boiler from that with which they had arrived. 17 spare boilers were built for the 258 Ivatt 2-6-0s and 2-6-2Ts to provide a float to cover repairs. The earlier engines generally had two and in some cases three boiler changes; the later engines mostly had just a single although a few had two changes.

Works...
The works visits for the class have been pieced together from four different sources: for the London Midland Region maintained engines the Engine History Cards (up to around the end of 1961) and the Engine Record Cards (up to withdrawal) recorded details of the repairs. For those on the Eastern, North Eastern and Scottish Regions the information was recorded on Repair Statistics cards, and similarly for Western Region maintained engines which each had an Engine History sheet.
Shopping was carried out at various works depending on where the engine was allocated. The London Midland engines were almost exclusively dealt with at Crewe, although in the early 1950s Derby carried out a handful of Non-Classified repairs and four Light repairs:

No.	Type	From	To
46404	LC	17/9/50	5/10/50
46494	LC EO *	18/3/52	21/4/52
46499	LI	23/5/55	12/7/55
46502	LI	8/10/54	11/11/54
*Collision damage			

Other exceptions to this were Light repairs for 6407 at Horwich in late 1947 and for 46406 in December 1950, and two Heavy repairs and at least eight Light repairs carried out at Rugby during the mid-1950s:

No.	Type	From	To
46402	HI	10/11/55	9/12/55
46404	LC EO	12/5/58	21/5/58
46433	LI	15/1/53	6/2/53
46440	LI	20/1/53	13/2/53
46449	LI	30/12/52	26/1/53
46451	LI	29/9/53	22/10/53
46458	HG	17/12/56	18/1/57
46483	LI	29/6/54	9/8/54
46490	LC EO	3/5/56	15/5/56
46492	NC	15/8/55	16/9/55
46492	LC EO	2/8/58	15/8/58

At least two LMR engines were also sent for repair to Cowlairs in 1964, 46406 from Bury (LC) and 46485 from Newton Heath (HC). Crewe took over the Heavy repairs on the engines previously maintained at Swindon from early 1960 and Light repairs formerly done at Oswestry from the end of 1962. It continued regular repairs on the class up to December 1964 with the final one recorded as late as 14/12/65-24/1/66 when 46505 had a Heavy Casual which included a boiler change.

Darlington did almost all of the General and Light repairs on Scottish, Eastern and North Eastern Region engines, including those transferred from the London Midland when the regional boundaries changed in the late-1950s. The last recorded were on 46422 and 46475 which were completed in July 1962. Exceptions were at least nine General repairs carried out at Gateshead between February 1957 and June 1958, and two repairs at Stratford in the late 1950s on 46468 (Light Casual 5/10-26/10/56) and 46466 (Unclassified 16/2-21/2/59). There were also three visits by 46460 to Inverurie in the early-1950s and one to Cowlairs, and a handful of Light and Non-Classified repairs on Scottish Region engines at Cowlairs in 1964/5.

Swindon did the Heavy repairs and some Light repairs on all of the engines it built for the Western Region until 1959; 46519 was the last one dealt with there, leaving on 14 March 1960. Wolverhampton and Caerphilly took over the Heavy repairs until the engines were transferred to the LMR at the end of 1962 and they came under Crewe's jurisdiction.

No.	Type	Works	From	To
46503	HI	Wolverhampton	11/4/60	17/6/60
46504	HI	Caerphilly	22/5/59	31/7/59
46505	HG	Wolverhampton	30/11/59	29/1/60
46507	HI	Wolverhampton	31/12/59	26/2/60
46508	HI	Wolverhampton	13/11/59	8/1/60
46515	HI	Caerphilly	1/12/59	22/1/60
46517	HC	Caerphilly	11/12/61	16/2/62
46521	HI	Caerphilly	9/7/59	25/9/59
46523	HI	Wolverhampton	9/10/59	27/11/59
46524	HI	Wolverhampton	1/6/59	27/8/59
46527	HG	Wolverhampton	26/9/60	18/11/60

Most of the Unclassified repairs were, sensibly, done locally at Oswestry between 1953 and the end of 1962. Oswestry and Wolverhampton also did a few LC repairs:

No.	Type	Works	From	To
46503	HI	Wolverhampton	11/4/60	17/6/60
46504	HI	Caerphilly	22/5/59	31/7/59
46505	HG	Wolverhampton	30/11/59	29/1/60
46507	HI	Wolverhampton	31/12/59	26/2/60
46508	HI	Wolverhampton	13/11/59	8/1/60
46515	HI	Caerphilly	1/12/59	22/1/60
46517	HC	Caerphilly	11/12/61	16/2/62
46521	HI	Caerphilly	9/7/59	25/9/59
46523	HI	Wolverhampton	9/10/59	27/11/59
46524	HI	Wolverhampton	1/6/59	27/8/59
46527	HG	Wolverhampton	26/9/60	18/11/60

Mileages

Total annual mileage was recorded on the Engine History Cards of LMR based engines, but only up to around 1960, and is not available for engines transferred to other Regions after 1957. There is no surviving information for most of those which worked on the Eastern, North Eastern or Scottish Regions. Total mileage was recorded on the Engine History sheets for the Western Region engines when they underwent a Heavy repair, which gives a good indication of the average annual mileages.

In any event, these were estimates based on diagrammed rather than actual mileages and were summarised from the mileage records kept by the Mechanical Foremen's clerks, a minor miracle of paperwork and not mechanically recorded. An allowance for light engine working was added to the distances for the revenue earning work. There were several ways in which the process could fail to record the actual mileages worked. The borrowing of an engine by another depot for a fill-in turn or a failure where the engine was "stopped" and did not complete the diagram are two of the most common examples. Only three engines, all from the first 1946 batch and based at Kettering, had total recorded mileages of over 400,000:

No.	Total	Average pa
46402	422,383	30,170
46403	479,601	34,257
46404	464,074	33,148

Average mileages for the LMR-allocated engines generally ranged from around 20,000 miles per annum up to 34,000 for 46403, with 46409 (31,043), 46428 (32,580), 46444 (30,884) and 46448 (31,809) and 46496 (33,736) also breaking the 30,000 mile barrier. The three lowest were the Central Division's 46485 (16,414) and 46486 (17,705) together with Aston's 46492 (18,451).

LMR - recorded mileages of over 300,000
The Western Region engines averaged

LMR - recorded mileages of over 300,000			
No.	Total	Average	Years
46400	313,454	28,496	11.0
46401	339,166	30,833	11.0
46402	422,383	30,170	14.0
46403	479,601	34,257	14.0
46404	464,074	33,148	14.0
46405	336,545	24,039	14.0
46406	360,202	25,729	14.0
46409	310,426	31,043	10.0
46410	353,351	25,239	14.0
46411	366,551	26,182	14.0
46412	319,011	22,787	14.0
46414	353,922	25,280	14.0
46416	358,322	25,594	14.0
46417	358,856	25,633	14.0
46418	334,799	23,914	14.0
46419	343,806	24,558	14.0
46422	314,911	24,224	13.0
46423	309,215	25,768	12.0
46428	390,958	32,580	12.0
46432	309,934	25,828	12.0
46434	356,049	29,671	12.0
46437	304,942	27,722	11.0
46444	339,723	30,884	11.0
46447	303,121	27,556	11.0
46448	349,898	31,809	11.0
46496	303,627	33,736	9.0

Western Region engines			
No.	Total	Average	Years
46503	193,117	26,449	7.3
46504	258,102	26,067	9.9
46505	187,313	26,833	7.0
46506	192,758	21,483	9.0
46507	174,432	24,754	7.0
46508	196,197	28,272	6.9
46509	210,721	24,891	8.5
46510	203,882	26,606	7.7
46511	196,138	27,684	7.1
46512	200,789	26,944	7.5
46513	198,451	27,180	7.3
46514	197,407	27,231	7.2
46515	192,026	27,880	6.9
46516	201,955	28,660	7.0
46517	159,751	18,086	8.8
46518	205,492	31,032	6.6
46519	203,748	30,566	6.7
46520	191,051	29,649	6.4
46521	188,754	29,556	6.4
46522	185,873	20,722	9.0
46523	194,885	29,663	6.6
46524	180,952	29,057	6.2
46525	127,763	15,927	8.0
46526	164,728	22,561	7.3
46527	174,519	23,402	7.5

Note – these figures are calculated from the mileages recorded at each Heavy General overhaul.

'Improvements, Etc'

The History Cards had a section headed 'Improvements, Etc.' that recorded brief details of modifications or improvements applied to the engines. What was recorded here for the Class 2s was almost exclusively confined to the replacement of the fabricated crossheads by cast steel crossheads, new chimney arrangements and fitting AWS equipment. The clerks responsible for the cards did not always record changes which must have taken place, nor were they necessarily consistent with the descriptions and Works Order numbers used as a shorthand for this purpose. That said, it is possible with a little detective work to get a reasonably accurate picture of what was done when. This book uses the relevant 'off works' date for each particular modification rather than the 'period ending' date which was actually written on the Improvements section of the cards because clearly this makes more sense.

Tabulated in the following pages for each engine are the most significant 'Improvements' together with tender changes. Where a tender change is known to have occurred or a modification applied but the date is not recorded a "?" is shown in the tables. The most common instance of this is the replacement chimney modification, 14 of which were not recorded; it is reasonable to assume most of these would have been done during the first works visit post-May 1952.

around 26,000 miles per annum with 46518 (31,032) and 46519 (30,566) the highest; 46517 (18,086) and 46525 (16,237) were the lowest.

To put these figures into some sort of context, these compare with averages of around 24,000 pa for the Ivatt Class 4s over the period 1953-60; the latter were generally employed on longer distance work than the Class 2s.

46516-46518 and 46521-46524 were reallocated from Oswestry to Brecon within a few weeks of entering service, and the shed always had half a dozen or so of the class on its books until late 1959. They were used on the Hereford and Mid-Wales services. Two of the Brecon allocation were sub-shedded at Builth Wells and exchanged fortnightly. 46521 was transferred back to Oswestry in October 1959 which dates this picture prior to then since it has an 89B shedplate. S.V. Blencowe.

The last of the class built for the LMR, 46502 at Hasland shed near Chesterfield on 23 March 1958 alongside 46497. It had been allocated to Nottingham since it was built in April 1952 but would move to Derby in January 1959. 46497 was shedded at Hasland from November 1956 until it moved to Derby with 46502, apart from three months at Nottingham in mid-1957. K.C.H. Fairey, ColourRail

All except the last three Western Region built engines were initially allocated to Oswestry, although 46516-46518 and 46521-46524 were reallocated to Brecon within a few weeks of entering service. 46510 was at Oswestry on 15 August 1957 and remained on its books until January 1965 when it moved to Shrewsbury for its last few months in service. The Oswestry engines were sub-shedded at Aberystwyth, Builth Road, Llanidloes and Moat Lane.

46400

Built at Crewe 11/12/46 as 6400
Renumbered w/e 29/7/50

Improvements and modifications

Chimney	17/10/52
Cast steel crossheads	11/11/54

Repairs

Crewe	NC	16/10/47	3/11/47
Shed	TRO	1/7/49	15/7/49
Shed	LC	23/3/50	21/4/50
Crewe	LI	19/6/50	28/7/50
Shed	LC	6/3/51	22/3/51
Crewe	HG	26/12/51	9/2/52
Crewe	LC EO	23/9/52	17/10/52
Crewe	LI	22/10/54	11/11/54
Gateshead	GEN	26/3/58	2/5/58
Crewe	HG	7/1/63	29/1/63

Boilers

New	12430
9/2/52	12435
2/5/58	13835
7/1/63	12431

Tenders

New	7000

Mileage/(weekdays out of service)

1946	194	0
1947	27,634	81
1948	32,910	50
1949	37,019	53
1950	34,051	94
1951	34,627	82
1952	30,468	79
1953	34,130	51
1954	15,081	51
1955	17,222	45
1956	23,827	66
1957	26,291	-

Sheds

Derby	11/12/46
Kettering (loan)	1/3/47
Derby	19/4/47
Kettering	9/8/47
Bournville	25/7/53
Kettering	12/9/53
Bristol Barrow Road	6/2/54
Sheffield Millhouses	2/6/56
Cambridge	7/10/61
March	23/6/62
Barrow in Furness	18/8/62
Carnforth	18/9/65

Stored

Serviceable	10/10/65	24/10/65
Serviceable	21/11/65	8/12/65
Serviceable	11/12/65	18/4/66
Serviceable	16/5/66	20/6/66
Serviceable	7/11/66	?

Withdrawn w/e 6/5/67

46400 at Holbeck in the early 1960s while allocated to Millhouses shed at Sheffield. It had a Heavy General repair at Gateshead in 1958 when its tender was given a large size BR crest. 46400 was transferred to Cambridge in October 1961. www.rail-online.co.uk

The final posting for 46400 was Carnforth in September 1965. It spent most of the time up to withdrawal in May 1967 in store, but it was back in service on 30 August 1966 here at Lancaster.

46401

Built at Crewe 10/12/46 as 6401
Renumbered w/e 18/3/50

Improvements and modifications

Chimney	12/7/52
Cast steel crossheads	20/6/56

Repairs

Crewe	LI	28/2/50	17/3/50
Crewe	HI	7/12/50	23/1/51
Crewe	NC	19/3/51	17/4/51
Crewe	HG	30/5/52	3/7/52
Crewe	LI	26/5/56	20/6/56
Crewe	HG	15/6/59	7/8/59
Crewe	LI	8/3/63	5/4/63

Boilers

New	12431
3/7/52	12430
7/8/59	12979

Tenders

New	7001

Mileage/(weekdays out of service)

1946	734	0
1947	30,911	40
1948	39,377	29
1949	33,778	94
1950	36,978	74
1951	33,661	76
1952	32,568	77
1953	37,391	35
1954	27,392	74
1955	23,564	90
1956	21,691	66
1957	21,121	38

Sheds

Kentish Town	10/12/46
Sheffield Millhouses	18/1/47
Kettering (loan)	21/6/47
Kettering	18/10/47
Gloucester Barnwood	28/7/56
Oswestry	28/11/59
Willesden	30/3/63
Buxton	25/5/63

Withdrawn w/e 7/5/66

46401 soon after renumbering in March 1950 and still with LMS on the tender. It kept its original chimney until July 1952. It was allocated to Kettering between July 1947 and July 1956. www.rail-online.co.uk

46401 at Crewe Gresty Lane in 1963 shortly before it was transferred from Oswestry to Willesden while it was in Crewe Works for a Light Intermediate repair in March 1963. www.rail-online.co.uk

46402

Built at Crewe 10/12/46 as 6402
Renumbered w/e 11/2/50

Improvements and modifications

Chimney	?
Cast steel crossheads	21/10/58

Repairs

Shed	TRO	29/12/48	10/1/49
Crewe	LI	16/1/50	10/2/50
Crewe	HG	10/12/51	22/1/52
Rugby	HI	10/11/55	9/12/55
Crewe	HG	12/9/58	21/10/58
Crewe	HI	26/10/64	4/12/64

Boilers

New	12434
22/1/52	13617
21/10/58	12434
4/12/64	13859

Tenders

New	7002
22/1/52	7015

Mileage/(weekdays out of service)

1946	241	0
1947	28,540	61
1948	35,894	38
1949	39,622	75
1950	35,948	81
1951	35,092	77
1952	35,757	53
1953	37,470	54
1954	29,132	75
1955	22,430	89
1956	33,233	48
1957	19,333	36
1958	18,267	61
1959	25,396	-
1960	26,028	-

Sheds

Kentish Town	10/12/46
Sheffield Millhouses	18/1/47
Kettering	9/8/47
Leicester Midland	10/11/56
Derby	10/1/59
Springs Branch (Wigan)	23/5/64
Bank Hall	3/7/65
Buxton	13/11/65

Stored

Serviceable	2/8/65	8/11/65

Withdrawn w/e 1/7/67

Above. Renumbered during a Light Intermediate repair at Crewe Works completed on 10 February 1950, 46402 is probably returning from a running-in trip down the Shrewsbury line. It has had a partial repaint confined mainly to the front end and cab sides. The tender has a couple of patches with new paint but retains its LMS lettering. It was allocated to Kettering from August 1947 until November 1956.

Left. Derby only ever had couple of the class on its books during the early 1950s but in January 1959, 46402 was one of six to arrive there. They worked on local duties including station pilot at Midland station – like 46402 in October 1963. www.rail-online.co.uk

46403

Built at Crewe 10/12/46 as 6403
Renumbered w/e 31/12/49

Improvements and modifications

Chimney	?	
Cast steel crossheads	2/3/55	

Repairs

Crewe	LI	5/12/49	29/12/49
Crewe	HG	23/10/51	26/11/51
Crewe	HI	14/1/55	17/2/55
Crewe	NC Rec	22/2/55	2/3/55
Crewe	HG	2/4/57	2/5/57
Crewe	LI	14/12/60	24/2/61

Boilers

New	12435
26/11/51	13589
2/5/57	13438

Tenders

New	7003

Mileage/(weekdays out of service)

1946	771	1
1947	33,591	42
1948	37,505	42
1949	37,437	55
1950	41,079	41
1951	30,408	105
1952	42,813	39
1953	37,908	51
1954	29,632	64
1955	29,710	80
1956	34,560	57
1957	33,546	67
1958	38,706	41
1959	26,306	-
1960	25,629	-

Sheds

Derby	10/12/46
Kettering (loan)	21/6/47
Kettering	18/10/47
Hasland (loan)	8/1/55
Kettering	15/1/55
Motherwell (loan)	23/3/63
Kettering	13/7/63
Motherwell (loan)	3/8/63
Motherwell	14/9/63
Stirling	12/10/63

Stored

Serviceable	10/9/62	28/2/63

Withdrawn w/e 4/7/64

46403 was one of seven of the class at Kettering during the 1950s where they were the mainstay on the Cambridge trains. It is passing Barnwell Junction with the 3.30pm from Kettering on 25 May 1957 with the paintwork still gleaming some two months after leaving Crewe Works after a Heavy General overhaul. G.W. Sharpe.

46403 at Barton-Seagrave on the outskirts of Kettering on 18 May 1959 still had another four years at Kettering before it was transferred to the Scottish Region in 1963.

46404

Built at Crewe 11/12/46 as 6404
Renumbered w/e 28/5/49

Improvements and modifications

Chimney	18/10/52
Cast steel crossheads	8/10/55

Repairs

Crewe	LC	8/8/49	2/9/49
Crewe	LC	27/10/49	7/12/49
Crewe	LC	21/3/50	17/4/50
Derby	LC	17/9/50	5/10/50
Crewe	HG	14/9/52	18/10/52
Crewe	HG	17/9/55	8/10/55
Crewe	HI	18/5/57	14/6/57
Rugby	LC EO	12/5/58	21/5/58
Crewe	HG	29/5/61	27/6/61

Boilers

New	12436
18/10/52	12439
8/10/55	13557
27/6/61	12436

Tenders

New	7004

Mileage/(weekdays out of service)

1946	416	-
1947	45,633	38
1948	34,955	46
1949	31,675	95
1950	36,243	81
1951	41,543	40
1952	28,254	80
1953	38,436	36
1954	30,451	57
1955	28,883	74
1956	37,537	33
1957	31,687	53
1958	33,975	49
1959	25,389	-
1960	18,997	-

Sheds

Bedford	11/12/46
Kettering	11/1/47
Nottingham	30/3/63
Aintree	23/5/64

Withdrawn w/e 8/5/65

With two horseboxes, one LMS and one NER leading, Kettering's 46404 heads a local service in the late 1950s. It was one of the final three to leave its former stronghold at the East Midlands shed, departing in March 1963. www.rail-online.co.uk

After more than sixteen years at Kettering, 46404 was transferred to Nottingham Midland shed in March 1963 where it was photographed soon after. Note the 16D shed code painted on the smokebox door although a proper cast shedplate had been added. www.rail-online.co.uk

46405

Built at Crewe 11/12/46 as 6405
Renumbered w/e 11/6/49

Improvements and modifications

Chimney	?
Cast steel crossheads	20/10/55

Repairs

Crewe	HI	21/5/49	10/6/49
Crewe	HG	31/1/52	18/3/52
Crewe	HI	3/10/55	20/10/55
Crewe	HG	24/6/58	1/8/58

Boilers

New	12432
18/3/52	12434
1/8/58	13841

Tenders

New	7005

Mileage/(weekdays out of service)

1946	1,930	-
1947	31,310	36
1948	23,899	59
1949	24,019	48
1950	30,614	36
1951	18,595	54
1952	34,867	61
1953	35,835	66
1954	15,670	80
1955	21,632	102
1956	26,239	39
1957	17,391	40
1958	17,180	60
1959	19,156	-
1960	18,208	-

Sheds

Goole	11/12/46
Farnley Junction	29/3/47
Bank Hall	24/12/49
Goole	28/1/50
Aintree	16/6/56
Bury	15/9/62
Bolton	10/4/65
Bank Hall	22/5/65
Northwich	5/3/66

Stored

Serviceable	12/7/65	2/8/65
Serviceable	8/11/65	14/2/66

Withdrawn w/e 12/11/66

6405 at Copley Hill shortly before its first Heavy overhaul at Crewe Works completed in June 1949 and from which it emerged with its BR number. It was at the former L&NWR Farnley Junction shed together with 6406 from March 1947 until December 1949.

Immaculate in its new BR lined livery, 46405 at Crewe after its first Heavy General repair completed in March 1952. It was at Goole from January 1950 until June 1956. www.rail-online.co.uk

46406

Built at Crewe 12/12/46 as 6406
Renumbered w/e 21/5/49

Improvements and modifications
Chimney	13/12/52
Cast steel crossheads	22/12/54

Repairs
Crewe	LI	14/4/49	18/5/49
Horwich	LC	15/12/50	23/12/50
Crewe	HG	17/11/52	13/12/52
Crewe	HC EO	20/11/54	22/12/54
Crewe	HG	2/4/57	4/5/57
Crewe	LI	13/9/61	13/10/61
Cowlairs	LC	7/8/64	22/8/64

Boilers
New	12433
13/12/52	13901
4/5/57	13254

Tenders
New	7006

Mileage/(weekdays out of service)
1946	668	0
1947	28,276	41
1948	28,164	34
1949	24,011	63
1950	31,464	38
1951	28,540	32
1952	18,064	61
1953	37,773	29
1954	23,603	69
1955	23,966	63
1956	24,694	59
1957	22,610	62
1958	23,464	52
1959	24,444	-
1960	20,461	-

Sheds
Goole	12/12/46
Farnley Junction	29/3/47
Bank Hall	24/12/49
Bury	22/1/55
Newton Heath	10/4/65

Withdrawn w/e 21/1/67

The second of the pair allocated to Farnley Junction between March 1947 and the end of 1949, 6406 has steam to spare at Leeds City. It was renumbered in May 1949. www.rail-online.co.uk

Piloting a Black Five with a summer holiday service from Rochdale to North Wales, 46406 blasts away from New Hey on the Oldham loop. It had been allocated to Newton Heath since April 1965 and was withdrawn there in January 1967. www.rail-online.co.uk

46407

Built at Crewe 11/12/46 as 6407
Renumbered w/e 6/5/50

Improvements and modifications

Chimney	4/12/53
Cast steel crossheads	4/12/53

Repairs

Horwich	LO	25/11/47	20/12/47
Crewe	LI	12/4/50	2/5/50
Shed	LC TO	12/12/52	12/12/52
Crewe	HG	7/11/53	4/12/53
Darlington	GEN	13/5/57	14/6/57

Boilers

New	12437
4/12/53	12974

Tenders

New	7007

Mileage/(weekdays out of service)

1946	758	-
1947	33,318	61
1948	36,106	60
1949	27,496	95
1950	23,773	45
1951	19,682	54
1952	17,884	40
1953	18,757	66
1954	31,208	73
1955	21,031	56
1956	17,917	41

Sheds

Goole	11/12/46

Withdrawn w/e 23/12/61

6407 departs from Wakefield on 29 April 1949. It was officially at the former L&YR Goole shed for its whole life, although it was seen in the North West in its first two months in service. H.C. Casserley, courtesy M. Casserley.

Goole had five of the first ten 2-6-0s on its books in years up to 1950. 46407 was one of two which stayed there until the early 1960s and was withdrawn from the shed in December 1961, the first of the class to be taken out of service. In this picture it is in unlined black with a large BR emblem following a General overhaul at Darlington completed in June 1957. www.rail-online.co.uk

46408

Built at Crewe 12/12/46 as 6408
Renumbered w/e 26/8/50

Improvements and modifications

Chimney	?
Cast steel crossheads	?
AWS	29/4/61

Repairs

Crewe	LI	1/8/50	22/8/50
Crewe	GEN	4/8/53	5/9/53
Gateshead	GEN	7/3/57	12/4/57
Darlington	CL	14/10/58	7/11/58
Darlington	NC	18/4/61	29/4/61

Boilers

New	12438
5/9/52	12975

Tenders

New	7008

Mileage/(weekdays out of service)

1946	391	0
1947	29,690	29
1948	30,391	45
1949	28,711	74
1950	25,471	42
1951	30,016	49
1952	28,366	41
1953	27,909	56
1954	23,090	63
1955	25,930	62
1956	16,721	52

Sheds

Wakefield	12/12/46
Goole	21/6/47
Malton	3/3/62

Withdrawn w/e 27/10/62

6408 working a local trip freight at Wakefield on 29 April 1949. Its first allocation was at Wakefield but it moved to Goole in June 1947. It gained its BR number during a Light Intermediate repair in August 1950. H.C. Casserley, courtesy M. Casserley.

At its home shed in the late 1950s; 46408 was at Goole from June 1947 until March 1962 when it went to Malton for its last six months in traffic. 46408 was one of the regular engines used on the severely weight restricted Isle of Axholme line. www.rail-online.co.uk

46409

Built at Crewe 12/12/46 as 6409
Renumbered w/e 16/9/50

Improvements and modifications

Chimney	5/7/52
Cast steel crossheads	9/4/56
AWS	4/4/61

Repairs

Crewe	LI	22/8/50	12/9/50
Crewe	HG	6/6/52	5/7/52
Crewe	HI	10/3/56	9/4/56
Darlington	GEN	29/6/59	14/8/59
Darlington	NC	16/3/61	4/4/61

Boilers

New	12439
5/7/52	12424

Tenders

New	7009

Mileage/(weekdays out of service)

1946	585	0
1947	33,591	29
1948	33,166	72
1949	38,577	73
1950	17,423	63
1951	31,887	48
1952	33,968	67
1953	37,587	49
1954	23,720	78
1955	29,588	65
1956	30,334	53

Sheds

Wakefield	12/12/46
Goole	28/1/50
Hull Springhead	17/5/58
Goole	11/10/58
Scarborough	27/1/62
Goole	13/10/62
Hurlford	9/11/63

Withdrawn w/e 18/7/64

After spending sixteen years in Yorkshire, 46409 was transferred to the Scottish Region at Hurlford in November 1963. It was photographed there on 6 June 1964, a month before its withdrawal. Note the later style of guard irons fitted to the front of the pony truck instead of on the frames. www.rail-online.co.uk

46409 at Skipwith on the Derwent Valley Light Railway during the first leg of the epic SLS/RCTS North Eastern Tour which lasted from 27 September until 1 October 1963. It worked the tour from York over the Derwent Valley line to Selby where a 4F took over. www.rail-online.co.uk

46410

Built at Crewe 18/1/47 as 6410
Renumbered w/e 28/10/50

Improvements and modifications
Chimney	2/1/54
Cast steel crossheads	2/1/54

Repairs
Crewe	LI	10/10/50	27/10/50
Crewe	HG	2/12/53	2/1/54
Crewe	HI	17/4/57	10/5/57
Crewe	HG	8/12/60	25/1/61
Crewe	LC EO	14/4/61	6/5/61

Boilers
New	12898
2/1/54	12905
25/1/61	12904

Tenders
New	7010

Mileage/(weekdays out of service)
1947	25,917	34
1948	33,313	39
1949	29,380	51
1950	28,036	43
1951	33,029	28
1952	25,820	42
1953	23,555	56
1954	24,710	24
1955	22,410	44
1956	24,318	36
1957	21,198	65
1958	23,847	35
1959	19,977	-
1960	17,841	-

Sheds
Blackpool Central	18/1/47
Newton Heath	21/11/53
Lancaster Green Ayre	22/6/57
Workington	11/5/63
Widnes	16/11/63
Speke Junction	18/4/64

Withdrawn w/e 19/3/66

Four of the ten engines built in 1947, 6410-6413, went from new to the Central Division at Blackpool. 46410 was at its home shed on 26 April 1953. It left there along with 46411 and 46412 in November of that year. H.K. Boulter.

46410 at Workington in September 1963; it spent six months there in 1963, leaving in November for Speke Junction.

46411

Built at Crewe 25/1/47 as 6411
Renumbered w/e 30/9/50

Improvements and modifications

Chimney	23/1/54
Cast steel crossheads	23/1/54

Repairs

Crewe	LI	31/8/50	26/9/50
Crewe	HG	31/12/53	23/1/54
Crewe	HI	16/4/57	11/5/57
Crewe	HG	10/12/60	15/2/61

Boilers

New	12899
23/1/54	14004
15/2/61	13868

Tenders

New	7011

Mileage/(weekdays out of service)

1947	26,973	27
1948	28,728	42
1949	30,177	22
1950	26,257	55
1951	26,060	39
1952	26,752	39
1953	28,522	36
1954	23,220	41
1955	23,871	45
1956	24,927	26
1957	23,292	40
1958	25,276	25
1959	27,968	-
1960	24,528	-

Sheds

Blackpool Central	25/1/47
Newton Heath	21/11/53

Withdrawn w/e 14/1/67

With its replacement tall chimney fitted in January 1954, 46411 runs under the overhead wires at Guide Bridge on 12 June 1954. The Union Jack hanging under one awning and St George's and Saltire flags under the other were in preparation for the opening of the new Woodhead Tunnel two days later. www.rail-online.co.uk

After its transfer from Blackpool in November 1953, 46411 spent the rest of its years until withdrawal in January 1967 at Newton Heath. One of its regular duties was as a Wallside pilot at Manchester Victoria where it was used to assist trains up Miles Platting bank. This is probably 1961, with 4F 44571 parked behind. www.rail-online.co.uk

46412

Built at Crewe 31/1/47 as 6412
Renumbered w/e 25/11/50

Improvements and modifications
Chimney	?
Cast steel crossheads	27/2/54

Repairs
Crewe	LI	27/10/50	21/11/50
Crewe	HG	1/2/54	27/2/54
Crewe	HI	18/12/57	11/1/58
Crewe	HG	27/2/61	11/4/61

Boilers
New	12900
27/2/54	12436
11/4/61	13432

Tenders
New	7012

Mileage/(weekdays out of service)
1947	24,529	31
1948	28,816	60
1949	37,076	37
1950	21,251	103
1951	24,251	42
1952	26,531	37
1953	25,838	40
1954	19,364	74
1955	18,375	48
1956	19,833	35
1957	17,438	49
1958	18,798	39
1959	18,467	-
1960	18,444	-

Sheds
Blackpool Central	31/1/47
Agecroft	21/11/53
Aintree	9/10/54
Bury	15/9/62
Newton Heath	10/4/65

Withdrawn w/e 6/8/66

46412 was at Aintree from October 1954 until September 1962 when it was transferred to Bury. On 22 September 1963 it is at Newton Heath, where it would be transferred in April 1965. www.rail-online.co.uk

46412 from Newton Heath heads Trafford Park Black 5 45352 at New Hey on Saturday 25 June 1966 with the 09.50 Llandudno-Manchester Victoria which had been extended to Oldham Mumps via Rochdale. www.rail-online.co.uk

46413

Built at Crewe 8/2/47 as 6413
Renumbered w/e 4/6/49

Improvements and modifications

Chimney	1/11/52
Cast steel crossheads	11/2/56
AWS	15/4/61

Repairs

Crewe	LI	25/4/49	3/6/49
Crewe	HG	18/8/52	1/11/52
Crewe	HI	13/1/56	11/2/56
Darlington	GEN	28/9/59	29/10/59
Darlington	NC	6/4/61	15/4/61

Boilers

New	12901
1/11/52	12431

Tenders

New	7013

Mileage/(weekdays out of service)

1947	25,548	24
1948	31,379	44
1949	16,059	61
1950	11,652	173
1951	24,255	57
1952	22,295	91
1953	28,126	34
1954	27,095	46
1955	23,150	41
1956	24,881	54

Sheds

Blackpool Central	8/2/47
Western Region (loan)	2/7/49
Blackpool Central	9/9/50
Bank Hall	9/10/54
Wakefield	15/1/55
Low Moor	14/11/59
Wakefield	3/12/60
Malton	3/3/62
Goole	20/4/63
Hurlford	9/11/63
Ardrossan	17/10/64
Ayr	20/2/65

Withdrawn w/e 23/10/65

46413 at its home shed Blackpool in April 1953 with the taller pattern chimney which had been fitted in late 1952 during a Heavy General repair when it also gained BR lined black livery.

46413 was the engine used in tests on the Western Region and the Swindon Stationary Test Plant in in 1949/50. Pictured at its home shed Blackpool in April 1953 with the taller pattern chimney which had been fitted in late 1952 during a Heavy General repair when it also gained BR lined black livery.

46414

Built at Crewe 13/2/47 as 6414
Renumbered w/e 2/6/51

Improvements and modifications

Chimney	1/5/53
Cast steel crossheads	1/5/53

Repairs

Crewe	LI	7/5/51	28/5/51
Crewe	HG	30/3/53	1/5/53
Crewe	LI	4/8/56	1/9/56
Crewe	HG	8/1/60	18/2/60

Boilers

New	12902
1/5/53	13439
18/2/60	12439

Tenders

New	7014
3/1/66	7096

Mileage/(weekdays out of service)

1947	23,832	28
1948	21,768	1
1949	26,017	31
1950	29,823	33
1951	27,263	69
1952	28,304	51
1953	28,576	61
1954	25,203	51
1955	23,434	63
1956	23,235	71
1957	23,003	55
1958	23,267	51
1959	26,791	-
1960	23,406	-

Sheds

Bank Hall	13/2/47
Swansea Paxton Street (loan)	20/12/47
Bank Hall	18/12/48
Bury	22/1/55
Bolton	10/4/65
Bank Hall	15/5/65
Northwich	5/3/66

Stored

Serviceable	8/11/65	15/11/65
Serviceable	7/2/66	14/2/66

Withdrawn w/e 11/6/66

6414 was at Bank Hall, the Central Division shed at Liverpool, from new in February 1947 until the end of the year when it was transferred to Swansea Paxton Street. It returned a year later and stayed until January 1955 when it moved to Bury.

46414 after arrival at the East Lancs (or L&YR) side of Preston station, in the period before its transfer from Bank Hall in January 1955.

46415

Built at Crewe 20/2/47 as 6415
Renumbered w/e 3/3/51

Improvements and modifications
Chimney	27/11/53
Cast steel crossheads	27/11/53
AWS	14/6/61

Repairs
Crewe	LI	5/2/51	5/3/51
Crewe	LC	19/11/51	29/12/51
Crewe	HG	30/10/53	27/11/53
Crewe	LC	25/8/55	24/9/55
Gateshead	GEN	21/5/58	27/6/58
Darlington	NC	1/6/61	14/6/61

Boilers
New	12903
27/11/53	14003

Tenders
New	7015
29/12/51	7029

Mileage/(weekdays out of service)
1947	19,626	27
1948	24,815	10
1949	22,857	28
1950	31,014	28
1951	28,273	89
1952	26,219	51
1953	17,115	81
1954	29,020	49
1955	20,136	78
1956	25,291	33

Sheds
Bank Hall	20/2/47
Swansea Paxton Street (loan)	20/12/47
Bank Hall	12/6/48
Huddersfield Hillhouse	26/9/53
Wakefield (loan)	17/10/53
Wakefield	21/11/53
Goole	31/1/59

Withdrawn w/e 3/11/62

6415 at Bank Hall in May 1950. It had spent six months at Swansea Paxton Street in the first half of 1948 and did not receive its BR number until March 1951.

46415 tender first on a local at Heyside just to the north of Oldham. It moved from Bank Hall to Wakefield in late 1953 via a few weeks at Huddersfield Hillhouse.

46416

Built at Crewe 22/2/47 as 6416
Renumbered w/e 3/12/49

Improvements and modifications
Chimney	9/2/54
Cast steel crossheads	9/2/54

Repairs
Crewe	LC	2/11/49	30/11/49
Crewe	LI	8/11/51	22/12/51
Crewe	HG	11/1/54	9/2/54
Crewe	HI	27/11/56	14/12/56
Crewe	HG	2/4/59	13/5/59
Crewe	LI	21/5/63	8/6/63

Boilers
New	12906
9/2/54	12901
13/5/59	13848

Tenders
New	7016

Mileage/(weekdays out of service)
1947	21,142	21
1948	26,652	42
1949	24,784	66
1950	32,896	43
1951	25,805	74
1952	35,273	40
1953	22,589	56
1954	26,361	71
1955	23,861	66
1956	22,936	70
1957	25,501	36
1958	23,842	55
1959	22,984	-
1960	23,696	-

Sheds
Bank Hall	22/2/47
Colwick (loan)	19/6/48
New England (loan)	10/7/48
Gorton (loan)	17/7/48
Bank Hall	7/8/48
Bury	22/1/55
Bolton	10/4/65

Withdrawn w/e 23/4/66

6416 on the turntable at Colwick. One of two Bank Hall engines loaned to the Eastern Region in mid-1948, it spent a month at the Nottingham shed.

46416 at Crewe, probably after a Light Intermediate repair completed in December 1951. 46416 had received its BR number during a Light Casual two years earlier and a new chimney at its next overhaul in early 1954.

46417

Built at Crewe 4/3/47 as 6417
Renumbered w/e 2/12/50

Improvements and modifications

Chimney	9/11/53
Cast steel crossheads	9/11/53

Repairs

Crewe	LI	2/11/50	29/11/50
Crewe	HG	14/10/53	9/11/53
Crewe	HI	25/10/56	20/11/56
Crewe	LC	19/11/57	2/1/58
Crewe	HG	20/4/60	26/5/60
Crewe	HI	20/12/62	17/1/63

Boilers

New	12905
9/11/53	12438
26/5/60	12968

Tenders

New	7017

Mileage/(weekdays out of service)

Year	Mileage	Days
1947	19,758	38
1948	28,703	32
1949	29,064	41
1950	28,193	56
1951	33,527	32
1952	25,231	51
1953	20,879	57
1954	36,858	29
1955	25,545	57
1956	20,216	84
1957	21,945	78
1958	21,641	77
1959	25,023	-
1960	22,273	-

Sheds

Bank Hall	4/3/47
Stratford (loan)	19/6/48
Bank Hall	24/7/48
Bury	22/1/55
Bolton	10/4/65
Newton Heath	3/9/66

Withdrawn w/e 18/2/67

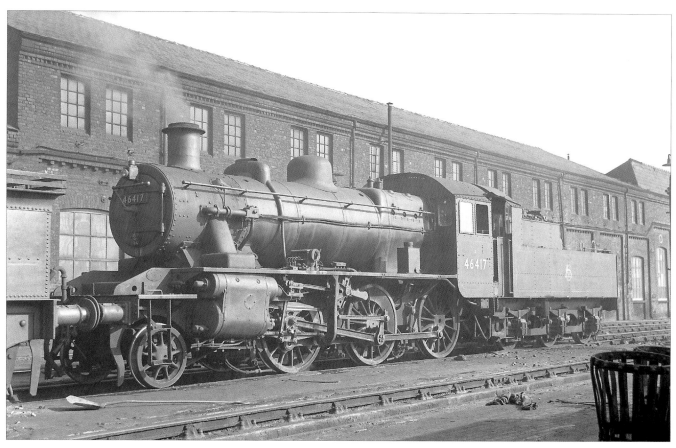

46417 at Bury in the mid-1950s. It was there for over a decade, from January 1955 until April 1965 when it was transferred to Bolton. Its main claim to fame was a loan spell on the Eastern Region at Stratford in 1948. www.rail-online.co.uk

At Bury in the early 1960s, 46417 has overhead warning flashes on its front frames and boiler and underneath the grime on the tender is the later BR crest. 46417 moved to Bolton then Newton Heath in its last two years in service and was withdrawn in February 1967. www.rail-online.co.uk

46418

Built at Crewe 13/3/47 as 6418
Renumbered w/e 24/2/51

Improvements and modifications

Chimney	?
Cast steel crossheads	16/3/54

Repairs

Crewe	LI	29/1/51	21/2/51
Crewe	HG	16/2/54	16/3/54
Crewe	LC EO	11/2/55	14/3/55
Crewe	LI	22/9/56	12/10/56
Crewe	HG	23/3/61	2/5/61

Boilers

New	12904
16/3/54	12906
2/5/61	12903

Tenders

New	7018

Mileage/(weekdays out of service)

1947	22,960	20
1948	25,400	60
1949	25,771	44
1950	27,029	39
1951	23,614	39
1952	25,334	34
1953	22,135	50
1954	23,091	52
1955	21,129	56
1956	21,847	45
1957	24,293	33
1958	25,250	32
1959	23,023	-
1960	23,923	-

Sheds

Newton Heath	13/3/47
Darlington (loan)	19/6/48
Newton Heath	24/7/48

Withdrawn w/e 21/1/67

Two weeks after completing its final Heavy General repair, 46418 was still 'running-in' at Crewe on 20 May 1961 before returning to Newton Heath where it had been allocated from new in 1947. It was one of the two engines loaned to the North Eastern Region in 1948 which led to the building of the batch for that Region in 1951.

Well into its second decade at Newton Heath, 46418 was on shed there on 20 August 1961. It was there until withdrawn in January 1967. www.rail-online.co.uk

46419

Built at Crewe 15/3/47 as 6419
Renumbered w/e 2/12/50

Improvements and modifications

Chimney	2/4/54
Cast steel crossheads	2/4/54

Repairs

Crewe	LI	8/11/50	1/12/50
Crewe	HG	5/3/54	2/4/54
Crewe	LI	7/1/57	30/1/57
Crewe	HG	23/6/60	26/8/60

Boilers

New	12907
2/4/54	12904
26/8/60	13874

Tenders

New	7019

Mileage/(weekdays out of service)

1947	22,593	29
1948	27,955	45
1949	29,945	50
1950	25,361	55
1951	27,328	25
1952	24,644	35
1953	21,181	59
1954	24,044	41
1955	21,602	39
1956	24,281	35
1957	22,330	45
1958	25,715	43
1959	25,734	-
1960	21,093	-

Sheds

Newton Heath	15/3/47
Crewe North (loan)	12/4/47
Newton Heath	26/4/47
Darlington (loan)	19/6/48
Newton Heath	24/7/48
Lees (Oldham)	15/9/62
Springs Branch (Wigan)	18/4/64
Aintree	22/1/66

Stored

Serviceable	3/1/66	10/1/66
Serviceable	9/5/66	23/5/66

Withdrawn w/e 27/8/66

The other half of the Newton Heath duo, 6419 runs through Manchester Victoria on 13 June 1947. What makes the picture interesting is the large figure '7' painted above the cab number which is presumably connected with the target on the smokebox displaying the same number. It had been on loan at Crewe North for two weeks in March and went to Darlington in June 1948 with 6418 where it worked mainly on passenger duties over the Stainmore line to Kirkby Stephen and Penrith. www.rail-online.co.uk

Still working as a Manchester Victoria pilot on 20 September 1960. 46419 was at Newton Heath until September 1962 when it was finally separated from 46418, moving to Oldham Lees shed.

46420

Built at Crewe 3/11/48

Improvements and modifications

Chimney	19/6/52
Cast steel crossheads	24/4/54
AWS	23/2/63

Repairs

Crewe	LC	12/9/50	29/9/50
Crewe	LI	30/5/52	19/6/52
Crewe	HG	29/3/54	24/4/54
Crewe	LC	26/5/56	12/6/56
Crewe	HG	6/10/58	31/10/58
Crewe	LC EO	6/3/59	6/5/59

Boilers

New	12982
24/4/54	13440
31/10/58	13830

Tenders

New	7020

Mileage/(weekdays out of service)

1948	4,070	4
1949	26,681	25
1950	22,347	52
1951	25,702	34
1952	27,798	49
1953	22,397	46
1954	22,667	53
1955	22,877	48
1956	21,424	34
1957	16,651	23
1958	15,272	53
1959	17,225	-
1960	19,421	-

Sheds

Widnes	6/11/48
Rhyl	12/7/52
Widnes	4/10/52
Coventry	28/4/56
Rugby	15/11/58
Llandudno Junction	18/6/60
Chester Midland	17/9/60
Nuneaton	10/12/60

Withdrawn w/e 16/1/65

The first of the 1948 engines, 46420, at its home shed Widnes on 24 April 1949. In addition to the BR numbers, it has several minor modifications from the first twenty engines including vertically rather than horizontally mounted injectors under the cab, draught screens between the two cab windows, and a raised cover over a modified top feed clack valve. The tender has BRITISH RAILWAYS lettering and a curved foothold at the front end of the frames.

46420 crossing the River Nene at Wellingborough on 12 May 1960. It had been transferred from Coventry to Rugby in November 1958.

46421

Built at Crewe 5/11/48

Improvements and modifications

Chimney	30/1/54
Cast steel crossheads	30/1/54

Repairs

Crewe	LC	12/6/50	1/7/50
Crewe	HI	15/11/51	7/12/51
Crewe	GEN	6/1/54	30/1/54
Crewe	LI	11/5/56	2/6/56
Crewe	HG	3/2/61	15/3/61

Boilers

New	12978
30/1/54	12437
15/3/61	12902

Tenders

New	7021

Mileage/(weekdays out of service)

1948	3,960	3
1949	26,369	27
1950	23,715	49
1951	23,241	50
1952	24,298	33
1953	22,894	40
1954	23,682	44
1955	22,578	43
1956	21,494	45
1957	19,909	32
1958	18,343	25
1959	17,904	-
1960	17,436	-

Sheds

Widnes	5/11/48
Llandudno Junction	26/6/54
Widnes	4/9/54
Bescot	28/4/56
Bushbury	30/6/62
Bescot	11/8/62
Saltley	26/3/66

Stored

Serviceable	10/1/66	?

Withdrawn w/e 8/10/66

46421 at Widnes on 12 September 1954. It had been allocated there since it was built in November 1948. It had been through Crewe Works for a Heavy General overhaul earlier in the year when it was fitted with the revised taller chimney and cast steel crossheads.

Bescot's immaculate 46421 on Crewe North shed fresh from Crewe Works Paint Shop after a Heavy General repair completed on 15 March 1961. It spent its last decade in the West Midlands. www.rail-online.co.uk

46422

Built at Crewe 8/11/48

Improvements and modifications
Chimney	22/6/56
Cast steel crossheads	25/2/54

Repairs
Crewe	LC	25/7/50	9/8/50
Crewe	LI	8/2/52	8/3/52
Crewe	HG	1/2/54	25/2/54
Crewe	LC	29/5/56	22/6/56
Crewe	HG	6/2/59	6/3/59
Crewe	HI	27/2/63	22/3/63

Boilers
New	12969
25/2/54	12899
6/3/59	13860

Tenders
New	7022

Mileage/(weekdays out of service)
1948	3,527	4
1949	26,688	24
1950	23,203	53
1951	25,756	31
1952	23,790	46
1953	23,769	33
1954	29,721	53
1955	20,779	52
1956	27,896	48
1957	33,175	45
1958	24,606	37
1959	30,080	-
1960	21,921	-

Sheds
Widnes	8/11/48
Crewe North (loan)	27/2/54
Widnes	20/3/54
Rhyl	29/5/54
Widnes	9/10/54
Springs Branch (Wigan)	28/4/56
Kirkby Stephen (loan)	9/4/60
Kirkby Stephen	30/4/60
Springs Branch (Wigan)	17/6/61
Lancaster Green Ayre	10/2/62
Carnforth	23/4/66

Withdrawn w/e 24/12/66

46422 a long way from home at Rugby MPD on 7 May 1961. Originally one of the five engines which went new to Widnes in 1948, 46422 was at Kirby Stephen from April 1960 until June 1961. www.rail-online.co.uk

46422 arriving at the north facing bay Platform No.2 at Lancaster Castle on 8 September 1963 with a local from Morecambe. It had been transferred from Springs Branch to Green Ayre shed in February 1962 and stayed until April 1966. www.rail-online.co.uk

46423

Built at Crewe 26/11/48

Improvements and modifications
Chimney	24/5/52
Cast steel crossheads	3/6/54

Repairs
Crewe	LC	16/8/50	5/9/50
Crewe	LI	5/5/52	24/5/52
Crewe	HG	23/4/54	3/6/54
Crewe	LC EO	3/4/56	26/4/56
Crewe	LI	17/12/57	9/1/58
Crewe	HG	13/1/61	21/2/61

Boilers
New	12973
3/6/54	12903
21/2/61	13869

Tenders
New	7023

Mileage/(weekdays out of service)
1948	1,875	2
1949	26,432	28
1950	23,224	48
1951	25,215	37
1952	24,100	44
1953	24,000	38
1954	22,981	57
1955	22,459	41
1956	32,657	69
1957	33,148	48
1958	32,686	48
1959	20,988	-
1960	19,450	-

Sheds
Widnes	27/11/48
Rhyl (loan)	6/6/53
Widnes	27/6/53
Rhyl	28/4/56
Springs Branch (Wigan)	22/3/58
Nuneaton	6/12/58
Aston	31/1/59
Watford	15/9/62
Widnes	25/5/63
Speke Junction	18/4/64

Withdrawn w/e 16/1/65

46423 passing Saltney Ferry with Mold Junction shed in the background in 1956. It had been transferred to Rhyl from Widnes in April 1956 and stayed there for almost two years before moving to Springs Branch. www.rail-online.co.uk

46423 at Blue Hand Bridge Bodfari between Denbigh and Chester on 4 July 1956 with a local train to Chester. C.M. Bentley.

46424

Built at Crewe 26/11/48

Improvements and modifications

Chimney	2/5/52
Cast steel crossheads	23/5/55

Repairs

Crewe	LI	25/10/50	18/11/50
Crewe	NC	22/4/52	2/5/52
Crewe	HG	9/2/53	6/3/53
Crewe	HI	28/4/55	23/5/55
Crewe	LC EO	16/11/56	11/12/56
Crewe	HG	20/5/59	20/6/59
Crewe	LI	12/2/63	7/3/63

Boilers

New	12979
6/3/53	12433
20/6/59	13845

Tenders

New	7024

Mileage/(weekdays out of service)

1948	2,270	2
1949	25,836	27
1950	23,167	54
1951	24,928	45
1952	22,951	52
1953	25,449	65
1954	25,853	31
1955	21,607	49
1956	20,762	41
1957	23,213	34
1958	22,308	43
1959	19,461	-
1960	20,082	-

Sheds

Widnes	27/11/48
Crewe North (loan)	14/3/53
Willesden (loan)	28/3/53
Rhyl (loan)	25/7/53
Widnes	26/9/53
Willesden	28/4/56
Widnes	25/5/63
Speke Junction	18/4/64
Workington	10/7/65

Stored

Serviceable	11/11/65	10/12/66

Withdrawn w/e 10/12/66

46424 running in from Crewe North on 15 March 1953 after completing a Heavy General repair during which its plain black LMS livery was replaced by BR lined black. It had been fitted with a tall chimney in May 1952 and was allocated to Widnes from new until April 1956, with the exception of three short loan spells in 1953. Initial Photographics.

46424 was transferred to Willesden from Widnes in April 1956 and stayed there until 1963 when it returned to Widnes. One of the duties of the Willesden allocation was on cross-London freights as demonstrated by 46424 at Acton Wells Junction in 1961. www.rail-online.co.uk

46425

Built at Crewe 29/11/48

Improvements and modifications
Chimney	20/6/53
Cast steel crossheads	7/11/53

Repairs
Crewe	LI	6/11/51	28/11/51
Crewe	NC EO	1/5/53	15/5/53
Crewe	LC EO	29/5/53	20/6/53
Crewe	HG	2/10/53	7/11/53
Crewe	HI	28/8/57	28/9/57
Crewe	HG	8/11/60	23/12/60
Crewe	LC	10/10/61	14/11/61

Boilers
New	12974
7/11/53	12902
23/12/60	12438

Tenders
New	7025

Mileage/(weekdays out of service)
1948	1,856	0
1949	23,303	25
1950	23,409	22
1951	20,962	51
1952	20,658	33
1953	17,458	86
1954	21,007	32
1955	21,019	25
1956	21,150	37
1957	17,838	46
1958	17,374	41
1959	17,330	-
1960	14,352	-

Sheds
Bescot	4/12/48
Rhyl (loan)	27/6/53
Bescot	25/7/53

Withdrawn w/e 11/9/65

46425 went new to Bescot shed where it remained until withdrawn in September 1965, apart from a month in North Wales on loan to Rhyl in summer 1953. Here it is on station pilot duty at Birmingham New Street some time after its later pattern chimney was fitted in November 1953. www.rail-online.co.uk

46425 at Crewe Works on 28 September 1957, newly released from the Paint Shop. It had been undergoing a Heavy Intermediate repair which took a month.

46426

Built at Crewe 3/12/48

Improvements and modifications

Chimney	18/9/54
Cast steel crossheads	18/9/54

Repairs

Crewe	LI	12/3/51	14/4/51
Crewe	HG	25/8/54	18/9/54
Crewe	HC	26/3/56	25/4/56
Crewe	HG	18/9/61	26/10/61

Boilers

New	12981
18/9/54	12900
26/10/61	13557

Tenders

New	7026

Mileage/(weekdays out of service)

1948	1,269	1
1949	24,505	24
1950	23,853	23
1951	20,389	53
1952	21,598	34
1953	19,531	32
1954	19,260	49
1955	19,361	27
1956	26,048	61
1957	24,021	42
1958	23,148	45
1959	21,544	-
1960	23,272	-

Sheds

Bescot	3/12/48
Rhyl	5/5/56
Lancaster Green Ayre	29/9/56
Carlisle Upperby	11/1/64

Withdrawn w/e 24/9/66

Officially into traffic on 3 December 1948, 46426 is still in Crewe Works two days later in shiny plain black with BR Gill Sans numbers and lettering. Together with 46425 and 46427, it was allocated to Bescot, the first West Midlands shed to receive any of the class.

46426 piloting a Stanier 2-6-4T at Sutton Coldfield was noted several times on the local passenger trains between Birmingham New Street and Lichfield in its early days. It left the Midlands in 1956, to Rhyl for the summer and then went on to Lancaster Green Ayre where is was based until 1964.

46427

Built at Crewe 3/12/48

Improvements and modifications
Chimney	5/1/55
Cast steel crossheads	5/1/55

Repairs
Crewe	LC	30/4/51	23/5/51
Crewe	HG	7/12/54	5/1/55
Crewe	HI	15/3/58	3/4/58
Crewe	HG	8/9/61	12/10/61
Crewe	NC	18/12/62	10/1/63

Boilers
New	12970
5/1/55	12969
12/10/61	12978

Tenders
New	7027

Mileage/(weekdays out of service)
1948	1,540	0
1949	23,419	24
1950	23,183	27
1951	16,753	42
1952	18,263	35
1953	19,073	29
1954	18,140	52
1955	16,573	32
1956	22,922	32
1957	20,163	28
1958	17,728	41
1959	21,780	-
1960	16,933	-

Sheds
Bescot	3/12/48
Monument Lane	30/9/50
Aston	17/3/51
Bescot	16/10/65
Stourbridge Junction	26/3/66
Tyseley	16/7/66

Stored
Serviceable	14/10/65	?

Withdrawn w/e 8/10/66

46427 in the late 1950s at Aston. It spent its whole life in the West Midlands, working from five different shed over the years. It left Bescot for Monument Lane in September 1950, then Aston in March 1951 before returning to Bescot in October 1965. 46427 went to Stourbridge Junction in March 1966 and finally to Tyseley in July before withdrawal in October 1966. It had been fitted with a replacement taller pattern chimney in January 1955.

46427 on the ashpit wagon road at Aston. This was one of allocated there in the late 1950s and early 1960s. They performed a range of light jobs including transfer workings in and out of Curzon Street and Windsor Street goods depots and were also used as bankers on the line from Perry Barr through Handsworth Park to Soho. www.rail-online.co.uk

46428

Built at Crewe 3/12/48

Improvements and modifications
Chimney	22/6/56
Cast steel crossheads	22/6/56

Repairs
Crewe	LC	1/2/49	4/3/49
Crewe	LI	2/4/51	27/4/51
Crewe	HG	11/6/53	4/7/53
Crewe	LI	31/5/56	22/6/56
Crewe	HG	2/4/59	30/4/59
Crewe	LI	4/6/63	28/6/63

Boilers
New	12975
4/7/53	12979
30/4/59	12899

Tenders
New	7028

Mileage/(weekdays out of service)
1948	1,133	0
1949	32,546	42
1950	19,772	44
1951	35,181	54
1952	39,724	51
1953	29,859	55
1954	34,964	21
1955	33,292	49
1956	36,061	44
1957	36,647	28
1958	29,967	46
1959	30,812	-
1960	31,000	-

Sheds
Preston	3/12/48
Heaton Mersey (loan)	19/3/49
Wigan CLC (loan)	9/7/49
Heaton Mersey (loan)	20/5/50
Preston	23/9/50
Springs Branch (Wigan)	24/3/51
Lower Ince	9/6/51
Springs Branch (Wigan)	29/3/52
Rhyl	5/6/54
Springs Branch (Wigan)	2/10/54
Bescot	10/2/62
Bushbury	24/3/62
Leamington	24/10/64
Tyseley	19/6/65
Crewe South	8/10/66

Withdrawn w/e 12/11/66

46428 spent its early years in the north west and was in its third spell at Springs Branch when photographed there on 2 March 1957. It was one of the last to receive a replacement chimney, fitted in June 1956. www.rail-online.co.uk

46428 has no shedplate but LEAMINGTON, all but invisible, is painted on the bufferbeam. This will be the period when 46428 was allocated there, from October 1964 until June 1965. It is the oldest example to be preserved; after fifty years it has still not been restored to working order, although this is now underway at Bury. www.rail-online.co.uk

46429

Built at Crewe 2/12/48

Improvements and modifications

Chimney	19/6/54
Cast steel crossheads	19/6/54

Repairs

Crewe	LI	27/11/51	7/1/52
Crewe	HG	20/5/54	19/6/54
Crewe	HI	13/9/57	4/10/57
Crewe	HG	18/3/61	24/6/61

Boilers

New	12977
19/6/54	12898
24/6/61	14004

Tenders

New	7029
7/1/52	7002

Mileage/(weekdays out of service)

1948	1,199	1
1949	21,729	36
1950	21,364	43
1951	22,205	51
1952	25,706	32
1953	22,209	44
1954	20,000	49
1955	20,061	43
1956	25,401	29
1957	22,443	45
1958	20,313	22
1959	17,830	-
1960	18,566	-

Sheds

Preston	2/12/48
Stoke	27/11/54
Bescot	28/4/62
Saltley	26/3/66

Stored

Serviceable	28/3/66	?

Withdrawn w/e 2/7/66

46429 at Stoke on 30 April 1960. It was one of two allocated there from November 1954 until April 1962, the other was 46430 and both were transferred from Preston.

46429 moved from Stoke to Bescot in April 1962. On 2 November 1963 it worked the Stephenson Locomotive Society Last Train on the Harborne Branch in the Birmingham suburb. www.rail-online.co.uk

46430

Built at Crewe 10/12/48

Improvements and modifications

Chimney	26/6/52
Cast steel crossheads	30/6/54
AWS	25/2/63

Repairs

Crewe	LI	5/6/52	26/6/52
Crewe	HG	5/6/54	30/6/54
Crewe	HI	11/11/57	30/11/57
Crewe	HG	5/1/61	3/2/61
Crewe	NC	7/2/63	25/2/63

Boilers

New	12976
30/6/54	12978
3/2/61	13884

Tenders

New	7030

Mileage/(weekdays out of service)

1948	873	1
1949	20,045	29
1950	22,526	34
1951	26,245	48
1952	26,506	61
1953	21,754	40
1954	20,556	47
1955	20,142	25
1956	24,973	30
1957	21,264	49
1958	21,088	28
1959	18,638	-
1960	19,359	-

Sheds

Preston	11/12/48
Springs Branch (Wigan)	24/3/51
Rhyl	7/7/51
Bangor (loan)	29/9/51
Rhyl	20/10/51
Springs Branch (Wigan)	27/10/51
Preston	15/12/51
Rhyl	12/7/52
Preston	18/10/52
Llandudno Junction	17/7/54
Preston	2/10/54
Stoke	27/11/54
Bescot	28/4/62
Buxton (loan)	25/8/62
Bescot	10/11/62
Rugby	18/5/63

Withdrawn w/e 9/10/65

46430 was loaned to Rhyl shed for the summer season in both 1951 and 1952. It was one of the engines used on the North Wales Land Cruise trains as shown by the W663 headcode on 14 September 1952 at Rhyl shed. It has a replacement tall chimney, fitted during a Light Intermediate in June of that year. 46430 was the first of the class to have a plain '2' power classification rather than the original '2F', reflecting its mixed traffic status. R.S. Carpenter Collection.

After almost eight years at Stoke, 46430 was transferred to Bescot in April 1962; shortly after this it was at Birmingham New Street on a special working comprising two inspection saloons. www.rail-online.co.uk

46431

Built at Crewe 14/12/48

Improvements and modifications

Chimney	12/11/52
Cast steel crossheads	20/5/55
AWS	9/1/63

Repairs

Crewe	LI	28/10/52	12/11/52
Crewe	HG	4/4/55	20/5/55
Crewe	LC	8/3/57	15/4/57
Crewe	HI	25/6/59	7/8/59
Crewe	HG	1/2/62	9/3/62
Crewe	NC	13/12/62	9/1/63

Boilers

New	12980
20/5/55	12907
9/3/62	?

Tenders

New	7031

Mileage/(weekdays out of service)

1948	572	0
1949	22,827	26
1950	20,123	32
1951	19,438	29
1952	18,113	59
1953	22,515	28
1954	20,510	40
1955	19,775	53
1956	21,634	29
1957	19,390	67
1958	21,321	57
1959	21,248	-
1960	24,961	-

Sheds

Willesden	18/12/48
Watford	29/11/58
Lancaster Green Ayre	25/5/63
Carnforth	23/4/66

Withdrawn w/e 25/3/67

46431 at Willesden on 31 August 1949. It was allocated there from December 1948 until November 1958, one of a batch of four arrived from new. They were used on empty coaching stock duties between Euston and Wembley, on cross-London freights, Permanent Way trains and for shed and yard pilot work. H.C. Casserley, courtesy M. Casserley.

46431 runs light through Willesden Junction station in 1959. It had been transferred to Watford in November 1958 and remained there until May 1963 when it moved on to Lancaster Green Ayre. www.rail-online.co.uk

46432

Built at Crewe 24/12/48

Improvements and modifications

Chimney	27/1/56
Cast steel crossheads	27/1/56

Repairs

Crewe	LI	5/8/53	27/8/53
Crewe	HG	24/12/55	27/1/56
Crewe	HI	24/4/59	23/5/59
Crewe	HG	10/8/62	7/9/62

Boilers

New	12968
27/1/56	13433
7/9/62	12980

Tenders

New	7032

Mileage/(weekdays out of service)

1948	188	0
1949	22,472	17
1950	20,588	35
1951	18,959	26
1952	24,306	48
1953	31,542	60
1954	36,080	42
1955	32,363	52
1956	37,296	65
1957	25,936	56
1958	23,461	61
1959	17,766	-
1960	18,977	-

Sheds

Willesden	25/12/48
Springs Branch (Wigan)	12/7/52
Rhyl	5/5/56
Workington	19/1/57
Springs Branch (Wigan)	30/4/66

Stored

Serviceable	21/11/66	?

Withdrawn w/e 6/5/67

46432 at Willesden on 30 April 1950, in lined black with **BRITISH RAILWAYS** on the tender. Its stay here was quite short, moving to Springs Branch in July 1952. www.rail-online.co.uk

46432 at Threlkeld, between Keswick and Troutbeck on the Cockermouth, Keswick and Penrith line, on 8 July 1965. It had been transferred to Workington in January 1957.

46433

Built at Crewe 29/12/48

Improvements and modifications
Chimney	4/2/56
Cast steel crossheads	4/2/56
AWS	1/2/63

Repairs
Crewe	LC	12/1/50	10/2/50
Rugby	LI	15/1/53	6/2/53
Crewe	HG	29/12/55	4/2/56
Crewe	LI	25/9/58	21/10/58
Crewe	HG	1/1/63	1/2/63

Boilers
New	12971
4/2/56	13451
1/2/63	12995

Tenders
New	7033

Mileage/(weekdays out of service)
1948	153	0
1949	24,207	27
1950	19,049	51
1951	18,386	39
1952	18,355	35
1953	20,241	40
1954	21,205	39
1955	19,180	52
1956	32,505	56
1957	39,497	44
1958	23,929	93
1959	21,114	-
1960	16,994	-

Sheds
Willesden	1/1/49
Rhyl	5/5/56
Stoke (loan)	21/9/57
Rhyl	12/10/57
Workington	14/6/58
Lancaster Green Ayre	11/5/63
Carnforth	23/4/66

Stored
Serviceable	13/3/67	20/3/67

Withdrawn w/e 6/5/67

46433 at Aber in the late 1950s; it was at Rhyl from May 1956 until June 1958. The station platforms are very low and are probably original Chester and Holyhead Railway. www.rail-online.co.uk

46433 at Newton Heath on 4 June 1966. It still has a 10J Lancaster Green Ayre shedplate although it had been transferred to Carnforth at the end of April. It had been fitted with AWS at Crewe Works in January 1963, one of the last to receive the equipment. www.rail-online.co.uk

46434

Built at Crewe 29/12/48

Improvements and modifications

Chimney	12/6/53
Cast steel crossheads	6/1/56

Repairs

Crewe	LI	21/3/51	14/4/51
Crewe	LI	23/5/53	12/6/53
Crewe	HG	6/12/55	6/1/56
Crewe	HI	6/1/58	25/1/58
Crewe	HG	27/8/59	30/9/59

Boilers

New	12972
6/1/56	12439
30/9/59	12433

Tenders

New	7034

Mileage/(weekdays out of service)

1949	35,780	30
1950	25,547	38
1951	23,278	50
1952	22,934	35
1953	28,464	53
1954	35,343	47
1955	30,365	69
1956	36,934	28
1957	35,374	33
1958	31,538	36
1959	27,886	-
1960	22,606	-

Sheds

Willesden	1/1/49
Wigan CLC (loan)	16/4/49
Heaton Mersey	22/5/50
Widnes	23/9/50
Rhyl	27/6/53
Springs Branch (Wigan)	24/10/53
Carlisle Upperby	7/5/60

Withdrawn w/e 24/9/66

The spotters at Crewe are not very interested in 46434 as it runs through the station in the early 1960s. www.rail-online.co.uk

46434 engaged on pilot work (see *Postscript* page 356) at Carlisle on 15 July 1964. It was at Upperby from May 1960 until withdrawn in September 1966. D. Forsyth, ColourRail

46435

Built at Crewe 4/1/50

Improvements and modifications
Chimney	17/1/53
Cast steel crossheads	25/2/56
AWS	14/6/61

Repairs
Crewe	LI	31/12/52	17/1/53
Crewe	HG	21/1/56	25/2/56
Darlington	GEN	26/1/60	25/2/60
Darlington	NC	1/6/61	14/6/61

Boilers
New	12676
25/2/56	13436

Tenders
New	7035

Mileage/(weekdays out of service)
1950	31,907	34
1951	30,858	31
1952	34,363	44
1953	30,515	55
1954	18,963	34
1955	22,636	49
1956	28,560	58

Sheds
Blackpool Central	7/1/50
Southport	30/6/51
Walton on the Hill	25/8/51
Blackpool Central	22/9/51
Bank Hall	29/9/51
Wakefield	15/1/55
Low Moor	14/11/59
Hurlford	9/11/63

Withdrawn w/e 18/7/64

46435, the first to be outshopped with the first BR emblem, at Blackpool North on 29 April 1951. It had been allocated there from new in January 1950 but would shortly move to Southport, in June. R. Carpenter Collection.

46435 at Wigan on 21 July 1952; it was at four different north west sheds in a period of three months in mid-1951 but had settled down at Bank Hall, staying there until January 1955.

46436

Built at Crewe 10/1/50

Improvements and modifications
Chimney	26/1/57
Cast steel crossheads	13/2/54

Repairs
Crewe	HI	25/1/54	13/2/54
Crewe	HG	20/12/56	26/1/57
Crewe	HI	29/11/60	13/1/61
Crewe	HG	18/3/64	21/5/64

Boilers
New	13254
26/1/57	13471
21/5/64	13548

Tenders
New	7036

Mileage/(weekdays out of service)
1950	32,368	30
1951	19,787	41
1952	19,129	43
1953	18,748	37
1954	22,733	64
1955	21,949	71
1956	24,651	53
1957	24,102	66
1958	24,693	55
1959	23,976	-
1960	20,009	-

Sheds
Fleetwood	10/1/50
Walton on the Hill	29/7/50
Goole	16/12/50
Bury	10/3/56
Bolton	10/4/65
Newton Heath	20/8/66

Stored
Serviceable	11/10/65	17/1/66
Serviceable	7/11/66	?

Withdrawn w/e 6/5/67

46436 posed in May 1952 highlights the detail of the lined black livery.

46436 running light into Manchester Exchange in the early 1960s. After spending over five years at Goole, it moved to Bury in March 1956.

46437

Built at Crewe 16/1/50

Improvements and modifications
Chimney	27/3/54
Cast steel crossheads	27/3/54

Repairs
Shed	LC EO	14/8/51	18/8/51
Crewe	LI	26/2/54	27/3/54
Crewe	HG	11/9/56	11/10/56
Crewe	LI	21/10/59	28/11/59
Crewe	HG	17/10/63	22/11/63

Boilers
New	13429
11/10/56	12676
22/11/63	13456

Tenders
New	7037

Mileage/(weekdays out of service)
1950	39,653	24
1951	30,328	55
1952	19,945	40
1953	19,836	61
1954	31,334	73
1955	34,391	70
1956	24,334	50
1957	26,460	21
1958	26,784	24
1959	24,271	-
1960	27,606	-

Sheds
Fleetwood	16/1/50
Goole	25/2/50
Walton on the Hill	16/12/50
Goole	31/12/50
Newton Heath	10/3/56

Stored
Serviceable	12/10/65	30/5/66

Withdrawn w/e 6/5/67

46437 on ECS duty at Newton Heath on 4 June 1966. It was at Newton Heath from March 1956 until withdrawn in May 1967. www.rail-online.co.uk

46437 pauses at Bacup with the LCGB Rossendale Forester Railtour on 3 December 1966. It was paired with Stanier 2-6-4T 42644 for most of the journey. www.rail-online.co.uk

46438

Built at Crewe 21/1/50

Improvements and modifications

Chimney	13/10/56
Cast steel crossheads	13/10/56
AWS	20/1/61

Repairs

Shed	LC EO	6/8/51	16/8/51
Crewe	LI	17/8/53	11/9/53
Crewe	HG	10/9/56	13/10/56
Darlington	GEN	5/12/60	20/1/61

Boilers

New	13430
13/10/56	13844

Tenders

New	7038
13/10/56	7095

Mileage/(weekdays out of service)

1950	25,686	23
1951	23,809	44
1952	20,509	38
1953	21,553	64
1954	28,748	48
1955	23,550	43
1956	22,213	72

Sheds

Fleetwood	21/1/50
Wakefield	18/2/50
Sowerby Bridge	14/11/59
Wakefield	17/3/62

Withdrawn w/e 9/2/63

Brand new 46438 in January 1950 at Crewe North after a running-in trip on the Shrewsbury line. Its first shed was Fleetwood and it remained on the Central Division until its withdrawal in 1963.

46438 at Sowerby Bridge on 29 September 1961. It has a number of features arising from its General overhaul at Darlington which was completed in January 1961. It has guard irons mounted on the pony truck instead of the frames and is unlined with large 10in cab numbers and large BR emblem on the tender. The latter was originally paired with Darlington-built 46495 and has a vertical handrail and footstep on the rear frame and a strengthened front step. www.rail-online.co.uk

46439

Built at Crewe 27/1/50

Improvements and modifications

Chimney	12/2/54
Cast steel crossheads	12/2/54

Repairs

Crewe	LI	18/1/54	12/2/54
Crewe	HG	28/1/57	16/2/57
Crewe	LC EO	17/12/57	17/1/58
Crewe	LI	4/5/59	12/6/59
Crewe	HG	2/1/63	26/1/63

Boilers

New	13431
16/2/57	13555
26/1/63	13885

Tenders

New	7039

Mileage/(weekdays out of service)

1950	23,323	20
1951	23,695	34
1952	25,282	39
1953	22,651	52
1954	23,225	74
1955	18,893	40
1956	19,558	31
1957	17,918	53
1958	17,970	40
1959	17,372	-
1960	18,543	-

Sheds

Fleetwood	27/1/50
Wakefield	18/2/50
Aintree	9/10/54
Bury	15/9/62
Bolton	10/4/65
Aintree	19/6/65

Stored

Serviceable	7/11/66	24/2/67

Withdrawn w/e 18/3/67

46439 at Bank Hall on 23 August 1955, with a replacement chimney fitted in February 1954. It was transferred from Wakefield to Aintree in October 1954 and stayed in Liverpool until September 1962.

46439 departs from Wigan Wallgate with the 2J58 Manchester Victoria stopping train in 1963. It was allocated to Bury shed at this date, moving to Bolton in April 1965 and then back to Aintree two months later. www.rail-online.co.uk

46440

Built at Crewe 2/2/50

Improvements and modifications
Chimney	8/12/55
Cast steel crossheads	8/12/55

Repairs
Rugby	LI	20/1/53	13/2/53
Crewe	HG	4/11/55	8/12/55
Crewe	LI	2/1/58	1/2/58
Crewe	LC EO	1/11/60	27/1/61
Crewe	HG	2/11/62	1/12/62

Boilers
New	13433
8/12/55	13443
1/12/62	13433

Tenders
New	7040

Mileage/(weekdays out of service)
1950	30,352	30
1951	28,783	62
1952	24,711	42
1953	23,043	74
1954	22,454	65
1955	21,107	122
1956	30,770	29
1957	23,470	52
1958	16,085	86
1959	27,110	-
1960	18,249	-

Sheds
Skipton	2/2/50
Holbeck	13/2/54
Derby	10/4/54
Toton (loan)	27/10/56
Derby	26/1/57
Toton (loan)	23/2/57
Derby	6/4/57
Burton	27/7/57
Derby	10/1/59
Springs Branch (Wigan)	23/5/64
Speke Junction	7/11/64
Northwich	18/6/66

Withdrawn w/e 25/3/67

46440 in March 1963 at Burton on Trent, working the 8.20am local to Walsall. It spent a decade in the East Midlands. www.rail-online.co.uk

46440 backing through Derby station in 1964 where it will probably have been on pilot duties. It moved to Springs Branch in May of that year. www.rail-online.co.uk

46441

Built at Crewe 9/2/50

Improvements and modifications

Chimney	26/5/54
Cast steel crossheads	26/5/54
AWS	?

Repairs

Crewe	HI	3/5/54	26/5/54
Crewe	HG	27/12/56	25/1/57
Crewe	HI	19/6/61	29/7/61
Crewe	NC	12/2/63	25/2/63
Crewe	GEN	18/2/64	28/4/64

Boilers

New	13434
25/1/57	13587

Tenders

New	7041

Mileage/(weekdays out of service)

1950	27,410	24
1951	30,618	28
1952	27,963	48
1953	27,578	41
1954	26,011	41
1955	27,173	38
1956	27,465	33
1957	26,070	46
1958	23,643	44
1959	24,208	-
1960	23,126	-

Sheds

Lancaster Green Ayre	9/2/50
Carnforth	23/4/66

Stored

Serviceable	10/10/65	14/12/65
Serviceable	24/1/66	?

Withdrawn w/e 15/4/67

46441 at Crewe North after a running-in turn in February 1950. It was allocated to Lancaster Green Ayre and stayed there until April 1966 when it moved to Carnforth for its last year in traffic.

There is very little space left on the running plate of 46441 at Lancaster Green Ayre in 1964. Nearest the cab is the AWS vacuum reservoir (the smaller timing reservoir is hidden by the cab at this angle), the rear sandbox and then further forward is the Silvertown mechanical lubricator which delivered oil to the cylinders and motion. 46441 was purchased for preservation out of BR service and after working regularly from Steamtown Carnforth was put on static display. However work is starting to return it to operation at the Lakeside & Haverthwaite Railway. www.rail-online.co.uk

46442

Built at Crewe 10/2/50

Improvements and modifications
Chimney	10/1/56
Cast steel crossheads	10/1/56

Repairs
Crewe	LI	5/6/63	26/6/63
Crewe	HG	9/12/55	10/1/56
Crewe	HG	31/8/59	6/10/59
Crewe	LI	31/7/63	20/8/63

Boilers
New	13436
10/1/56	13453
6/10/59	13554

Tenders
New	7042

Mileage/(weekdays out of service)
1950	28,579	34
1951	34,029	46
1952	27,527	57
1953	23,827	60
1954	25,433	75
1955	19,195	90
1956	28,973	61
1957	26,469	53
1958	18,969	97
1959	20,322	-
1960	21,157	-

Sheds
Skipton	10/2/50
Kirkby Stephen (loan)	7/5/60
Kirkby Stephen	25/6/60
Workington	9/7/60
Bescot	6/1/62
Rugby	1/12/62
Bangor	9/3/63
Croes Newydd (loan)	1/2/64
Leamington	24/10/64
Tyseley	19/6/65

Stored
Serviceable	24/11/63	27/1/64

Withdrawn w/e 8/10/66

46442 in the early 1950s at Skipton, where it was shedded for its first decade in service. www.rail-online.co.uk

46442 departing from Bradford Forster Square, probably in 1956 after it received a tall chimney in January of that year. Its 20F shedplate dates the period as no later than February 1957 when the code was changed to 24G.

46443

Built at Crewe 20/2/50

Improvements and modifications
Chimney	9/1/54
Cast steel crossheads	9/1/54

Repairs
Crewe	LI	12/12/53	9/1/54
Crewe	HG	5/12/56	11/1/57
Crewe	LI	6/4/61	8/5/61

Boilers
New	13438
11/1/57	13442

Tenders
New	7043

Mileage/(weekdays out of service)
1950	23,598	33
1951	30,167	43
1952	29,735	61
1953	24,284	88
1954	28,958	58
1955	25,724	80
1956	18,353	113
1957	31,888	38
1958	23,548	39
1959	26,011	-
1960	21,024	-

Sheds
Derby	20/2/50
Saltley	18/11/61
Newton Heath	15/10/66

Stored
Serviceable	7/11/66	?

Withdrawn w/e 25/3/67

46443 working as a Birmingham New Street station pilot, probably in 1965 as rebuilding of the station is underway. 46443 was transferred from Saltley to Newton Heath in October 1966 but went into store within three weeks and may not have worked again up to its withdrawal in March 1967, although it was fit to run in steam to the Severn Valley Railway the following month. www.rail-online.co.uk

The now preserved 46443 at Crewe soon after completion of an unrecorded repair from which it emerged in unlined black. The 2E shedplate indicates the date as post-September 1963 when Saltley's code changed from 21A; 46443 was there from November 1961 until October 1966. www.rail-online.co.uk

46444

Built at Crewe 22/2/50

Improvements and modifications
Chimney	9/12/53
Cast steel crossheads	9/12/53

Repairs
Derby	NC EO	7/5/53	11/5/53
Crewe	HI	18/11/53	9/12/53
Crewe	HG	24/1/55	4/3/55
Crewe	LI	29/7/57	17/8/57
Crewe	HG	23/5/60	5/7/60

Boilers
New	13432
4/3/55	12976
5/7/60	13439

Tenders
New	7044

Mileage/(weekdays out of service)
1950	24,691	38
1951	29,977	55
1952	28,991	50
1953	31,469	75
1954	35,156	47
1955	33,698	73
1956	37,672	50
1957	30,968	48
1958	39,663	43
1959	25,547	-
1960	21,891	-

Sheds
Derby	22/2/50
Leicester Midland	27/10/51
Kettering	19/1/52
Nottingham	23/3/63
Bank Hall	23/5/64

Withdrawn w/e 10/7/65

46444 at Crewe North on 26 February 1950, four days after it officially entered service. It has no shedplate – this would have been fitted when it arrived at its first posting, Derby, where it stayed until October 1951 when it was transferred to Kettering. L.W. Perkins.

After joining the first four of the class at Kettering, 46444 settled down to work alongside them on the service to Cambridge, staying until March 1963. On 21 August 1959 it was departing from St Ives to Cambridge.

46445

Built at Crewe 27/2/50

Improvements and modifications
Chimney	18/12/52
Cast steel crossheads	19/4/56

Repairs
Shed	LC	3/4/52	10/4/52
Crewe	HG	26/11/52	18/12/52
Crewe	HI	17/3/56	19/4/56
Crewe	HG	24/10/58	22/11/58
Crewe	HI	8/8/62	30/8/62
Crewe	NC Rec	5/9/62	12/9/62

Boilers
New	13439
18/12/52	12422
22/11/58	13849

Tenders
New	7045

Mileage/(weekdays out of service)
1950	17,341	13
1951	20,596	18
1952	19,379	43
1953	24,947	18
1954	22,635	39
1955	24,336	38
1956	30,224	58
1957	37,090	47
1958	32,479	58
1959	33,285	-
1960	17,846	-

Sheds
Coventry	27/2/50
Rhyl	5/5/56
Stoke (loan)	23/11/57
Rhyl	14/12/57
Rugby	20/6/59
Bescot	25/5/63
Saltley	26/3/66

Stored
Serviceable	10/1/66	?

Withdrawn w/e 2/7/66

46445 shortly after it entered traffic on 27 February 1950. It was sent to Coventry within a few days and remained there until May 1956.

After leaving the industrial Midlands for the North Wales coast in May 1956, 46445 stayed at Rhyl until June 1959 when it went back, this time to Rugby. Shortly before this, on 23 April 1959, 46445 takes on water at Denbigh while working the 3pm Ruthin to Chester. R.J. Buckley, Initial Photographics.

46446

Built at Crewe 4/3/50

Improvements and modifications

Chimney	2/10/52
Cast steel crossheads	19/4/56

Repairs

Shed	LC EO	18/4/52	30/4/52
Crewe	HG	6/9/52	2/10/52
Crewe	NC EO	5/5/53	15/5/53
Shed	LC	11/4/55	20/4/55
Crewe	LI	20/3/56	19/4/56
Crewe	HG	25/9/59	12/11/59

Boilers

New	13440
2/10/52	13900
12/11/59	12430

Tenders

New	7046

Mileage/(weekdays out of service)

1950	17,351	16
1951	19,121	32
1952	20,752	48
1953	23,508	20
1954	28,698	22
1955	26,547	49
1956	21,025	44
1957	15,862	33
1958	16,965	32
1959	17,709	-
1960	19,712	-

Sheds

Crewe North	4/3/50
Coventry	25/3/50
Nuneaton	15/11/58
Rugby	31/1/59
Machynlleth	25/5/63
Shrewsbury	10/12/66

Withdrawn w/e 17/12/66

Rugby's 46446 waits at Leire Halt on 25 March 1961. Note the flatbottom rail at this back-water on the Leicester to Rugby line. 46446 spent most of the 1950s at Coventry, arriving at Rugby in January 1959. www.rail-online.co.uk

46446 in late 1963 or 1964 at Morfa Mawddach on a Barmouth-Dolgellau local. It had been transferred to Machynlleth in May 1963 from Rugby and was withdrawn in December 1966, after a 'paper transfer' to Shrewsbury. www.rail-online.co.uk

46447

Built at Crewe 15/3/50

Improvements and modifications
Chimney	13/6/53
Cast steel crossheads	24/9/55

Repairs
Crewe	LI	27/5/53	13/6/53
Crewe	HG	23/8/55	24/9/55
Crewe	HI	23/4/59	22/5/59
Crewe	HG	21/5/62	16/6/62

Boilers
New	13435
24/9/55	13445
16/6/62	12969

Tenders
New	7047

Mileage/(weekdays out of service)
1950	26,453	27
1951	32,551	27
1952	30,133	28
1953	31,799	44
1954	32,718	37
1955	27,492	55
1956	29,367	34
1957	26,652	62
1958	24,453	59
1959	20,243	-
1960	21,260	-

Sheds
Crewe North	15/3/50
Workington	27/5/50
Springs Branch (Wigan)	12/12/59
Llandudno Junction	18/6/60
Bangor	17/9/60
Nuneaton	16/9/61
Derby	25/5/63
Springs Branch (Wigan)	23/5/64

Stored
Serviceable	22/11/65	26/3/66

Withdrawn w/e 31/12/66

Three of the Workington allocation headed by 46447 on shed on 14 April 1957. Although the Derby Lightweight DMUs like the one on the left had revolutionised the Cumbrian passenger services after 1955, the 2-6-0s continued to work in the area until the mid-1960s. www.rail-online.co.uk

Nuneaton's 46447 on the Crewe North turntable on 23 June 1962 after a Heavy General repair completed the week before. After withdrawal in December 1966, 46447 went to Woodham's scrapyard from where it was rescued in 1972 by the Ivatt Locomotive Trust. It was eventually restored to working order in 2014.

46448

Built at Crewe 21/3/50

Improvements and modifications
Chimney	?
Cast steel crossheads	9/10/53

Repairs
Crewe	LI	15/9/53	9/10/53
Crewe	HG	31/10/56	1/12/56
Crewe	HG	4/6/59	25/7/59
Crewe	LI	13/12/63	12/2/64

Boilers
New	13442
1/12/56	13554
25/7/59	12972

Tenders
New	7048

Mileage/(weekdays out of service)
1950	29,807	24
1951	37,526	40
1952	29,216	37
1953	26,824	52
1954	34,595	30
1955	34,606	42
1956	33,214	51
1957	35,306	32
1958	31,631	31
1959	29,053	-
1960	28,120	-

Sheds
Crewe North	21/3/50
Workington	27/5/50
Springs Branch (Wigan)	13/2/54
Rhyl	29/5/54
Springs Branch (Wigan)	5/6/54
Uttoxeter (loan)	16/1/60
Springs Branch (Wigan)	12/3/60
Bescot	10/2/62
Bushbury	24/3/62
Saltley	7/12/63
Newton Heath	15/10/66

Stored
Serviceable	1/10/63	2/12/63

Withdrawn w/e 6/5/67

With SALTLEY painted on the bufferbeam in LNER style, 46448 works a Birmingham transfer freight at Landor Street Junction in 1965. After spending its early years in the north west, it reached Saltley in December 1963 via Bescot and Bushbury. www.rail-online.co.uk

Still with its allocation on the buffer beam, 46448 works a parcels train at Manchester Victoria on 25 February 1967. It was had been transferred to Newton Heath in October 1966 and would remain in service until May 1967. www.rail-online.co.uk

46449

Built at Crewe 28/3/50

Improvements and modifications

Chimney	9/9/55
Cast steel crossheads	9/9/55

Repairs

Rugby	LI	30/12/52	26/1/53
Crewe	NC EO	3/2/54	15/2/54
Crewe	HG	16/8/55	9/9/55
Crewe	HI	4/12/59	15/1/60
Crewe	HG	4/5/62	1/6/62

Boilers

New	13443
9/9/55	12980
1/6/62	12906

Tenders

New	7049

Mileage/(weekdays out of service)

1950	25,170	21
1951	35,707	20
1952	36,462	14
1953	31,568	52
1954	35,320	34
1955	22,053	58
1956	17,056	87
1957	17,879	73
1958	13,234	127
1959	21,118	-
1960	15,623	-

Sheds

Crewe North	28/3/50
Penrith	27/5/50
Carlisle Upperby	23/4/55
Kirkby Stephen	30/4/60
Preston	17/9/60
Lostock Hall	16/9/61
Lees (Oldham)	14/9/63
Newton Heath	18/4/64

Withdrawn w/e 6/5/67

46449 at Penrith in the early 1950s before its chimney was replaced (in September 1955). It was allocated here from 1950 until April 1955 when it moved to Carlisle Upperby. Note long ladder and absence of rear footstep and vertical handrail on the tender. www.rail-online.co.uk

46449 returning to Durham on 19 August 1960 after turning on the Baxter Wood triangle to the south east of the station. It had been at Kirkby Stephen since April but would move away to Preston in September. It was one of five engines fitted to take the No.3A snowplough for working over the CK&P line and still has the thrust strips for this protruding above the buffers.

46450

Built at Crewe 3/4/50

Improvements and modifications
Chimney	1/4/54
Cast steel crossheads	19/1/55

Repairs
Derby	NC EO	6/5/53	13/5/53
Crewe	LI	2/3/54	1/4/54
Crewe	LC	21/12/54	19/1/55
Crewe	HG	3/4/57	27/4/57
Darlington	GEN	2/8/61	4/4/62

Boilers
New	13255
27/4/57	13434

Tenders
New	7050
19/1/55	7089

Mileage/(weekdays out of service)
1950	14,806	20
1951	19,102	50
1952	18,807	22
1953	18,399	58
1954	16,004	71
1955	17,339	53
1956	16,108	43
1957	16,442	0

Sheds
Sheffield Grimesthorpe	5/4/50
Sheffield Millhouses	1/4/61
Canklow	6/1/62
Dumfries (loan)	14/4/62
Canklow	21/4/62
Dumfries (loan)	12/5/62
Dumfries	26/5/62

Withdrawn w/e 22/1/66

With new lagging on the ejector pipework, 46450 has finished a Light Intermediate overhaul at Crewe Works on 28 March 1954 during which its chimney was replaced. www.rail-online.co.uk

46450 at Grindleford about to enter the 3½ mile long Totley Tunnel on the Hope Valley line to Sheffield. It was allocated to Grimesthorpe throughout the 1950s along with 46451. www.rail-online.co.uk

46451

Built at Crewe 11/4/50

Improvements and modifications

Chimney	11/2/57
Cast steel crossheads	11/2/57

Repairs

Derby	NC EO	6/5/53	12/5/53
Rugby	LI	29/9/53	22/10/53
Crewe	HG	17/1/57	11/2/57
Darlington	LC	8/12/59	2/2/60
Darlington	GEN	12/5/60	30/6/60
Darlington	NC Rec	13/6/62	13/6/62
Cowlairs	LC EO	28/10/64	26/12/64
Cowlairs	NC	5/11/65	6/11/65

Boilers

New	13441
11/2/57	13583

Tenders

New	7051
?	7076
?	7051

Mileage/(weekdays out of service)

1950	14,971	16
1951	20,197	30
1952	18,055	33
1953	17,633	63
1954	17,860	43
1955	18,941	41
1956	16,624	31
1957	18,896	0

Sheds

Sheffield Grimesthorpe	11/4/50
Sheffield Millhouses	15/4/61
Hurlford (loan)	7/10/61
Hurlford	14/10/61

Withdrawn w/e 3/12/66

46451 at Sheffield Grimesthorpe where it was allocated from new in April 1950 until April 1961 when it went to Millhouses for six months before transferring to Hurlford. This period is pre-January 1951 because Jinty 7236 in the background was renumbered then. www.rail-online.co.uk

46451 at Hurlford, its home from October 1961. Note the unusual position of the overhead warning flash, on the steampipe rather than on the front frame. 46451 was withdrawn at Hurlford in December 1966. www.rail-online.co.uk

46452

Built at Crewe 17/4/50

Improvements and modifications
Chimney	27/11/53
Cast steel crossheads	27/11/53

Repairs
Derby	NC EO	12/5/53	14/5/53
Crewe	LI	9/11/53	27/11/53
Crewe	HG	1/10/56	27/10/56
Crewe	HI	16/5/60	17/6/60
Crewe	HG	11/11/63	16/12/63

Boilers
New	13545
27/10/56	13548
17/12/63	13801

Tenders
New	7052

Mileage/(weekdays out of service)
1950	21,117	18
1951	29,283	23
1952	25,387	29
1953	21,712	46
1954	24,061	58
1955	20,196	94
1956	19,103	109
1957	26,309	48
1958	22,880	74
1959	21,898	-
1960	24,913	-

Sheds
Manningham	17/4/50
Skipton	26/9/53
Lostock Hall	15/9/62
Lees (Oldham)	11/1/64
Newton Heath	18/4/64
Workington	4/9/65

Stored
Serviceable	11/11/65	?

Withdrawn w/e 6/5/67

Manningham's 46452 with a local train at Hirstwood between Bingley and Saltaire. It was at the Bradford shed from new in April 1950 until September 1953. R. Butterfield, Initial Photographics.

46452 was transferred to Newton Heath in April 1964 and stayed there until September 1965. The class had a long history as station pilots at Manchester Victoria; 46452 is standing on the banking engine line there in 1964. www.rail-online.co.uk

46453

Built at Crewe 18/4/50

Improvements and modifications
Chimney   22/5/54
Cast steel crossheads   22/5/54

Repairs
Crewe   LI   22/4/54   22/5/54
Darlington   GEN   14/3/57   18/4/57

Boilers
New   13546

Tenders
New   7053

Mileage/(weekdays out of service)
1950	21,931	20
1951	28,973	33
1952	24,744	38
1953	20,340	24
1954	22,803	50
1955	29,153	45
1956	26,841	32

Sheds
Manningham   18/4/50
Holbeck   10/4/54

Withdrawn w/e 21/4/62

46452 running in at Crewe in April 1950. It would spend all of its life on the North Eastern Region, starting at Manningham and moving to Holbeck in 1954.

46453 soon after a General repair at Darlington from 14 March to 18 April 1957 during which it was fitted with the later pattern of guard irons mounted on the pony truck. It also has the 2MT power classification on the bufferbeam in LNER style. 46453 was transferred to Holbeck from Manningham in April 1954 and was one of the early withdrawals, in April 1962.

46454

Built at Crewe 24/4/50

Improvements and modifications
Chimney	?
Cast steel crossheads	15/9/53

Repairs
Crewe	LI	11/8/53	15/9/53
Crewe	HG	4/5/56	1/6/56
Crewe	LI	19/9/60	21/10/60
Crewe	HG	28/8/62	27/9/62

Boilers
New	13548
1/6/56	12971
27/9/62	12907

Tenders
New	7054

Mileage/(weekdays out of service)
1951	31,580	37
1952	30,888	53
1953	24,495	108
1954	27,903	64
1955	24,197	80
1956	25,729	76
1957	26,179	47
1958	21,869	41
1959	25,990	-
1960	21,543	-

Sheds
Derby	27/4/50
Burton	15/6/57
Leicester Midland	21/6/58
Derby	24/9/60
Saltley	18/11/61

Withdrawn w/e 8/10/66

46454 was only a few weeks old when it was photographed at Derby on 10 May 1950 departing to New Street. R.J. Buckley, Initial Photographics.

Ex-works 46454 at Crewe, probably after a Heavy General in mid-1956, showing the reinforced front steps on the tender which were retro-fitted to LMR based engines. 46454 was always on the Midland Division and was shedded at Derby at this date. R.S. Carpenter Collection.

46455

Built at Crewe 28/4/50

Improvements and modifications
Chimney	23/9/52
Cast steel crossheads	7/1/56
AWS	22/2/63

Repairs
Crewe	LI	2/9/52	23/9/52
Crewe	NC EO	26/4/53	12/5/53
Crewe	LC EO	5/2/54	19/2/54
Crewe	LC EO	13/3/54	9/4/54
Crewe	HG	8/12/55	7/1/56
Crewe	HI	17/9/60	29/10/60
Crewe	HG	29/1/63	22/2/63

Boilers
New	13553
7/1/56	13435
22/2/63	13443

Tenders
New	7055

Mileage/(weekdays out of service)
1950	24,498	19
1951	34,578	26
1952	34,996	34
1953	33,267	44
1954	33,191	51
1955	22,741	60
1956	27,548	37
1957	26,072	43
1958	14,908	98
1959	18,893	-
1960	23,293	-

Sheds
Crewe North	28/4/50
Penrith	10/6/50
Workington	30/1/54
Penrith	20/2/54
Carlisle Upperby	2/4/55
Workington	23/4/55
Carlisle Upperby	30/1/60
Carlisle Kingmoor	17/12/66

Stored
Serviceable	7/2/66	23/9/66
Serviceable	11/11/66	?

Withdrawn w/e 6/5/67

46455 at Carlisle Upperby on 17 August 1961; it had been transferred there in January 1960 from Workington. In addition to local freight work, it was occasionally employed on the Silloth branch passenger trains. www.rail-online.co.uk

46455 spent most of its time on the Cockermouth, Keswick and Penrith line, based at either Penrith or Workington throughout the 1950s. This continued after its transfer to Upperby in 1960 and on 13 June 1964 it was at Penrith with a Keswick train. 46455 was modified in February 1954 with stronger pony truck springs and thrust strips on top of the bufferbeam to allow it to be used with a large No.3A snowplough during the winter. www.rail-online.co.uk

46456

Built at Crewe 9/5/50

Improvements and modifications

Chimney	?
Cast steel crossheads	15/9/53

Repairs

Shed	LC EO	23/10/52	3/11/52
Crewe	LI	25/8/53	15/9/53
Crewe	HG	11/6/56	21/7/56
Crewe	LC EO	30/11/57	1/1/58
Crewe	HG	18/1/60	4/3/60

Boilers

New	13554
21/7/56	12968
4/3/60	12901

Tenders

New	7056

Mileage/(weekdays out of service)

1950	20,177	35
1951	31,003	26
1952	27,836	40
1953	29,448	50
1954	32,895	46
1955	26,816	47
1956	23,655	92
1957	22,360	91
1958	28,674	47
1959	21,669	-
1960	15,353	-

Sheds

Crewe North	9/5/50
Workington	1/7/50
Bescot	23/9/61

Withdrawn w/e 25/9/65

46456, tender first, crosses Mosedale Viaduct on the Cockermouth, Keswick and Penrith line in 1961. The 12-arch stone viaduct over Mosedale Beck was two miles east of Threlkeld, with Blencathra Mountain in the background. The express headlamps and the carriage destination boards suggest the three rear coaches are the Workington/Keswick portion of the 'Lakes Express' heading towards Penrith. 46456 was allocated to Workington from July 1950 until September 1961. www.rail-online.co.uk

46456 at Bescot in the 1960s. It had been transferred there in September 1961 after more than a decade at Workington. Note the LMR modified reinforced steps at the front of the tender and the long ladder projecting down below the bufferbeam. www.rail-online.co.uk

46457

Built at Crewe 12/5/50

Improvements and modifications

Chimney	?
Cast steel crossheads	23/9/53

Repairs

Crewe	LI	28/8/53	23/9/53
Crewe	HG	4/3/57	30/3/57
Crewe	LI	24/11/60	6/1/61
Crewe	HI	11/3/64	6/5/64

Boilers

New	13437
30/3/57	13855

Tenders

New	7057

Mileage/(weekdays out of service)

1950	16,628	19
1951	33,442	30
1952	27,944	36
1953	25,103	50
1954	31,512	36
1955	25,000	41
1956	25,870	36
1957	24,533	72
1958	19,638	70
1959	18,867	-
1960	18,339	-

Sheds

Crewe North	12/5/50
Workington	30/9/50
Springs Branch (Wigan) (loan)	10/12/55
Workington	24/12/55
Carlisle Upperby	29/3/58
Bescot	13/1/62
Chester Midland	18/7/64
Leamington	24/10/64
Tyseley	19/6/65
Carlisle Upperby	15/10/66
Carlisle Kingmoor	17/12/66

Stored

Serviceable	28/11/66	?

Withdrawn w/e 6/5/67

46457 at Penrith on 18 July 1951. It was one of the few to stay at Crewe North for more than a short time after completion. It was there until the end of September before moving to Workington. H.K. Boulter.

46457 at Workington, where it was allocated for nearly a decade (apart from a two-week loan to Springs Branch in 1955) on 16 April 1960. It subsequently moved to Carlisle Upperby and then to the West Midlands before returning to Upperby in October 1966. www.rail-online.co.uk

46458

Built at Crewe 22/5/50

Improvements and modifications
Chimney	18/1/57
Cast steel crossheads	18/1/57

Repairs
Crewe	LI	5/10/53	3/11/53
Rugby	HG	17/12/56	18/1/57
Crewe	HI	30/8/59	31/10/59
Crewe	HG	4/10/63	13/11/63

Boilers
New	13555
18/1/57	13429

Tenders
New	7058

Mileage/(weekdays out of service)
1950	16,068	16
1951	31,104	27
1952	29,398	31
1953	24,169	63
1954	36,753	34
1955	22,915	41
1956	20,542	36
1957	23,958	34
1958	22,040	43
1959	17,838	-
1960	15,029	-

Sheds
Crewe North	22/5/50
Workington	18/11/50
Willesden	17/9/55
Kirkby Stephen	30/4/60
Carlisle Upperby	11/11/61

Stored
Serviceable	11/11/66	16/11/66

Withdrawn w/e 17/12/66

46458 at Workington in the early 1950s, still with its original chimney, which was not replaced until 1957. It was allocated there from November 1950 until September 1955 when it was transferred to Willesden. Behind it is Furness Railway 0-6-0 52501, withdrawn in 1957. www.rail-online.co.uk

Upperby's 46458 at Braithwaite near Keswick on the Cockermouth, Keswick and Penrith line. It returned to the area after nearly five years at Willesden, firstly at Kirkby Stephen in April 1960 then at Carlisle Upperby from November 1961. www.rail-online.co.uk

46459

Built at Crewe 23/5/50

Improvements and modifications
Chimney	14/6/52
Cast steel crossheads	25/8/55
AWS	10/1/63

Repairs
Crewe	LI	26/5/52	14/6/52
Crewe	HG	2/8/55	25/8/55
Crewe	HG	7/11/60	21/12/60
Crewe	NC	17/12/62	10/1/63

Boilers
New	13557
25/8/55	13432
21/12/60	12976

Tenders
New	7059

Mileage/(weekdays out of service)
1950	18,720	20
1951	33,300	38
1952	34,202	35
1953	34,204	38
1954	32,472	44
1955	23,635	71
1956	25,251	39
1957	19,808	22
1958	17,899	36
1959	18,294	-
1960	14,168	-

Sheds
Crewe North	23/5/50
Rugby (loan)	19/8/50
Crewe North	23/9/50
Penrith	18/11/50
Workington	20/2/54
Chester Midland	12/5/56
Springs Branch (Wigan) (loan)	2/6/56
Chester Midland	7/7/56
Bescot	29/9/56
Rugby	18/5/63
Nuneaton	5/12/64

Withdrawn w/e 2/10/65

46459 departing from the goods loop at the east end of Keswick on the Cockermouth, Keswick and Penrith Railway, looking towards Penrith in the early 1950s. It was allocated to Penrith between November 1950 and February 1954. The local crews apparently used to call the Ivatts 'Spivs', a nickname derived (somewhat opaquely) from the difference between working on their predecessors, the LNWR Cauliflowers, and the Ivatts with their enclosed tender cabs. www.rail-online.co.uk

46459 waits to depart from Whitehaven in 1953. After spending its first six months at Crewe North or Rugby, 46453 moved to Penrith in November 1950 and Workington in February 1954 but left the area in May 1956 for Chester. R.S. Carpenter Collection.

46460

Built at Crewe 31/5/50

Improvements and modifications
Chimney	?
Cast steel crossheads	?

Repairs
Inverurie	NC	11/1/52	18/1/52
Inverurie	LC EO	18/2/53	13/3/53
Darlington	LI	14/1/54	13/2/54
Darlington	LC EO	30/10/54	10/12/54
Inverurie	NC	18/5/56	18/5/56
Cowlairs	LC EO	15/6/56	7/7/56
Gateshead	GEN	9/8/57	13/9/57
Darlington	LC EO	8/5/59	3/7/59
Darlington	GEN	27/12/61	5/5/62

Boilers
New	13556

Tenders
New	7060

Mileage/(weekdays out of service)
1950	18,627	4

Sheds
St Margarets	31/5/50
Kittybrewster	26/1/52
Keith	16/4/60
Aberdeen Ferryhill	24/6/61
Oban	5/8/61
Perth South	11/5/63
Grangemouth	23/11/63
Ayr	30/10/65

Withdrawn w/e 27/8/66

46460 at Crewe in June 1950 before it went to Scotland, initially to St. Margarets and then Kittybrewster in 1952.

Before it was transferred to Kittybrewster, 46460 was fitted with cow-catchers at front and rear so it could be used on the St. Combs branch where the line was unfenced. It was on shed at Fraserburgh on 17 May 1953 where it was based when it worked the branch.

46461

Built at Crewe 5/6/50

Improvements and modifications

Chimney	19/8/53
Cast steel crossheads	?

Repairs

Darlington	LI	29/6/53	19/8/53
Darlington	LC	14/10/55	28/11/55
Darlington	LC EO	27/3/56	7/5/56
Darlington	GEN	21/7/59	1/9/59
Cowlairs	LC	3/4/64	16/4/64

Boilers

New	13558
1/9/59	12424

Tenders

New	7061

Mileage/(weekdays out of service)

1950	22,886	3
1951	28,648	44
1952	18,029	27
1953	16,730	56
1954	19,555	5
1955	16,291	64
1956	20,191	69
1957	18,138	24
1958	12,693	41
1959	11,298	-
1960	15,308	-
1961	13,788	-
1962	9,731	-

Sheds

St Margarets	5/6/50
Kittybrewster (loan)	13/11/54
St Margarets	22/1/55
Kittybrewster (loan)	26/3/55
St Margarets	9/4/55
Kittybrewster (loan)	9/1/60
Keith (loan)	16/1/60
St Margarets	16/4/60
Bathgate	25/1/64

Stored

Unserviceable	9/4/61	1/10/61

Withdrawn w/e 1/8/64

46461 at Joppa, south of Portobello, in April 1956. It was allocated to St.Margarets from new in June 1950 until January 1964, apart from three spells on loan to Kittybrewster as substitute for 46460 on the St.Combs branch. Normally, it worked on local passenger and freight duties. www.rail-online.co.uk

46461 runs through Prestonpans in 1962 with a short freight. When it left St.Margarets in January 1964 it moved to Bathgate but was withdrawn six months later. www.rail-online.co.uk

46462

Built at Crewe 9/6/50

Improvements and modifications

Chimney	?
Cast steel crossheads	?

Repairs

Darlington	LI	24/9/53	17/10/53
Darlington	GEN	13/7/56	12/9/56
Darlington	GEN	5/3/62	3/7/62

Boilers

New	13559
?	13528

Tenders

New	7062
3/7/62	7076

Mileage/(weekdays out of service)

1950	20,724	2

Sheds

St Margarets	10/6/50
Bathgate	1/1/66

Withdrawn w/e 27/8/66

46462 in showroom condition, at Crewe in June 1950 before it went north to St.Margarets. The infamous forward-facing lion on the BR emblem shows up clearly. www.rail-online.co.uk

46462 emerges from the Mound Tunnel outside Edinburgh Waverley with a Down local passenger train on 29 July 1954. Peter Groom.

46463

Built at Crewe 19/6/50

Improvements and modifications
Chimney	?
Cast steel crossheads	?

Repairs
Darlington	HI	3/8/53	3/9/53
Darlington	GEN	12/11/56	14/12/56
Darlington	GEN	21/12/59	29/1/60
Crewe	HI	16/1/63	22/2/63

Boilers
New	13551
?	13827

Tenders
New	7063
5/9/53	7071
?	7064

Mileage/(weekdays out of service)
1950	17,977	3

Sheds
Dundee Tay Bridge	24/6/50
Motherwell	11/5/63

Withdrawn w/e 12/2/66

Below. The last two of the five engines built for the Scottish Region in 1950 went to Dundee Tay Bridge where 46463 was photographed on 8 April 1951. It regularly worked the Tayport and St.Andrews branch services. M. Bentley.

46463 was at Dundee Tay Bridge until May 1963 when it was transferred to Motherwell; it stayed there until withdrawal in February 1966. A.G. Forsyth, Initial Photographics.

46464

Built at Crewe 22/6/50

Improvements and modifications

Chimney	?
Cast steel crossheads	?

Repairs

Darlington	LI	1/10/53	29/10/53
Gateshead	GEN	4/2/57	8/3/57
Darlington	GEN	13/2/60	22/3/60
Cowlairs	NC EO	10/10/62	10/10/62

Boilers

New	13550
?	13823

Tenders

New	7064

Mileage/(weekdays out of service)

1950	13,765	7

Sheds

Dundee Tay Bridge	22/6/50
St Margarets	16/12/50
Dundee Tay Bridge	27/1/51
Kittybrewster	30/4/55
Dundee Tay Bridge	5/11/55
Kittybrewster	31/8/57
Dundee Tay Bridge	2/11/57

Withdrawn w/e 20/8/66

46464 at Newcastle Central in late 1953. Although always allocated to Scottish Region sheds, it was repaired at both Darlington and Gateshead during the 1950s. Its paintwork suggests that it may have recently emerged from overhaul at Darlington.

The RCTS/SLS Scottish railtour at Carmyllie on 16 June 1960 headed by 46464 with the two preserved Caledonian Railway coaches at the front. It was the regular engine on the line up to closure in May 1965 and was nicknamed 'The Carmyllie Pilot' by the locals. 46464 was the first of the class to be purchased for preservation and ran for a few years on the Strathspey Railway, but has been out of use since 1980.

46465

Built at Darlington 20/6/51
Makers no. 2157

Improvements and modifications
Cast steel crossheads   ?

Repairs
Darlington	GEN	22/1/54	26/2/54
Darlington	ADJ	28/2/54	3/3/54
Darlington	ADJ	8/3/54	10/3/54
Darlington	C/L	6/9/55	8/10/55
Darlington	GEN	5/10/56	12/11/56
Darlington	GEN	4/5/59	5/6/59
Crewe	HG	10/9/62	12/10/62
Crewe	LC	5/12/63	28/12/63

Boilers
New	13823
12/11/56	13825
5/6/59	13857
12/10/62	13445

Tenders
New	7065

Sheds
Cambridge	20/6/51
March	23/6/62
Buxton	18/8/62

Stored
Serviceable	30/1/67	4/3/67

Withdrawn w/e 4/3/67

Below. The changes to the tenders built at Darlington can be seen on 46465 at Chapel and Wakes Colne in the mid-1950s. The ladder has been shortened and stops above the bufferbeam and vertical handrails added above footsteps at the rear of the sideframes.
www.rail-online.co.uk

The first of the Darlington-built engines, 46465 at Ipswich (fish van at the front) in the 1950s. Changes from the Crewe-built engines include a tall chimney incorporating the revised draughting following the tests at Swindon with 46413, guard irons on the pony truck and 10in cab numbers. 46465 was allocated to Cambridge from new in June 1951 until June 1962. www.rail-online.co.uk

46466

Built at Darlington 22/6/51
Makers no. 2158

Improvements and modifications
Cast steel crossheads   ?

Repairs
Darlington	LI	27/5/53	4/7/53
Darlington	GEN	7/9/55	7/10/55
Darlington	GEN	1/3/58	3/4/58
Stratford	U/C	16/2/59	21/2/59
Darlington	HC	19/8/59	29/10/59

Boilers
New	13824
4/10/55	13835
3/4/58	13827
28/10/59	13558

Tenders
New	7066

Sheds
Cambridge	22/6/51
March	23/6/62

Withdrawn w/e 1/9/62

46466 on 14 August 1954 at Coldham's Lane on the northern edge of Cambridge. Although heading north out of the city it is about to turn almost 180 degrees south towards Newmarket and Bury. www.rail-online.co.uk

46466 at Colchester North in 1952 after arriving with a train from the Stour Valley line. It was shedded at Cambridge from new in June 1951 until June 1962 when it moved, on paper at least, to March where it was withdrawn soon afterwards. www.rail-online.co.uk

233

46467

Built at Darlington 29/6/51
Makers no. 2159

Improvements and modifications

Cast steel crossheads	?

Repairs

Darlington	C (H)	10/7/51	17/7/51
Darlington	HI	29/9/53	6/11/53
Darlington	HC	10/10/55	8/12/55
Darlington	LI	3/9/56	10/10/56
Darlington	GEN	17/5/58	17/6/58
Darlington	GEN	7/3/62	9/5/62
Cowlairs	LC EO	19/5/64	23/5/64

Boilers

New	13825
10/10/56	13824
17/6/58	13846

Tenders

New	7067

Sheds

Cambridge	29/6/51
Hurlford	14/10/61
Stranraer	9/2/63
Dumfries	22/2/64

Stored

Unserviceable	6/11/61	10/3/62

Withdrawn w/e 25/7/64

46467 on shed at Kettering after working in from Cambridge. When it moved from 31A in October 1961 it went to the Scottish Region, at Hurlford, then Stranraer in February 1963. www.rail-online.co.uk

46467 at Cowlairs Works for a Light Casual repair 19-23 May 1964. It had been transferred from Stranraer to its final shed Dumfries in February 1964. The works visit was largely in vain because 46467 was withdrawn by the end of July. www.rail-online.co.uk

46468

Built at Darlington 6/7/51
Makers no. 2160

Improvements and modifications
Cast steel crossheads   ?

Repairs
Darlington	C/L	29/9/52	31/10/52
Darlington	LI	7/9/53	22/10/53
Darlington	ADJ	24/10/53	28/10/53
Darlington	ADJ	29/10/53	31/10/53
Darlington	ADJ	5/11/53	8/11/53
Darlington	LC	21/2/56	13/4/56
Stratford	LC	5/10/56	26/10/56
Darlington	GEN	10/7/57	24/8/57
Darlington	GEN	4/4/61	4/5/61

Boilers
New	13826
24/8/57	13834

Tenders
New	7068

Sheds
Colchester	6/7/51
Parkeston Quay	7/11/59
Stratford	7/1/61
Cambridge	14/1/61
Oban	25/3/61
Perth South	27/5/61
Oban	1/7/61
Perth South	14/7/62
Grangemouth	23/11/63

Withdrawn w/e 23/10/65

Initially an Eastern Region engine, 46468 was one of three transferred to Scotland in March 1961. It went to Oban, where this picture was taken, and stayed until July 1962 except for a month at Perth South in mid-1961. Amongst their other duties, the Oban engines worked the Ballachulish branch. www.rail-online.co.uk

With Oban painted on its bufferbeam, 46468 leaves Connel Ferry in early 1962. It was transferred to Perth South for the second time in July 1962 and thence to Grangemouth in November 1963. www.rail-online.co.uk

46469

Built at Darlington 10/7/51
Makers no. 2161

Improvements and modifications
Cast steel crossheads   ?

Repairs
Darlington	C/L	18/7/51	20/7/51
Darlington	LI	1/11/54	10/12/54
Darlington	ADJ	16/12/54	21/12/54
Gateshead	GEN	3/2/58	7/3/58

Boilers
New	13827
7/3/58	13837

Tenders
New	7069

Sheds
Colchester	10/7/51
Parkeston Quay	7/11/59
Stratford	7/1/61
Cambridge	14/1/61
March	23/6/62

Stored
Unserviceable	10/6/62	12/8/62

Withdrawn w/e 1/9/62

The last of the five engines built for the Eastern Region, 46469 works tender first on a freight through Stratford on 5 March 1960. It was then allocated to Parkeston Quay but moved to the London shed for one week in January 1961. www.rail-online.co.uk

46469 at Newmarket in 1961 after it had been transferred from Stratford in January 1961. It worked until June 1962 when it was stored unserviceable, to be withdrawn at the end of August.
www.rail-online.co.uk

46470

Built at Darlington 16/7/51
Makers no. 2162

Improvements and modifications

Cast steel crossheads ?

Repairs

Darlington	NC	26/11/51	16/12/51
Darlington	GEN	20/10/53	28/11/53
Darlington	HG	29/9/56	26/10/56
Crewe	HG	7/7/59	20/8/59
Crewe	HG	24/6/63	7/8/63

Boilers

New	13828
26/10/56	13829
20/8/59	12422
7/8/63	13883

Tenders

New	7070

Mileage/(weekdays out of service)

Cumulative to 31/12/57	193,807	
1958	13,953	111
1959	19,240	-
1960	20,824	-

Sheds

West Auckland	16/7/51
Kirkby Stephen	22/1/55
Springs Branch (Wigan)	17/9/60
Aston	10/2/62
Watford	23/6/62
Chester Midland	9/3/63
Leamington	24/10/64
Tyseley	19/6/65
Carlisle Upperby	15/10/66
Carlisle Kingmoor	17/12/66

Stored

Serviceable	26/12/66	?

Withdrawn w/e 6/5/67

46470 outside Crewe Paint Shop on 8 August 1963 at the end of a Heavy General which started officially on 24 June. It was originally a North Eastern engine until September 1960 when it was transferred to Springs Branch.

46470 at Old Hill banking a freight up towards Cradley Hill, shortly before it was transferred from Tyseley to Carlisle Upperby.

46471

Built at Darlington 18/7/51
Makers no. 2163

Improvements and modifications
Cast steel crossheads　　　　?

Repairs
Darlington	NC	21/4/52	3/5/52
Darlington	GEN	14/7/53	31/8/53
Darlington	GEN	14/8/56	22/9/56

Boilers
New　　　　13829

Tenders
New	7071
?	7063

Sheds
Kirkby Stephen	18/7/51
West Auckland	15/1/55
Darlington	4/6/55
West Auckland	12/11/55
Northallerton	5/4/58
West Auckland	9/4/60
Blyth (South)	17/9/60
Gateshead	29/4/61
Tweedmouth	17/2/62

Withdrawn w/e 20/10/62

46471 at South Blyth shed in 1960 or early 1961; it had been transferred there from West Auckland in September 1960. It stayed until April 1961 when it went to Gateshead and then finally to Tweedmouth in February 1962, from where it was withdrawn that October.

46471 on 22 May 1955 at West Auckland with several other Ivatts for company during the first of three spells at the shed. It stayed in the north east until withdrawn in 1962. R. Butterfield, Initial Photographics.

46472

Built at Darlington 20/7/51
Makers no. 2164

Improvements and modifications
Cast steel crossheads   ?

Repairs

Darlington	HI	16/3/54	15/4/54
Darlington	LC	22/3/56	12/4/56
Darlington	LC	19/12/57	24/1/58
Crewe	HG	1/7/58	9/8/58

Boilers

New	13830
9/8/58	13852

Tenders

New	7072

Mileage/(weekdays out of service)

Cumulative to 31/12/57	135,045	
1958	15,496	108
1959	19,866	-
1960	20,486	-

Sheds

Darlington	20/7/51
West Auckland	13/11/54
Kirkby Stephen	15/1/55
Rugby	20/12/58
Chester Midland	9/1/60
Willesden	30/4/60
Northwich	25/5/63
Newton Heath	8/8/64

Withdrawn w/e 16/1/65

46472 was in the north east at Darlington, West Auckland and Kirkby Stephen until the end of 1958 when it was transferred to Chester Midland. On 26 March 1960, it was working the RCTS 'Cheshire District Railtour' when photographed at Dee Junction at the west end of Bidston station. www.rail-online.co.uk

On special duties with plenty of steam to spare, 46472 is at Bedford on 1 March 1962 with the LMS Inspection Saloon. It was transferred from Chester to Willesden in April 1960 where it stayed until April 1963 when it went to Northwich. www.rail-online.co.uk

46473

Built at Darlington 18/8/51
Makers no. 2165

Improvements and modifications
Cast steel crossheads   ?

Repairs
Darlington	GEN	21/10/53	21/11/53
Darlington	LC	10/1/57	7/2/57
Darlington	GEN	25/7/57	31/8/57

Boilers
New   13831

Tenders
New   7073

Sheds
West Auckland	18/8/51
Darlington	4/6/55
Blyth (South)	17/9/60
Heaton	21/1/61
Blyth (South)	8/4/61
Gateshead	29/4/61
Tweedmouth	14/4/62
Malton	11/8/62
York	20/4/63
Goole	9/11/63

Withdrawn w/e 21/12/63

46473 with the Gateshead breakdown crane at Low Fell in 1961. It was at the shed from April 1961 until the following April when it went to Tweedmouth.

New to West Auckland in August 1951, 46473 is shunting at Tebay later that year. It moved to no less than eight other NER sheds over the following years.

46474

Built at Darlington 1/9/51
Makers no. 2166

Improvements and modifications
Cast steel crossheads	?
AWS	?

Repairs
Darlington	NC	18/1/52	30/1/52
Darlington	LI	17/8/53	16/9/53
Darlington	C/L	23/1/56	20/3/56
Gateshead	GEN	9/12/57	10/1/58
Gateshead	C/L	3/6/58	27/6/58
Darlington	NC	27/3/61	14/4/61

Boilers
New	13832

Tenders
New	7074

Sheds
Kirkby Stephen	1/9/51
Darlington	4/6/55
Blyth (South)	17/9/60
Heaton	21/1/61
Tweedmouth	17/2/62
Dumfries	9/11/63

Withdrawn w/e 25/7/64

Working hard with a reasonable load, 46474 departs from Norham near Berwick in 1961. At this time it was allocated to Heaton, from January 1961 until February 1962. www.rail-online.co.uk

Darlington's 46474 departs from Lartington, south of Barnard Castle, in the late 1950s with a westbound train over the Stainmore line to Penrith. It had been at Kirkby Stephen from new in 1951 and moved to South Blyth in 1960.

46475

Built at Darlington 1/9/51
Makers no. 2167

Improvements and modifications
Cast steel crossheads	?
AWS	18/3/61

Repairs
Darlington	NC	5/12/51	18/12/51
Darlington	GEN	4/5/54	5/6/54
Darlington	GEN	23/11/59	24/12/59
Darlington	NC	7/3/61	18/3/61
Darlington	CH	25/5/62	4/7/62

Boilers
New	13833

Tenders
New	7075

Sheds
Darlington	1/9/51
Tweedmouth	1/12/62
Dumfries	9/11/63

Withdrawn w/e 1/8/64

At Tebay on 1 August 1953, 46475 is adorned with the cable-operated, rather crude front slip coupling mechanism used to uncouple from the train in front while still on the move when banking over Stainmore summit.

46475 at Darlington shed on 30 April 1952; it had been allocated there from new in September 1951 and stayed until November 1962 when it moved away to Tweedmouth.

46476

Built at Darlington 8/9/51
Makers no. 2168

Improvements and modifications
Cast steel crossheads	?
AWS	17/6/61

Repairs
Darlington	NC	5/5/52	13/5/52
Darlington	GEN	28/9/53	22/10/53
Darlington	GEN	29/10/56	30/11/56
Darlington	NC	8/6/61	17/6/61

Boilers
New	13834

Tenders
New	7076

Sheds
Kirkby Stephen	8/9/51
West Auckland	9/4/55
Darlington	4/6/55
Tweedmouth	25/1/58

Withdrawn w/e 5/1/63

46476 outshopped from Darlington Works on 8 September 1951 and not yet carrying its Kirkby Stephen shedplate. The new engines ran their first thousand miles from Darlington Bank Top, mainly on the Darlington-Tebay line. Note the LNER-style engraved brass worksplate which records this engine as maker's number 2168. E. Haigh.

A rare instance of Ivatts double-heading a passenger train. On 16 August 1952 at Tebay, 46476 is in front of 46480.

253

46477

Built at Darlington 15/9/51
Makers no. 2169

Improvements and modifications

Cast steel crossheads	?
AWS	18/3/61

Repairs

Darlington	I/H	13/10/53	11/11/53
Gateshead	GEN	8/4/57	10/5/57
Darlington	NC	7/3/61	18/3/61

Boilers

New   13835

Tenders

New   7077

Sheds

Darlington	15/9/51
Kirkby Stephen	28/3/53
Darlington	4/6/55

Withdrawn w/e 22/12/62

46477 at Darlington where it was allocated from new in 1951 to March 1953 and again from June 1955 until withdrawn in December 1962. It was one of almost twenty NER 2-6-0s fitted with AWS in early 1961. In addition to the AWS, it has small 8in cab numbers, rather than the original 10in size, which were applied during a General overhaul at Gateshead in 1957. www.rail-online.co.uk

46477 from Darlington shed approaches Stainmore summit with an eastbound train from Penrith on 25 July 1952. T.G. Hepburn, Rail Archive Stephenson.

46478

Built at Darlington 22/9/51
Makers no. 2170

Improvements and modifications

Cast steel crossheads	?

Repairs

Darlington	NC	2/5/52	9/5/52
Darlington	I/L	16/2/53	21/3/53
Darlington	GEN	29/4/55	28/5/55

Boilers

New	13836

Tenders

New	7078

Sheds

Kirkby Stephen	22/9/51
Darlington	4/6/55
Stockton	23/3/57
Thornaby	20/6/59
Goole	12/3/60

Withdrawn w/e 5/5/62

46478 at Darlington North Road on 4 September 1955, newly repainted in unlined black during a General overhaul completed on 28 May. It was transferred from Kirkby Stephen to Darlington immediately after the works visit. N. Preedy.

A rare view at Epworth in 1962 on the former L&Y/NER Joint line from Goole to Haxey Junction. 46478 was allocated to Goole from March 1960 until withdrawn in May 1962. www.rail-online.co.uk

46479

Built at Darlington 22/9/51
Makers no. 2171

Improvements and modifications
Cast steel crossheads	?
AWS	8/4/61

Repairs
Darlington	NC	21/5/52	29/5/52
Darlington	GEN	8/12/53	15/1/54
Darlington	GEN	2/6/58	10/7/58
Darlington	NC	28/3/61	8/4/61

Boilers
New	13837

Tenders
New	7079

Sheds
West Auckland	22/9/51
Darlington	13/11/54
Blyth (South)	17/9/60
Heaton	29/4/61
Tweedmouth	17/2/62
Stranraer	9/11/63
Dumfries	22/2/64

Withdrawn w/e 3/7/65

After more than a decade on the North Eastern Region, 46479 was transferred to Stranraer in November 1963 and then on to Dumfries in February 1964. It is running light through the station there on 11 June 1965, just a few days before it was withdrawn. It was fitted with AWS at Darlington in April 1961. www.rail-online.co.uk

46479 with a westbound freight passing Coal Road signalbox, two miles east of Barnard Castle. This is the period when it was allocated to West Auckland, between September 1951 and November 1954.

259

46480

Built at Darlington 29/9/51
Makers no. 2172

Improvements and modifications

Cast steel crossheads	?
AWS	24/3/61

Repairs

Darlington	NC	31/1/52	8/2/52
Darlington	I/L	3/11/53	5/12/53
Darlington	GEN	21/10/57	15/11/57
Darlington	NC	17/3/61	24/3/61
Darlington	LC	20/6/61	21/11/61
Crewe	HG	12/2/63	11/3/63

Boilers

New	13838
15/11/57	13826

Tenders

New	7080

Mileage/(weekdays out of service)

1959	14,487	-
1960	13,384	-
Cumulative to 12/8/62	201,240	

Sheds

Darlington	29/9/51
Kirkby Stephen	7/3/53
West Auckland	15/1/55
York	2/8/58
Buxton	18/8/62

Withdrawn w/e 6/5/67

46480 working the ash road shunt at York MPD on 20 April 1959. One of the engines that went to York in the late 1950s, it is in unlined black following a General overhaul at Darlington in late 1957. www.rail-online.co.uk

46480 at Chinley in late 1962 following its move from York to Buxton in August of that year. It was withdrawn at the end of April 1967, a month before the final five were withdrawn from Buxton. www.rail-online.co.uk

46481

Built at Darlington 6/10/51
Makers no. 2173

Improvements and modifications

Cast steel crossheads	?		
AWS	17/6/61		

Repairs

Darlington	NC	9/1/52	17/1/52
Darlington	I/L	14/9/53	10/10/53
Gateshead	GEN	5/2/57	22/3/57
Darlington	NC	8/6/61	17/6/61

Boilers

New   13839

Tenders

New   7081

Sheds

Kirkby Stephen	6/10/51
West Auckland	9/4/55
York	2/8/58
Malton	4/8/62

Withdrawn w/e 15/12/62

46481 was withdrawn at Malton in December 1962; by April 1963 it was at Crewe Works for scrapping with Jubilee 45691 behind. It had been fitted with AWS in June 1961. www.rail-online.co.uk

46481 with an eastbound train at Kirkby Stephen on 1 August 1953. It went new to the shed there in October 1951 and moved to West Auckland in April 1955.

46482

Built at Darlington 13/10/51
Makers no. 2174

Improvements and modifications

| Cast steel crossheads | ? |
| AWS | 15/4/61 |

Repairs

Darlington	NC	27/12/51	4/1/52
Darlington	GEN	14/12/53	20/1/54
Darlington	GEN	29/8/58	25/9/58
Darlington	NC	6/4/61	15/4/61

Boilers

| New | 13840 |

Tenders

| New | 7082 |

Sheds

West Auckland	3/10/51
Tweedmouth	17/10/59
Darlington	1/12/62
Polmadie (loan)	24/2/63
Polmadie	17/8/63
Ardrossan	11/10/63
Ayr	20/2/65

Withdrawn w/e 28/8/65

46482 at Ayr on 21 August 1965, the week before it was withdrawn. It had transferred there from Ardrossan six months earlier. It had moved to Scotland from the North Eastern Region in early 1963, initially to Polmadie.

West Auckland's 46482 has just arrived at Stainmore summit with a westbound coke train banked by a class J21 0-6-0 on 25 July 1952. T.G. Hepburn, Rail Archive Stephenson.

46483

Built at Darlington 16/10/51
Makers no. 2175

Improvements and modifications

Cast steel crossheads	?
AWS	22/4/61

Repairs

Rugby	LI	29/6/54	9/8/54
Darlington	C/L	23/5/57	11/7/57
Darlington	GEN	16/6/58	1/8/58
Darlington	NC	17/4/61	22/4/61

Boilers

New	13847

Tenders

New	7083

Mileage/(weekdays out of service)

1951	5,463	8
1952	27,880	51
1953	25,337	51
1954	19,737	65
1955	23,126	62
1956	22,631	28

Sheds

Blackpool Central	16/10/51
Bank Hall	22/3/52
Wakefield	15/1/55
Low Moor	15/3/58
Wakefield	11/7/59
Sowerby Bridge	14/11/59
Wakefield	17/3/62

Withdrawn w/e 23/11/63

Wakefield's 46483 working a pick-up goods at Dewsbury on 10 August 1962. The first of the engines built at Darlington for the LMR and originally at Blackpool Central, it had been allocated to Wakefield on three occasions since January 1955, sandwiching spells at Low Moor and Sowerby Bridge.

46483 with plenty of WD Austerity 2-8-0s for company at Wakefield in the snow of February 1963. It would work until November that year. www.rail-online.co.uk

46484

Built at Darlington 27/10/51
Makers no. 2176

Improvements and modifications
Cast steel crossheads	12/6/54

Repairs
Crewe	LI	25/5/54	12/6/54
Crewe	HG	29/7/57	30/8/57
Crewe	HI	31/5/61	1/7/61
Crewe	HI	30/9/64	20/11/64

Boilers
New	13841
30/8/57	13255
20/11/64	?

Tenders
New	7084

Mileage/(weekdays out of service)
1951	3,372	2
1952	28,392	22
1953	26,212	23
1954	21,048	59
1955	23,341	41
1956	24,201	27
1957	22,280	54
1958	26,320	21
1959	29,889	-
1960	25,532	-

Sheds
Newton Heath	27/10/51
Lees (Oldham)	9/6/62
Springs Branch (Wigan)	18/4/64
Bank Hall	3/7/65
Buxton	13/11/65

Stored
Serviceable	26/7/65	8/11/65

Withdrawn w/e 1/7/67

A few days after completing its first works overhaul, a Light Intermediate at Crewe, 46484 was at Derby on 22 June 1954, possibly working from Crewe until it was passed fit to return to its home at Newton Heath. Its Darlington origin is shown by the brass maker's plate and 10in cab numbers. R.J. Buckley, Initial Photographics.

After spending its first decade at Newton Heath, 46484 moved to Oldham Lees in June 1962 and then to Springs Branch in April 1964. On 9 July 1964 it was passing through Wigan North Western station. It was one of the final five engines in the class taken out of service at Buxton in mid-1967, having moved there in November 1965. www.rail-online.co.uk

46485

Built at Darlington 6/11/51
Makers no. 2177

Improvements and modifications

Cast steel crossheads	5/6/54

Repairs

Crewe	LI	14/5/54	5/6/54
Crewe	HG	4/3/57	3/4/57
Crewe	HI	8/12/61	6/1/62
Cowlairs	HC	3/7/64	15/8/64

Boilers

New	13843
3/4/57	13431

Tenders

New	7085

Mileage/(weekdays out of service)

1951	3,037	1
1952	25,664	22
1953	24,699	36
1954	18,539	79
1955	21,957	52
1956	22,366	33
1957	14,168	102
1958	16,035	43
1959	10,268	-
1960	7,405	-

Sheds

Newton Heath	6/11/51
Agecroft	14/11/53
Lees (Oldham)	9/6/62
Newton Heath	18/4/64
Workington	10/7/65
Buxton	18/6/66

Stored

Serviceable	11/11/65	16/5/66

Withdrawn w/e 1/7/67

46485 from Agecroft shed at Lichfield in 1957 shortly after a Heavy General repair at Crewe completed on 3 April. It has lost its Darlington 10in cab numbers in favour of the 8in variety and has the small version of the final BR emblem.

46485, one of the final five in traffic, at Buxton. It had gone there from Workington in June 1966 after spending six months in store. It is one of the few examples, and possibly the only one, with the '2MT' power classification above the cab number, courtesy of a repaint during a Heavy Casual overhaul at Cowlairs in 1964. G.W. Sharpe.

46486

Built at Darlington 1/11/51
Makers no. 2178

Improvements and modifications
Cast steel crossheads 10/5/56

Repairs
Crewe	HG	10/4/56	10/5/56
Crewe	LI	8/12/58	3/1/59
Crewe	HG	11/3/63	13/4/63

Boilers
New	13850
10/5/56	13553
13/4/63	13867

Tenders
New	7086

Mileage/(weekdays out of service)
1951	5,032	0
1952	25,100	36
1953	24,536	44
1954	19,457	62
1955	20,801	54
1956	20,822	50
1957	21,257	39
1958	13,240	76
1959	10,756	-
1960	16,044	-

Sheds
Newton Heath	1/11/51
Blackpool Central	12/1/52
Agecroft	13/2/54
Lees (Oldham)	9/6/62
Springs Branch (Wigan)	18/4/64
Lancaster Green Ayre	14/8/65
Carnforth	23/4/66

Stored
Serviceable	20/2/67	?

Withdrawn w/e 6/5/67

46486 at its fourth Central Division shed, Oldham Lees, on 29 July 1962. Prior to June 1962 it had been at Agecroft for almost eight years. www.rail-online.co.uk

At Crewe North after completing its last Heavy General repair on 13 April 1963, 46486 is ready to return to Oldham Lees where it would remain for the following twelve months. www.rail-online.co.uk

46487

Built at Darlington 9/11/51
Makers no. 2179

Improvements and modifications
| Cast steel crossheads | 2/1/54 | | |

Repairs
Crewe	HI	5/12/53	2/1/54
Crewe	HG	30/3/57	8/5/57
Crewe	LC EO	8/5/58	9/6/58
Crewe	LI	12/4/61	17/5/61
Crewe	LC	13/12/62	11/1/63
Crewe	HI	8/6/64	7/10/64

Boilers
| New | 13851 |
| 8/5/57 | 13437 |

Tenders
| New | 7087 |

Mileage/(weekdays out of service)
1951	3,063	1
1952	32,234	22
1953	24,936	65
1954	25,433	42
1955	21,832	45
1956	25,874	25
1957	22,716	53
1958	23,357	47
1959	27,932	-
1960	25,459	-

Sheds
Newton Heath	9/11/51
Blackpool Central	12/1/52
Huddersfield Hillhouse	26/9/53
Goole (loan)	17/10/53
Goole	7/11/53
Newton Heath	13/11/54
Lees (Oldham)	14/9/63
Springs Branch (Wigan)	18/4/64
Northwich	19/2/66

Stored
| Serviceable | 9/5/66 | ? |

Withdrawn w/e 6/5/67

Everything is gleaming including the brass worksplate on 46487 in Crewe Works after a Heavy General repair completed on 8 May 1957. It was allocated to Newton Heath from November 1954 until September 1963. www.rail-online.co.uk

46487 on station pilot/banking duty at Manchester Victoria in the early 1960s some time before it was transferred to Oldham Lees in September 1963.

46488

Built at Darlington 15/11/51
Makers no. 2180

Improvements and modifications

Cast steel crossheads

20/11/54

Repairs

Crewe	NC EO	22/1/54	6/2/54
Crewe	LI	29/10/54	20/11/54
Crewe	HG	14/5/58	6/6/58

Boilers

New	13849
6/6/58	13854

Tenders

New	7088

Mileage/(weekdays out of service)

1951	4,214	2
1952	39,002	27
1953	36,512	18
1954	28,005	67
1955	23,036	59
1956	27,885	42
1957	19,951	97
1958	19,224	71
1959	23,700	-
1960	13,817	-

Sheds

Workington	15/11/51
Carlisle Upperby	20/6/59
Workington	18/6/60

Withdrawn w/e 12/6/65

46488 at Penrith in the early 1950s with a 12D Workington shedplate and without the modification for a No.3A snowplough which dates the picture no later than December 1953. It was there until June 1959 when it was transferred to Carlisle Upperby, spending a year there before moving back to Workington in June 1960. The engraved brass Darlington worksplate is filthy and unreadable on the front frame, in contrast to the large 10in cab numbers. www.rail-online.co.uk

Outside Crewe Works Erecting Shop in November 1962, near the end of a works visit for 46488 not recorded on its Engine History Card. By this date 46488 had returned to Workington which had the 12F code from June 1960 onwards. The thrust plates for the No.3A snowplough are visible above the buffers. www.rail-online.co.uk

46489

Built at Darlington 21/11/51
Makers no. 2181

Improvements and modifications
Cast steel crossheads   2/12/53

Repairs

Crewe	LC EO	4/11/53	2/12/53
Crewe	NC EO	10/1/54	28/1/54
Crewe	LI	2/12/54	8/2/55
Crewe	HG	28/4/57	30/5/57
Crewe	HI	3/1/61	25/2/61

Boilers

New	13842
30/5/57	13441

Tenders

New	7089
8/2/55	7050

Mileage/(weekdays out of service)

1951	1,614	0
1952	26,375	28
1953	29,663	66
1954	26,854	54
1955	23,142	71
1956	26,372	50
1957	22,054	76
1958	22,913	82
1959	24,445	-
1960	25,680	-

Sheds

Preston	21/11/51
Springs Branch (Wigan)	29/11/52
Workington	30/1/54
Carlisle Upperby	20/6/59

Withdrawn w/e 16/11/63

46489 at Whitehaven Bransty on 25 August 1956. It had been at Workington since January 1954. It has one of the earlier type of tenders with long ladder and no rear handrail or footstep which it exchanged with 46450 in February 1955 while in Crewe Works for a Light Intermediate repair. 46489 was modified in February 1954 with stronger pony truck springs and thrust strips on top of the bufferbeam to allow it to be used with a large No.3A snowplough.

The large Darlington 10in cab numbers on 46489 were replaced by the 8in version used by Crewe Works during its first Heavy General repair in 1957. It was allocated to Carlisle Upperby, where it is pictured on 13 July 1963, from June 1959 until withdrawn in November 1963.

46490

Built at Darlington 28/11/51
Makers no. 2182

Improvements and modifications

Cast steel crossheads	11/9/54

Repairs

Crewe	LI	24/8/54	11/9/54
Rugby	LC EO	3/5/56	15/5/56
Crewe	HG	24/2/58	22/3/58
Crewe	GEN	3/1/64	12/3/64

Boilers

New	13853
22/3/58	13856

Tenders

New	7090

Mileage/(weekdays out of service)

1951	1,687	0
1952	22,946	22
1953	20,588	40
1954	21,978	37
1955	20,282	31
1956	20,693	52
1957	19,872	35
1958	16,953	49
1959	19,650	-
1960	16,816	-

Sheds

Bescot	28/11/51
Saltley	26/3/66
Newton Heath (loan)	6/8/66
Newton Heath	20/8/66

Stored

Serviceable	28/3/66	1/8/66

Withdrawn w/e 6/5/67

46490 at Bescot in the early 1960s after the engine had acquired overhead warning flashes and before it was transferred to Saltley in March 1966. It had gone new to Bescot in November 1951, joining the original trio 46425-46427 which had replaced ex-L&NWR Webb 0-6-0s at the shed. At Saltley it went immediately into store until August when it was transferred to Newton Heath. 46490 was the last Darlington-built engine to have a tall thin chimney.

46490 in its final year in service, on a parcels train at Manchester Exchange. It was withdrawn from Newton Heath in May 1967. M. Bentley.

46491

Built at Darlington 4/12/51
Makers no. 2183

Improvements and modifications

Cast steel crossheads	23/6/54

Repairs

Crewe	NC EO	17/12/53	19/1/54
Crewe	LI	31/5/54	23/6/54
Crewe	HG	20/7/57	21/8/57
Crewe	HI	26/6/61	23/8/61
Crewe	HC	18/9/64	6/11/64

Boilers

New	13854
21/8/57	13901
6/11/64	13587

Tenders

New	7091

Mileage/(weekdays out of service)

1951	1,114	0
1952	38,144	33
1953	37,227	32
1954	30,101	60
1955	21,997	51
1956	22,872	78
1957	21,605	58
1958	26,134	-
1959	20,957	-
1960	16,790	-

Sheds

Workington	4/12/51
Penrith (loan)	23/1/54
Carlisle Upperby	2/4/55
Workington	23/4/55

Stored

Serviceable	14/3/66	?

Withdrawn w/e 6/5/67

46491 at Crewe Works on 19 August 1961 after a Heavy Intermediate repair. 46491 was the first engine built with the revised tall but wide chimney produced following the redraughting of 46413 at Swindon in 1950. 46491 is almost ready to return home; it spent its whole life in that area, mostly at Workington with spells at Penrith and Carlisle Upperby in the mid-1950s. It was one of five engines modified in 1954 with stronger pony truck springs and thrust strips on top of the bufferbeam to allow them to be used with a large No.3A snowplough.

46491 working a freight at Cockermouth on 14 May 1962. Although not formally withdrawn until May 1967 it went into store at Workington in March 1966. www.rail-online.co.uk

46492

Built at Darlington 19/12/51
Makers no. 2184

Improvements and modifications
Cast steel crossheads   12/1/57

Repairs
Crewe	LI	1/1/55	18/1/55
Rugby	NC	15/8/55	16/9/55
Crewe	HG	22/11/56	12/1/57
Rugby	LC EO	2/8/58	15/8/58
Crewe	HI	16/9/60	13/10/60
Crewe	HG	30/1/64	14/4/64

Boilers
New	13855
12/1/57	13859
14/4/64	13861

Tenders
New	7092

Mileage/(weekdays out of service)
1951	123	0
1952	20,985	14
1953	18,438	18
1954	18,066	24
1955	16,417	72
1956	16,213	70
1957	22,015	36
1958	15,894	63
1959	20,085	-
1960	17,824	-

Sheds
Aston	19/12/51
Saltley	16/10/65
Buxton	15/10/66

Stored
Serviceable	29/10/65	3/10/66

Withdrawn w/e 1/7/67

In unlined black after a Heavy General repair completed on 14 April 1964, 46492 is dwarfed by Coronation 46254 at Crewe North on 25 April. Having gone to Aston when new in December 1951, it stayed in Birmingham until October 1966, moving to Saltley in October 1965. www.rail-online.co.uk

Although still with a 2E Saltley shedplate, 46492 had been transferred to Buxton in October 1966, hence its appearance at Edale on the Hope Valley line between Hope and Chinley. It was one of the five engines which lasted until w/e 1 July 1967. The large building on the left was the Church Hotel now The Rambler Inn. www.rail-online.co.uk

46493

Built at Darlington 21/12/51
Makers no. 2185

Improvements and modifications

Cast steel crossheads	14/12/54
AWS	4/5/61

Repairs

Crewe	LI	20/11/54	14/12/54
Darlington	GEN	31/3/58	3/5/58
Darlington	ADJ	5/5/58	6/5/58
Darlington	NC	18/4/61	4/5/61

Boilers

New	13846
3/5/58	?

Tenders

New	7093

Mileage/(weekdays out of service)

1951	115	0
1952	27,433	23
1953	28,533	31
1954	26,579	70
1955	29,170	46
1956	24,095	51

Sheds

Burton	21/12/51
Holbeck	12/7/52

Withdrawn w/e 20/10/62

At Burton for its first six months in service, 46493 went to Holbeck in July 1952 and stayed there for the next decade. It was on a local passenger working from Leeds when photographed at Sheffield Midland in the mid-1950s.

In grimy plain black but still with large 10in numbers, 46493 was at Holbeck its home shed on 17 June 1961. It had been fitted with AWS the previous month, which was a waste since it was withdrawn the following year, in October 1962. A.G. Ellis.

46494

Built at Darlington 27/12/51
Makers no. 2186

Improvements and modifications
Cast steel crossheads 6/1/55

Repairs
Derby	LC EO	18/3/52	21/4/52
Crewe	LI	9/12/54	6/1/55
Darlington	GEN	10/11/58	12/12/58

Boilers
New	13858
12/12/58	13824

Tenders
New	7094

Mileage/(weekdays out of service)
1951	149	0
1952	21,446	47
1953	22,522	43
1954	16,490	66
1955	17,189	46
1956	22,663	75
1957	24,035	-

Sheds
Burton	27/12/51
Bristol Barrow Road	6/2/54
Sheffield Millhouses	2/6/56
Cambridge	1/4/61
March	23/6/62

Withdrawn w/e 15/9/62

46494 at Derby on 20 April 1952. The second of a pair of engines delivered new to Burton in December 1951, it was one of the class which moved around the country, with allocations at Bristol Barrow Road, Sheffield Millhouses and in East Anglia at Cambridge and March. R.J. Buckley, Initial Photographics.

46494 at Millhouses in the late 1950s, having been transferred to the Sheffield shed from Bristol in June 1956. While at Millhouses it was used on local passenger and freight work as well as pilot duties.

46495

Built at Darlington 30/1/52
Makers no. 2187

Improvements and modifications

Cast steel crossheads	7/1/54
AWS	23/2/63

Repairs

Crewe	LI	5/12/53	7/1/54
Crewe	LC EO	12/1/55	17/2/55
Crewe	HG	13/9/56	18/10/56
Crewe	LI	5/9/59	9/10/59
Crewe	HG	30/1/63	23/2/63

Boilers

New	13859
18/10/56	13850
23/2/63	13576

Tenders

New	7095
18/10/56	7038

Mileage/(weekdays out of service)

1952	36,321	39
1953	21,778	65
1954	32,559	52
1955	28,099	75
1956	28,032	64
1957	37,608	31
1958	32,221	57
1959	25,368	-
1960	26,048	-

Sheds

Kettering	30/1/52
Derby	25/2/61
Nuneaton	25/5/63
Crewe South	4/6/66

Withdrawn w/e 8/10/66

46495 at Newmarket Road Cambridge on 14 August 1954. As with the other engines at Kettering, 46495 was there for almost a decade, leaving for Derby in February 1961. www.rail-online.co.uk

With its 5E shedcode painted on, 46495 waits at Nuneaton with a short parcels train probably bound for Coventry. It had been transferred there from Derby in May 1963 and stayed until June 1966, moving to Crewe South for its last few months in service. www.rail-online.co.uk

46496

Built at Darlington 5/2/52
Makers no. 2188

Improvements and modifications
Cast steel crossheads   14/3/55

Repairs

Crewe	HI	12/2/55	14/3/55
Crewe	HG	16/1/56	29/2/56
Crewe	HG	26/2/59	3/4/59
Crewe	LI	15/5/62	4/6/62

Boilers

New	13844
29/2/56	12972
3/4/59	13617

Tenders

New	7096
3/1/66	7014

Mileage/(weekdays out of service)

1952	36,657	22
1953	35,971	58
1954	30,807	41
1955	25,970	74
1956	35,560	63
1957	42,357	43
1958	35,917	46
1959	33,933	-
1960	26,455	-

Sheds

Kettering	5/2/52
Nottingham	23/3/63
Bank Hall	23/5/64

Stored

Serviceable	8/11/65	2/4/66

Withdrawn w/e 2/4/66

Another long-serving Kettering engine, 46496 at Wellingborough in the late 1950s or early 1960s. It eventually moved to Nottingham in March 1963, after eleven years at Kettering. www.rail-online.co.uk

46496 at Rochdale after its transfer to Bank Hall in May 1964. It is on the north side, probably on a Wigan Wallgate to Rochdale service which was a rostered Bank Hall locomotive working at this time. 46496 went into store at Bank Hall in November 1965 and did not turn a wheel again before it was withdrawn in April 1966. www.rail-online.co.uk

46497

Built at Darlington 13/2/52
Makers no. 2189

Improvements and modifications

Cast steel crossheads	27/8/58

Repairs

Crewe	LI	10/12/55	27/1/56
Crewe	HG	23/7/58	27/8/58

Boilers

New	13860
27/8/58	13853

Tenders

New	7097

Mileage/(weekdays out of service)

1952	30,859	14
1953	29,704	28
1954	27,707	41
1955	23,881	73
1956	28,841	66
1957	17,193	85
1958	14,369	85
1959	26,165	-
1960	24,072	-

Sheds

Holbeck	13/2/52
Nottingham	24/3/56
Hasland	10/11/56
Nottingham	22/6/57
Hasland	21/9/57
Derby	10/1/59
Nottingham	23/11/63
Bank Hall	23/5/64

Withdrawn w/e 24/4/65

46497 was always on the Midland Division, variously at Holbeck, Hasland, Nottingham and Derby before ending up at Bank Hall in 1964. On 7 July 1960 it was at Derby where it was allocated between January 1959 and November 1963. R.J. Buckley, Initial Photographics.

46497 with empty coaching stock at Derby on 8 July 1962. The first coach is an ex-LMS TPO to diagram 1792 and shows the 'bulges' for the letter sorting racks. There were several postal services that either started or exchanged vehicles at Derby and the 2-6-0 is marshalling one such train and displays one headlamp over each buffer indicating station pilot duties. The BR Research headquarters and depot is under construction in the background. www.rail-online.co.uk

46498

Built at Darlington 27/2/52
Makers no. 2190

Improvements and modifications

Cast steel crossheads	20/9/55
AWS	23/6/61

Repairs

Crewe	LI	22/8/55	20/9/55
Darlington	GEN	23/2/59	23/3/59
Darlington	NC	13/6/61	23/6/61

Boilers

New	13857
23/3/59	?

Tenders

New	7098

Mileage/(weekdays out of service)

1952	27,635	14
1953	31,322	19
1954	29,566	55
1955	24,134	72
1956	26,716	44

Sheds

Holbeck	27/2/52
Polmadie (loan)	2/3/63
Polmadie	13/4/63
Ardrossan	12/10/63
Ayr	20/2/65

Withdrawn w/e 25/9/65

Holbeck's 46498 at Skipton MPD in the mid-1950s while the Leeds shed was still part of the LMR. It went there when new in February 1952 and stayed until 1963 when it was transferred to the Scottish Region, initially to Polmadie.

In February 1965 46498 was transferred to Ayr, its final shed, from Ardrossan. It has retained large Darlington applied 10in cab numbers and intriguingly has AWS fitted in June 1961 while it was still at Holbeck. The tender has strengthened front footsteps. www.rail-online.co.uk

46499

Built at Darlington 5/3/52
Makers no. 2191

Improvements and modifications

Cast steel crossheads	26/10/57

Repairs

Shed	LC EO	10/6/54	21/6/54
Derby	LI	23/5/55	12/7/55
Crewe	HG	19/9/57	26/10/57
Crewe	LI	11/9/61	11/10/61
Crewe	HC	16/11/64	12/12/64

Boilers

New	13848
26/10/57	13842
12/12/64	13442

Tenders

New	7099

Mileage/(weekdays out of service)

1952	16,887	25
1953	23,452	48
1954	23,978	55
1955	18,713	99
1956	25,202	51
1957	16,236	90
1958	16,644	70
1959	24,551	-
1960	23,060	-

Sheds

Toton	5/3/52
Hasland	2/5/53
Derby	10/1/59
Nottingham	23/11/63
Springs Branch (Wigan)	23/5/64
Barrow in Furness	27/6/64
Carnforth	2/10/65

Stored

Serviceable	24/10/65	3/11/65

Withdrawn w/e 6/5/67

The main activities of the 2-6-0s allocated to Derby were as passenger pilots as shown by 46499 on 27 May 1961. The watching youngster seems more interested in the photographer than 46499. It was one of only a handful of the class to be repaired at Derby Works, having a Light Intermediate in 1955 but was not allocated to Derby until 7 January 1959, moving from Hasland.

46499 at Barrow MPD in 1965. After working on the Midland Division until November 1963, 46499 was quickly transferred from Springs Branch to Barrow in December 1964 and remained there until September 1965 when it moved to Carnforth. www.rail-online.co.uk

46500

Built at Darlington 13/3/52
Makers no. 2192

Improvements and modifications

Cast steel crossheads	16/6/55

Repairs

Crewe	LI	20/5/55	16/6/55
Crewe	HG	17/10/58	15/11/58
Crewe	LI	28/5/63	18/6/63

Boilers

New	13845
15/11/58	13560

Tenders

New	7100

Mileage/(weekdays out of service)

1952	14,185	27
1953	23,892	42
1954	26,269	42
1955	21,583	73
1956	23,187	54
1957	17,174	85
1958	12,729	111
1959	27,899	-
1960	24,884	-

Sheds

Toton	13/3/52
Westhouses	26/4/52
Toton	17/5/52
Hasland	2/5/53
Derby	10/1/59
Aintree	23/5/64

Stored

Serviceable	24/1/66	?

Withdrawn w/e 7/1/67

46500 from Hasland had been in Crewe Works for a Light Intermediate repair in mid-1955 and appears to have just returned to Crewe North after a running-in trip. It appears to have been partially repainted, at the front end, but retains its original Darlington cab numbers. 46500 was at the Chesterfield shed from May 1953 until January 1959 when it moved to Derby. R.S. Carpenter Collection.

Inevitably on station pilot duties, 46500 at Derby in October 1963. It moved away to Aintree in May 1964 and was withdrawn at the end of 1966. www.rail-online.co.uk

46501

Built at Darlington 24/4/52
Makers no. 2193

Improvements and modifications

Cast steel crossheads	26/3/55

Repairs

Crewe	LI	28/2/55	26/3/55
Crewe	NC EO	29/3/55	30/3/55
Crewe	HG	6/9/57	10/10/57
Crewe	HI	12/4/61	19/5/61
Crewe	LI	13/11/64	10/12/64

Boilers

New	13851
10/10/57	13471

Tenders

New	7101

Mileage/(weekdays out of service)

1952	16,879	20
1953	36,946	50
1954	27,847	63
1955	27,840	67
1956	27,098	38
1957	25,815	65
1958	28,273	38
1959	28,233	-
1960	22,562	-

Sheds

Nottingham	24/4/52
Mansfield	21/11/53
Kirkby in Ashfield	9/4/60
Skipton (loan)	18/6/60
Skipton	23/7/60
Lostock Hall	15/9/62
Bury	11/1/64
Newton Heath	10/4/65

Stored

Serviceable	15/11/65	23/3/66
Serviceable	7/11/66	?

Withdrawn w/e 6/5/67

46501 at Nottingham in May 1958 working a local passenger train. It was at Mansfield from November 1953 until April 1960 having started off at Nottingham in April 1952.

46501 rounds Farington Curve near Preston with a Class J freight on 2 March 1963. It had been transferred from the Midland Division at Skipton in September 1962. www.rail-online.co.uk

303

46502

Built at Darlington 30/4/52
Makers no. 2194

Improvements and modifications

Cast steel crossheads	17/8/57

Repairs

Derby	LI	8/10/54	11/11/54
Derby	NC EO	17/11/54	22/11/54
Shed	LC EO	22/11/56	28/11/56
Crewe	HG	20/7/57	17/8/57
Crewe	HI	25/5/61	3/7/61

Boilers

New	13589

Tenders

New	7102

Mileage/(weekdays out of service)

1952	18,212	15
1953	30,693	43
1954	19,780	93
1955	38,442	60
1956	34,088	48
1957	23,094	69
1958	25,392	32
1959	21,736	-
1960	22,992	-

Sheds

Nottingham	30/4/52
Derby	10/1/59
Aintree	23/5/64

Stored

Serviceable	7/11/66	19/12/66
Serviceable	30/1/67	?

Withdrawn w/e 25/2/67

The last of the class built at Darlington, 46502 has just left Millhouses station with a Sheffield to Nottingham stopping train on the Up Fast line in the early 1950s. It was allocated to Nottingham from new until January 1959 when it went to Derby. www.rail-online.co.uk

A very work-stained 46502 working as Derby station pilot in early 1964, shortly before it moved to Aintree in May. www.rail-online.co.uk

46503

Built at Swindon 5/11/52

Repairs

Swindon	U	20/1/53	27/2/53
Craven Arms	U	18/5/54	14/7/54
Wolverhampton	LC	4/10/54	15/10/54
Swindon	HG	9/10/56	6/12/56
Oswestry	U	15/1/58	1/2/58
Oswestry	U	3/4/59	20/4/59
Wolverhampton	HI	11/4/60	17/6/60
Oswestry	U	10/8/62	24/8/62
Crewe	HG	19/12/63	22/1/64

Boilers

New	13861
6/12/56	14096
22/1/64	13784

Tenders

New	7103

Mileage

Cumulative to 6/12/56	104,510
Cumulative to 17/6/60	193,117

Sheds

Oswestry	5/11/52
Willesden	30/3/63
Northwich	25/5/63
Springs Branch (Wigan)	8/8/64
Speke Junction	7/11/64
Northwich	19/11/66

Withdrawn w/e 6/5/67

The first Swindon-built engine, 46503 with the 1.20pm Brecon-Moat Lane at Talyllyn Junction on 27 July 1959. R. Darlaston.

After leaving the Western Region in March 1963, 46503 had two months at Willesden before moving to Northwich in May. Pictured there in April 1964, it had reverted to plain black livery after a Heavy General repair at Crewe completed three months earlier. 46503 had been built in this unlined livery but from its first Heavy General in late 1956 it was in lined black. It left Northwich for Springs Branch and then Speke Junction during 1964 but returned there in November 1966 for its final six months in traffic.

46504

Built at Swindon 19/11/52

Repairs

Swindon	LC	12/6/53	25/6/53
Oswestry	LC	19/1/56	3/2/56
Swindon	HI	12/5/56	17/7/56
Caerphilly	HI	22/5/59	31/7/59
Crewe	LI	12/10/62	2/11/62

Boilers

New	13862

Tenders

New	7104

Mileage

Cumulative to 17/7/56	99,057
Cumulative to 31/7/59	177,052
Cumulative to 2/11/62	258,102

Sheds

Oswestry	19/11/52
Willesden	30/3/63
Barrow in Furness	25/5/63
Bury	10/10/64
Bolton	10/4/65
Newton Heath	13/8/66

Withdrawn w/e 15/10/66

46504 had been repainted in lined green during a Heavy Intermediate overhaul at Caerphilly completed on 31 July 1959. Six weeks later, on 13 September, it was photographed at Llanidloes.

While still allocated to Oswestry, 46504 had a Light Intermediate repair at Crewe Works in October 1962. Someone has chalked 'OK' on the freshly painted smokebox and the lined green paintwork has been left untouched, so 46504 appears to be ready to go back to Wales. It still has the GWR pattern ejector with a control valve on the top of the ejector body and an additional short exhaust pipe into the smokebox.

46505

Built at Swindon 21/11/52

Improvements and modifications

Repairs

Swindon	LC	4/9/53	21/9/53
Swindon	HI	21/5/56	14/8/56
Oswestry	U	31/1/59	16/2/59
Wolverhampton	HG	30/11/59	29/1/60
Oswestry	U	6/12/61	24/1/62
Crewe	LI	3/6/63	22/6/63
Crewe	HC	14/12/65	24/1/66

Boilers

New	13863
29/1/60	13440

Tenders

New	7105

Mileage

Cumulative to 14/8/56	98,885
Cumulative to 31/12/59	187,313

Sheds

Oswestry	21/11/52
Willesden	30/3/63
Chester Midland	25/5/63
Saltley	7/12/63
Leamington	24/10/64
Saltley	19/6/65
Newton Heath (loan)	6/8/66
Newton Heath	20/8/66
Buxton	6/5/67

Stored

Serviceable	29/9/63	2/12/63
Serviceable	7/11/66	13/2/67

Withdrawn w/e 1/7/67

Still in its original unlined black despite a Heavy Intermediate repair at Swindon in mid-1956, 46505 rests at its home shed, Oswestry, on 18 September 1958. It finally left there, for Willesden, in March 1963 after the London Midland Region had taken over the WR allocation on 1 January 1963. A.R. Goult.

46505 moved around the LMR from Willesden to Chester, Leamington and Saltley before reaching Newton Heath in August 1966. There are traces of the lined green livery applied at Wolverhampton in 1960 under the grime as it stands in the familiar Manchester Victoria pilot road on 15 March 1967. 46505 had been in store from November 1966 until February and moved to Buxton in May for its final two months in service. A.G. Forsyth, Initial Photographics.

46506

Built at Swindon 27/11/52

Repairs

Shrewsbury	U	2/12/52	24/12/52
Swindon	LC	9/4/53	6/5/53
Oswestry	U	17/1/55	1/2/55
Swindon	HG	28/9/56	12/12/56
Bristol St Philips Marsh	U	28/4/58	12/5/58
Bristol St Philips Marsh	U	20/6/58	8/7/58
Bristol St Philips Marsh	U	19/3/59	2/4/59
Bristol St Philips Marsh	U	7/7/59	1/8/59
Oswestry	LC	5/12/59	8/1/60
Bristol St Philips Marsh	U	29/11/60	30/12/60
Crewe	HG	15/11/61	20/12/61

Boilers

New	13864
12/12/56	14095
20/12/61	12905

Tenders

New	7106
8/7/65	7044

Mileage

Cumulative to 12/12/56	110,229
Cumulative to 15/11/61	192,758

Sheds

Oswestry	27/11/52
Bristol St Philips Marsh	29/12/56
Oswestry	31/10/59
Bristol St Philips Marsh	13/8/60
Bristol Barrow Road	3/11/62
Stourbridge Junction	15/12/62
Willesden	30/3/63
Chester Midland	25/5/63
Nottingham	7/12/63
Springs Branch (Wigan)	23/5/64
Barrow in Furness	27/6/64
Bury	10/10/64
Bolton	10/4/65
Newton Heath	13/8/66

Stored

Serviceable	29/9/63	21/11/63

Withdrawn w/e 6/5/67

46506 at Moat Lane on 13 April 1955, about to take the Mid-Wales Line down to Brecon. It is interesting because the Ivatt is facing in the 'Down' direction towards Machynlleth with a train of non-corridor stock. However, it seems possible that 46506 is propelling the stock back up the main line so that it can run forward into the Mid-Wales platform facing towards Llanidloes, a manoeuvre that took place regularly at this location. For some unknown reason 46506 does not appear to have the GWR pattern ejector – there is no control valve on the top of the ejector body. www.rail-online.co.uk

As with several of the other former Western Region engines, 46506 had numerous postings around the Region after it came under LMR control in January 1963. Its final destination was Newton Heath, in August 1966, and it had joined the ranks of Manchester Victoria pilots, resting there on 19 March 1967. R.K. Blencowe.

46507

Built at Swindon 28/11/52

Repairs

Swindon	LC	18/9/53	6/10/53
Bristol Bath Road	U	6/1/55	4/2/55
Bristol Bath Road	U	20/4/55	6/5/55
Bristol Bath Road	U	18/1/56	17/2/56
Swindon	U	21/3/56	29/3/56
Swindon	HI	30/6/56	20/9/56
Oswestry	U	25/2/59	11/3/59
Wolverhampton	HI	31/12/59	26/2/60
Shrewsbury	U	21/3/63	19/4/63

Boilers

New	13865
26/2/60	13829

Tenders

New	7107

Mileage

Cumulative to 20/9/56	84,017
Cumulative to 14/12/59	174,432

Sheds

Oswestry	28/11/52
Bristol Bath Road	1/1/55
Oswestry	16/6/56
Croes Newydd	9/2/63
Willesden (loan)	6/2/65
Croes Newydd	26/6/65

Withdrawn w/e 26/6/65

46507 at Rhayader, between Builth Wells and Llanidloes, 25 May 1957. It is uncertain whether it was built with unlined black livery but it definitely had lined black after its first Heavy repair in late 1956. It was one of a handful of engines to move away from Oswestry in the 1950s, to Bristol Bath Road between January 1955 and June 1956, when it returned to its original shed. N.L. Browne.

46507 is enveloped in steam on a cold winter's day at Builth Wells (Low level), looking towards Three Cocks Junction and Brecon, in the late 1950s. It ended its days at Croes Newydd in June 1965 after leaving Oswestry in February 1963. www.rail-online.co.uk

46508

Built at Swindon 2/12/52

Repairs

Oswestry shed	U	5/8/53	8/10/53
Oswestry	U	19/12/53	2/1/54
Swindon	HI	20/8/56	15/10/56
Wolverhampton	HI	13/11/59	8/1/60
Crewe	GEN	4/3/63	5/4/63

Boilers

New	13866
5/4/63	12975

Tenders

New	7108

Mileage

Cumulative to 15/10/56	98,748
Cumulative to 31/12/59	196,197

Sheds

Oswestry	2/12/52
Brecon	1/1/55
Oswestry	28/11/59
Croes Newydd	9/2/63
Willesden (loan)	6/2/65
Croes Newydd	7/8/65
Machynlleth	6/8/66
Shrewsbury	10/12/66

Stored

Serviceable	17/8/65	25/7/66
Serviceable	27/8/66	7/11/66

Withdrawn w/e 17/12/66

46508 was transferred to Brecon from Oswestry in January 1955, replacing 46523 which went in the other direction. It has plenty of steam to spare as it waits to depart from Builth Wells (Low level), probably in 1958. Brecon shed was closed in November 1959 and 46508 returned to Oswestry.

46508 at Oswestry between February and September 1963, after it had been transferred from there to Croes Newydd in February. The Wrexham shed was 89B from January 1961 until September 1963, taking over the code previously used for Brecon. www.rail-online.co.uk

46509

Built at Swindon 5/12/52

Repairs

Wolverhampton	LC	24/11/54	16/2/55
Oswestry	U	26/8/55	9/9/55
Swindon	HI	31/12/56	29/3/57
Crewe	HI	22/5/61	20/6/61
Crewe	HG	16/9/63	22/10/63

Boilers

New	13867
29/3/57	13861

Tenders

New	7109
16/7/60	7126

Mileage

Cumulative to 29/3/57	104,466
Cumulative to 20/6/61	210,721

Sheds

Oswestry	5/12/52
Croes Newydd	9/2/63
Willesden (loan)	6/2/65
Bescot	2/10/65
Tyseley	3/1/66

Stored

Serviceable	18/1/66	?

Withdrawn w/e 8/10/66

46509 waits at Hay-on-Wye with a Hereford to Brecon train in 1961 or 1962. It was at Oswestry from new in December 1952 until 1963 when it moved to Croes Newydd. 46509 had been repainted in lined green with an early BR emblem in 1957. M. Brown, www.rail-online.co.uk

Ivatt 2-6-0s worked on the Llanfyllin branch up to its closure in January 1965. The terminus had no turntable and so they ran tender-first from Oswestry towards Llanfyllin as demonstrated by 46509 at Llanmynech, the junction where the line left the Whitchurch to Welshpool line, on 15 June 1962. www.rail-online.co.uk

46510

Built at Swindon 9/12/52

Repairs

Swindon	HI	11/9/56	11/12/56
Swindon	LC	23/3/53	2/4/53
Oswestry shed	U	6/8/53	30/8/53
Brecon	U	6/7/54	27/7/54
Oswestry shed	U	6/12/54	22/12/54
Swindon	HI	11/9/56	11/12/56
Oswestry	U	14/3/58	28/3/58
Crewe	HG	25/8/60	28/9/60

Boilers

New	13868
28/9/60	13872

Tenders

New	7110

Mileage

Cumulative to 11/12/56	101,504
Cumulative to 28/9/60	203,882

Sheds

Oswestry	9/12/52
Shrewsbury	23/1/65

Withdrawn w/e 2/10/65

46510 with a freight on 31 May 1963 at Tinkers Green Halt on the former Cambrian line between Oswestry and Whitchurch. The halt was opened in October 1939 to serve a military training camp at Park Hall that had been used in the Great War, and which was reactivated at the start of the Second World War. The camp was a short walk from the station.

46510 at Oswestry in the early 1960s, probably with a train to Llanfyllin. It was allocated to Oswestry up until January 1965 when it moved to Shrewsbury for its last few months in service.
www.rail-online.co.uk

46511

Built at Swindon 12/12/52

Repairs

Swindon	U	6/3/53	24/3/53
Oswestry	U	18/1/54	20/2/54
Swindon	HI	28/4/56	29/6/56
Crewe	HG	26/2/60	31/3/60

Boilers

New	13869
31/3/60	13579

Tenders

New	7111

Mileage

Cumulative to 29/6/56	96,810
Cumulative to 21/3/60	196,138

Sheds

Oswestry	12/12/52
Shrewsbury	23/1/65

Withdrawn w/e 2/10/65

46511 at Builth Wells on 9 July 1960 with the 1.20pm Brecon-Moat Lane. The 89A shed code it displays was used for Oswestry until January 1961 when Shrewsbury took it over. R. Darlaston.

Moat Lane Junction was where the line from Whitchurch and Oswestry to Machynlleth and Aberystwyth met the Mid Wales line from Three Cocks Junction and Llanidloes. 46511 waits there in 1961/2 with a train to Brecon. www.rail-online.co.uk

46512

Built at Swindon 16/12/52

Repairs

Oswestry shed	U	14/2/53	15/4/53
Oswestry shed	U	23/4/53	28/5/53
Oswestry shed	U	4/1/54	22/1/54
Swindon	HI	3/11/56	10/1/57
Crewe	HI	23/6/60	2/8/60
Oswestry	U	20/4/61	4/5/61
Crewe	HG	20/3/63	30/3/63

Boilers

New	13870
10/1/57	13864
30/3/63	13448

Tenders

New	7112

Mileage

Cumulative to 31/12/56	104,988
Cumulative to 2/8/60	200,789

Sheds

Oswestry	16/12/52
Shrewsbury	23/1/65
Willesden (loan)	6/2/65
Shrewsbury	26/6/65
Nuneaton	2/10/65
Crewe South	4/6/66

Withdrawn w/e 12/11/66

46512 at Llansantffraid, the principal intermediate station on the Llanfyllin branch with a train to Oswestry in the early 1960s. www.rail-online.co.uk

46512 waits in the loop at Moat Lane Junction during the mid-1950s. After it was withdrawn in November 1966, 46512 went to Woodham's scrapyard at Barry. It was originally purchased from there to provide a replacement boiler for preserved 46464 but it is now being restored at the East Lancs Railway. www.rail-online.co.uk

46513

Built at Swindon 19/12/52

Repairs

Oswestry	U	25/6/55	17/8/55
Swindon	HI	23/6/56	7/9/56
Oswestry	U	3/1/58	17/1/58
Oswestry	U	17/4/59	30/4/59
Crewe	HG	25/5/60	28/6/60

Boilers

New	13871
28/6/60	13876

Tenders

New	7113

Mileage

Cumulative to 7/9/56	100,681
Cumulative to 28/6/60	198,451

Sheds

Oswestry	19/12/52
Newton Heath (loan)	23/1/65
Newton Heath	6/2/65
Carlisle Upperby	19/6/65

Withdrawn w/e 16/7/66

Upperby kept a cluster of Ivatt 2MT 2-6-0s till late on, seeming to use them in place of the traditional 3F 0-6-0Ts for pilot work at Citadel, its Jinties having all departed. 46513 is in the modern Upperby roundhouse on 7 August 1965; behind is another Ivatt and over on the left one of the Brush Type 4s increasingly in evidence by this time. D. Forsyth, ColourRail

46513 at the western end of Brecon station, probably in 1961. It was allocated to Oswestry from new in December 1952 until January 1965 when it moved to Newton Heath. www.rail-online.co.uk

327

46514

Built at Swindon 23/12/52

Repairs

Brecon	U	4/5/53	18/5/53
Brecon	U	19/6/53	7/8/53
Oswestry shed	U	2/6/54	21/6/54
Swindon	HI	20/7/56	11/9/56
Oswestry	U	3/10/57	18/10/57
Oswestry	LC	11/12/58	20/1/59
Crewe	HG	27/5/60	27/6/60
Oswestry	U	23/2/62	11/4/62
Oswestry	NC	?	10/1/63
Crewe	HG	?	27/6/63

Boilers

New	13872
27/6/60	13863

Tenders

New	7114

Mileage

Cumulative to 11/9/56	99,684
Cumulative to 27/6/60	197,407

Sheds

Oswestry	23/12/52
Newton Heath (loan)	30/1/65
Lancaster Green Ayre	26/6/65
Carnforth	23/4/66

Withdrawn w/e 25/6/66

Less than six months old, 46514 at Llanidloes on 5 April 1953 with a train to Builth Wells and Brecon.

A far cry from its days in mid-Wales, 46514 in the bay platform at Lancaster Castle. After a few months on loan at Newton Heath in early 1965, it was transferred to Lancaster Green Ayre in June and was there until April 1966 when it moved to Carnforth, from where it was withdrawn two months later. www.rail-online.co.uk

46515

Built at Swindon 6/1/53

Repairs

Swindon	HI	1/3/56	24/5/56
Oswestry	U	8/7/58	24/7/58
Caerphilly	HI	1/12/59	22/1/60
Oswestry	LC	31/7/62	15/8/62
Crewe	INT	2/4/63	2/5/63

Boilers

New	13873

Tenders

New	7115

Mileage

Cumulative to 24/5/56	89,814
Cumulative to 31/12/59	192,026

Sheds

Oswestry	6/1/53
Speke Junction (loan)	23/1/65
Speke Junction	6/2/65
Springs Branch (Wigan)	28/5/66

Stored

Serviceable	21/11/66	?

Withdrawn w/e 6/5/67

The crew prepare 46515 for duty at Oswestry shed on 23 June 1956. It had recently returned from Swindon after a Heavy Intermediate repair completed at the end of May. www.rail-online.co.uk

46515 in around 1963 at Welshampton near Ellesmere between Oswestry and Whitchurch. Note the GWR Iron Mink body supported on blocks used as a store. www.rail-online.co.uk

46516

Built at Swindon 13/1/53

Repairs

Oswestry shed	U	9/2/53	23/2/53
Swindon	HI	21/11/55	23/1/56
Oswestry	U	3/7/58	16/7/58
Oswestry	U	5/12/58	24/12/58
Crewe	HG	8/3/60	14/4/60
Crewe	LI	12/6/63	19/7/63

Boilers

New	13874
14/4/60	13002

Tenders

New	7116
23/1/56	7118

Mileage

Cumulative to 31/12/55	82,376
Cumulative to 14/4/60	201,955

Sheds

Oswestry	13/1/53
Brecon	8/8/53
Oswestry	31/10/59
Speke Junction (loan)	23/1/65
Speke Junction	6/2/65
Northwich	19/11/66

Stored

Serviceable	17/10/66	16/4/67

Withdrawn w/e 29/4/67

46516 on 23 May 1962 at Brecon. This is the east end of the station, looking towards Talyllyn Junction with the carriage sidings at the very right edge of the picture; the engine shed was also over to the right. www.rail-online.co.uk

46516 with a train from Hereford at Three Cocks Junction on 18 July 1962, less than six months before the line was closed. It was transferred from Oswestry to Speke Junction in early 1965, and then to Northwich in November 1966 although the records show it was stored from October 1966 until withdrawal in April 1967. www.rail-online.co.uk

46517

Built at Swindon 22/1/53

Repairs

Oswestry shed	U	23/9/53	25/11/53
Oswestry	U	25/3/54	8/4/54
Hereford	U	2/12/54	3/1/55
Worcester	U	1/6/56	16/6/56
Swindon	HI	13/11/57	3/1/58
Bristol St Philips Marsh	U	20/11/59	29/12/59
Bristol St Philips Marsh	U	27/9/60	11/10/60
Bristol St Philips Marsh	U	18/4/61	6/5/61
Caerphilly	HC	11/12/61	16/2/62

Boilers

New	13875
3/1/58	13867
16/2/62	13865

Tenders

New	7117

Mileage

Cumulative to 31/12/57	100,524
Cumulative to 16/2/62	159,751

Sheds

Oswestry	22/1/53
Brecon	8/8/53
Bristol St Philips Marsh	13/7/57
Bristol Barrow Road	3/11/62
Stourbridge Junction	15/12/62
Willesden	30/3/63
Northwich	25/5/63
Springs Branch (Wigan)	8/8/64

Stored

Serviceable	20/3/66	17/4/66

Withdrawn w/e 26/11/66

46517 on a short freight, probably between Whitney and Eardisley on the Hereford to Brecon line. The period is prior to its transfer from Brecon to Bristol St Philips Marsh in July 1957. M. Brown, www.rail-online.co.uk

On 16 June 1962, 46517 heads down the Western Region main line towards Bristol at Oldfield Park just to the west of Bath Spa. It was still allocated at that date to St Philips Marsh, but was transferred to Bath Road in November 1962. www.rail-online.co.uk

46518

Built at Swindon 27/1/53

Repairs

Swindon	HI	28/11/55	1/2/56
Oswestry	U	19/12/57	7/1/58
Oswestry	U	23/9/58	14/10/58
Oswestry	U	21/1/59	6/2/59
Swindon	HI	10/9/59	2/12/59
Crewe	LI	18/4/63	21/5/63

Boilers

New	13876
2/12/59	13875

Tenders

New	7118
1/2/56	7116

Mileage

Cumulative to 31/12/55	88,642
Cumulative to 2/12/59	205,492

Sheds

Oswestry	27/1/53
Brecon	16/5/53
Oswestry	31/10/59
Speke Junction (loan)	23/1/65
Speke Junction	6/2/65

Withdrawn w/e 19/3/66

Aberystwyth was a long way from 46518's home shed of Oswestry. The class was less common this far west with the GWR Manors and then BR Standard Class 4 4-6-0s working most of the passenger trains. However, they were reported there near the end of steam on the Cambrian lines, 46518 moving away to Speke Junction in January 1965. www.rail-online.co.uk

46518 with a southbound train to Brecon at Newbridge on Wye, north of Builth Wells on the line to Llanidloes and Moat Lane Junction in 1958; 46518 was transferred from Brecon to Oswestry in October 1959. www.rail-online.co.uk

46519

Built at Swindon 3/2/53

Repairs

Brecon	U	15/2/55	2/3/55
Swindon	HI	19/11/55	18/1/56
Oswestry	U	12/11/58	28/11/58
Swindon	HG	18/11/59	14/3/60
Oswestry	U	9/6/61	5/7/61
Oswestry	U	20/2/62	9/3/62
Machynlleth	U	12/3/63	8/4/63
Crewe	LI	29/5/64	1/7/64
Crewe	LC	5/10/64	23/10/64

Boilers

New	13877
14/3/60	13878

Tenders

New	7119

Mileage

Cumulative to 31/12/55	85,451
Cumulative to 14/3/60	203,748

Sheds

Oswestry	3/2/53
Machynlleth	9/3/63
Shrewsbury	27/2/65
Nuneaton	2/10/65
Stoke	4/6/66

Withdrawn w/e 8/10/66

46519 on 28 September 1957 at Moat Lane Junction. The Swindon pattern ejector with control valve on top of the ejector body and an additional short exhaust pipe, and the AWS battery box below the platform immediately in front of the cab show up particularly clearly. R.J. Buckley, Initial Photographics.

Brecon shed houses at least three Ivatt 2-6-0s on 28 June 1958, with 46519 nearest as a group of enthusiasts wander around. 46519 was allocated to Oswestry until March 1963 when it was transferred to Machynlleth. www.rail-online.co.uk

46520

Built at Swindon 9/2/53

Repairs
Oswestry	U	13/9/55	3/10/55
Swindon	HI	10/12/55	17/2/56
Oswestry	U	16/10/56	7/11/56
Oswestry	U	22/1/58	17/2/58
Oswestry	U	21/6/58	1/8/58
Swindon	HI	20/7/59	28/9/59
Crewe	LI	24/2/64	30/5/64

Boilers
New	13878
28/9/59	13880

Tenders
New	7120

Mileage
Cumulative to 31/12/55	86,051
Cumulative to 28/9/59	191,051

Sheds
Oswestry	9/2/53
Machynlleth	9/3/63
Nuneaton	23/1/65
Stoke	4/6/66
Northwich	15/10/66

Stored
Serviceable	20/2/66	4/6/66
Serviceable	26/3/67	?

Withdrawn w/e 6/5/67

The running-in board proclaims Builth Road Low Level – change for Llandrindod, Llanwrtyd, Llancammarch – '&C' because no more long names could be fitted on! 46520 passes through with a Down freight on 15 July 1957. The former L&NWR Central Wales line from Craven Arms to Carmarthen ran over the bridge in the background.

Leaving the Western Region, 46520 went initially to Nuneaton, in January 1965. It was in store from February 1966 until June when it went to Stoke and then it moved again in October, to Northwich. On 18 February 1967 46520 worked the British Transport Enthusiasts Guild/LCGB (North West Branch) Liverpool & Warrington Area Rail Tour which visited both Sutton Oak and Warrington Dallam sheds. Here it is at Broad Oak Junction with Sutton Oak shed in the background. 46520 was in lined green from September 1959 and had been specially cleaned up for the tour. M. Brown, www.rail-online.co.uk

46521

Built at Swindon 19/2/53

Repairs

Oswestry	U	20/1/55	4/2/55
Oswestry	LC	17/8/55	14/9/55
Swindon	HI	16/2/56	20/4/56
Oswestry	U	22/6/57	30/7/57
Oswestry	U	6/2/58	20/2/58
Caerphilly	HI	9/7/59	25/9/59
Crewe	LI	30/4/63	1/6/63

Boilers

New	13879

Tenders

New	7121

Mileage

Cumulative to 20/4/56	93,825
Cumulative to 25/9/59	188,754

Sheds

Oswestry	19/2/53
Brecon	21/3/53
Oswestry	31/10/59
Machynlleth	9/3/63

Withdrawn w/e 29/10/66

46521 on a Barmouth-Dolgellau local, at Penmaenpool, probably in 1964 since it has a 6F Machynlleth shedplate which did not come into effect until September 1963. After withdrawal from Machynlleth in October 1966 it went to Woodham's scrapyard from where it was purchased for preservation in 1971. It was restored at the Severn Valley Railway and is currently operational. www.rail-online.co.uk

46521 in 1961 or 1962 with a southbound train at Talgarth, between Three Cocks Junction and Talyllyn Junction. It was allocated to Oswestry from the October 1959 until March 1963 when it moved to Machynlleth. Now preserved. M. Brown, www.rail-online.co.uk

46522

Built at Swindon 3/3/53

Repairs

Swindon	HI	25/1/56	20/3/56
Oswestry	U	18/2/58	6/3/58
Swindon	HG	18/2/59	12/5/59
Oswestry	U	10/1/62	24/1/62
Oswestry	U	24/1/62	12/2/62
Crewe	HG	27/3/63	27/4/63

Boilers

New	13880
12/5/59	13883

Tenders

New	7122

Mileage

Cumulative to 20/3/56	92,296
Cumulative to 12/5/59	185,873

Sheds

Oswestry	9/3/53
Brecon	14/3/53
Oswestry	10/10/59
Machynlleth	9/2/63
Bescot	25/5/63
Tyseley (loan)	5/3/66
Banbury	26/3/66
Tyseley (loan)	2/4/66
Banbury	16/7/66
Carnforth	15/10/66

Stored

Serviceable	20/2/67	?

Withdrawn w/e 6/5/67

46522 at Llanidloes with a Moat Lane-Brecon train during the time it was allocated to Brecon, from March 1953 until October 1959. www.rail-online.co.uk

In the lined green livery it received during a Heavy General overhaul earlier in the year, 46522 waits at Hay-on-Wye with a train to Hereford in September 1959.

46523

Built at Swindon 5/3/53

Repairs

Oswestry	U	6/12/54	20/12/54
Swindon	HI	5/4/56	18/6/56
Oswestry	U	18/6/58	2/7/58
Wolverhampton	HI	9/10/59	27/11/59
Oswestry	U	14/6/62	28/6/62
Oswestry	U	30/8/62	18/9/62
Crewe	HI	31/8/63	9/10/63

Boilers

New   13881

Tenders

New   7123

Mileage

Cumulative to 18/6/56	99,517
Cumulative to 27/11/59	194,885

Sheds

Oswestry	5/3/53
Brecon	18/4/53
Oswestry	1/1/55
Machynlleth	9/2/63
Newton Heath	17/8/63
Aintree	19/6/65

Stored

Serviceable	19/6/66	24/2/67

Withdrawn w/e 6/5/67

46523 at Hay-on-Wye with an Up passenger working to Hereford in the late 1950s. www.rail-online.co.uk

'THREE COCKS - CHANGE FOR BUILTH WELLS, LLANDRINDOD WELLS, LLANIDLOES AND THE CAMBRIAN COAST' proclaims the vast running-in board. 46523 waits at the Junction with a Brecon train. It was at Brecon until the end of 1954 when it moved to Oswestry. www.rail-online.co.uk

46524

Built at Swindon 11/3/53

Repairs

Oswestry	LC	9/8/55	14/9/55
Swindon	HI	18/9/56	21/11/56
Oswestry	LC	12/7/58	21/8/58
Wolverhampton	HI	1/6/59	27/8/59
Oswestry	LC	18/9/59	25/9/59
Crewe	CAS	22/7/64	23/9/64

Boilers

New	13882

Tenders

New	7124
21/11/56	7127

Mileage

Cumulative to 21/11/56	103,678
Cumulative to 27/8/59	180,952

Sheds

Oswestry	11/3/53
Brecon	18/4/53
Oswestry	21/3/59
Shrewsbury	9/3/63

Withdrawn w/e 20/2/65

46524 on 20 July 1955 in front of Dean Goods 2538, a type which the Ivatt design was to replace on the Western Region lines in mid-Wales. It had been transferred from Brecon to Oswestry in January 1955 but still has an 89B shed plate.

348

46524 heads a southbound goods at Newbridge-on-Wye on 2 June 1961. This was the first station north of Builth Wells on the line up to Moat Lane Junction. 46524 was transferred from Oswestry to Machynlleth in February 1963 and saw out its final year at Aintree before withdrawal in May 1967. L.R. Freeman, transporttreasury

46525

Built at Swindon 17/3/53

Repairs

Swindon	LC	11/4/53	25/5/53
Bristol St Philips Marsh	U	30/1/55	4/3/55
Bristol St Philips Marsh	U	2/5/55	19/5/55
Bristol St Philips Marsh	U	9/8/55	7/9/55
Bristol St Philips Marsh	U	19/3/56	14/4/56
Bristol St Philips Marsh	U	5/11/56	19/11/56
Bristol St Philips Marsh	U	31/3/57	15/4/57
Swindon	HI	6/8/57	11/10/57
Swindon	LC	15/10/57	22/10/57
Crewe	LI	23/3/61	24/4/61
Oswestry	U	25/9/62	11/10/62
Oswestry	U	27/10/62	15/11/62

Boilers

New	13883
11/10/57	13870

Tenders

New	7125

Mileage

Cumulative to 11/10/57	74,195
Cumulative to 24/4/61	127,763

Sheds

Bristol St Philips Marsh	17/3/53
Oswestry	6/10/62
Shrewsbury	9/3/63

Withdrawn w/e 12/12/64

The last three engines built at Swindon went new to Bristol St Philips Marsh and 46525, photographed there on 27 August 1961, stayed until March 1963 when it was transferred to Shrewsbury. R.K. Blencowe.

46525 on a Welshpool-Shrewsbury train in 1963 near Shrewsbury, looking towards Welshpool at Redhill between mileposts 2 and 2¼; on the left is Hookagate Rail Welding Depot. 46525 had been allocated to Shrewsbury since March 1963 and was withdrawn from there in December 1964. www.rail-online.co.uk

46526

Built at Swindon 25/3/53

Repairs

Swindon	LC	5/8/53	25/8/53
Swindon	U	8/3/54	25/3/54
Bristol St Philips Marsh	U	24/4/54	16/5/54
Bristol St Philips Marsh	U	1/1/55	17/1/55
Bristol St Philips Marsh	U	24/6/55	28/7/55
Bristol St Philips Marsh	U	15/5/56	1/6/56
Swindon	HI	11/10/56	28/11/56
Oswestry	U	27/3/58	11/4/58
Crewe	HG	17/8/60	21/9/60
Oswestry	U	27/9/62	15/10/62

Boilers

New	13884
21/9/60	13871

Tenders

New	7126
16/7/60	7109

Mileage

Cumulative to 28/11/56	65,933
Cumulative to 21/9/60	164,728

Sheds

Bristol St Philips Marsh	25/3/53
Oswestry	29/12/56
Gloucester Barnwood	24/3/62
Oswestry	6/10/62
Stourbridge Junction	12/1/63
Watford	30/3/63
Saltley	7/12/63

Stored

Serviceable	20/5/63	2/12/63

Withdrawn w/e 16/7/66

When 46526 left Oswestry in March 1962 it went to Gloucester Barnwood along with 46527. They worked local passenger and freights from Ashchurch and also appeared on the Dursley branch, replacing GWR 16xx panniers, as indicated by 46526 near Dursley which evokes memories of a scene in the film 'The Titfield Thunderbolt'. W. Potter.

Two green former Western Region engines at Bescot on 7 April 1963. In front is 46526, which has no shedplate, and behind is 46517. Both were officially transferred from Stourbridge Junction, to Watford and Willesden respectively, in w/e 30 March 1963 but did not arrive there until 9 April. www.rail-online.co.uk

46527

Built at Swindon 1/4/53

Repairs

Swindon	LC	8/5/53	8/6/53
Bristol St Philips Marsh	U	2/3/54	9/4/54
Bristol St Philips Marsh	U	28/9/54	11/11/54
Bristol St Philips Marsh	U	30/5/55	21/6/55
Swindon	HI	8/9/56	8/11/56
Oswestry	U	25/2/58	13/3/58
Wolverhampton	HG	26/9/60	18/11/60
Gloucester Barnwood	U	17/7/62	10/8/62

Boilers

New	13885
18/11/60	13877

Tenders

New	7127
8/11/56	7124

Mileage

Cumulative to 8/11/56	73,494
Cumulative to 18/11/60	174,519

Sheds

Bristol St Philips Marsh	1/4/53
Bristol Bath Road	29/1/55
Bristol St Philips Marsh	23/3/57
Oswestry	25/1/58
Gloucester Barnwood	24/3/62
Oswestry	6/10/62
Stourbridge Junction	12/1/63
Bescot	30/3/63

Withdrawn w/e 9/10/65

Last of the class, 46527 calls at Hay-on-Wye station with a Down passenger working in 1961/62. Like 46526 it was based at Bristol in its early years, with two spells at St Philips Marsh and one at Bath Road, before moving to Oswestry in March 1957. M. Brown, www.rail-online.co.uk

46527 working a Down passenger train from Hereford at Three Cocks Junction in 1961/62. It moved from Oswestry to Gloucester Barnwood along with 46526 in March 1962, but both returned in October. M. Brown, www.rail-online.co.uk

355

46424 on pilot duty at Euston in May 1958. Hitherto Willesden had used a succession of superannuated pre-Group 0-6-0s, ex-LNW and ex-MR, on these empty stock jobs, or latterly anything that was to hand, including 8Fs – usually pinched engines you'd suspect – that should have been sent back north the day before. The Ivatts were far superior to the 0-6-0s, especially. There was no trouble with steaming but the clincher was – crew comfort. Standing in the rain and wind like this, in an ancient 0-6-0 was bad enough but running tender-first could be dismal indeed. Funnily enough the work latterly passed to BR versions of the Ivatts, the 2-6-0s in the 78000 series. F. Hornby, ColourRail

Postscript – The Perfect Pilot

After a year or two an official eye was cast over the performance of the new 2-6-0s. They had been designed for maximum utilisation, to be out any number of hours at a stretch and suited to any duties in their power range. In between pick up goods their designers envisaged them bounding along, fleet of foot, across miles of rural routes. So there was consternation when (admittedly at some sheds more than others) the Ivatts were found to be doing... not very much. Upon investigation they were found to be employed on station or other pilot duties which involved a minimum of miles worked and a maximum of standing around. Compared to the various locomotives up till then available at the sheds for such work, the Ivatts were infinitely preferable, simply on the grounds of comfort in poor weather. An edict of sorts went out but this proved impossible to enforce; if nothing else the sheds would simply 'adjust' the recorded mileages. After a while, with Modernisation announced, the 'problem' simply went away of its own accord.

PASSENGER ENGINE WORKINGS COMMENCING 2 NOVEMBER 1959				
DERBY TURN 50 ONE CLASS 2MT (EX LMS 2-6-0)				
	Shed	6.30am	LE	D
6.35am	Park Sdgs.			
6.35	SHUNT (Pass)	6.0pm		D
	Park Sdgs.	-	LE	D
6.5pm	Shed			
DERBY TURN 64 ONE CLASS 2MT (EX LMS 2-6-0)				
DERBY PARK SIDINGS SHUNT				
	Shed	5.45am	LE	MO
-	Park Sidings			
6.0am	SHUNT (Pass)	12.45		MO

Left. 46402 arranging stock at Derby station, 27 May 1961. D. Forsyth, ColourRail

Below. 46437 at Manchester Victoria on 3 July 1961. All the advantages of crew comfort working empty stock at Euston applied equally of course in Manchester; more so, maybe, given the higher rainfall... D. Forsyth, ColourRail

Left. 46426 at Carlisle pauses in its piloting, 31 July 1964. D. Forsyth, ColourRail

Bottom left. 46437 on 21 August 1961. Ivatt 2MT 2-6-0s waiting on the banking engine spur at Manchester Victoria constitute the classic view of these engines; there are very many such pictures, for they stood in a very visible, photographically congenial spot as they waited to help a train up to Miles Platting. In earlier times, typically, we'd have seen an old Lanky A class 0-6-0 standing here and the reason for the crews' preference is obvious – where would you rather be in January, cosy as you like in one of these or shivering in the 'barely there' yawningly open cab of an 0-6-0, helpless against the icy blasts? ColourRail

Below. 46411 in between banking turns at Manchester Victoria while an express pulls out beyond. This Ivatt became almost an institution – see page 123 for instance. ColourRail

Endpiece

Coming soon – the tank version. Upperby's 41217, still wreathed in push/pull pipes and linkage it will never use again, pauses with a train of tanks in Carlisle Citadel, 6 August 1965. *The Book of the Ivatt 2-6-2Ts* will be available early in 2020. D. Forsyth, ColourRail